Mastering Software Engineering

From Basics to Expert Proficiency

Contents

Introduction

Software engineering is a fundamental discipline in the field of computer science that focuses on the systematic development and maintenance of software systems. As modern life increasingly depends on software for various applications, the demand for high-quality, reliable, and scalable software has never been greater. This book, "Mastering Software Engineering: From Basics to Expert Proficiency," is designed to provide a comprehensive understanding of the core principles, methodologies, and practices essential for mastering software engineering.

Software engineering encompasses various processes and practices that ensure the efficient and effective creation of software systems. These include requirements engineering, system design and architecture, construction, implementation, testing, quality assurance, maintenance, and project management. Each of these areas plays a critical role in the development of robust software systems that meet user requirements and perform reliably in diverse operating environments.

One of the fundamental aspects of software engineering is the Software Development Life Cycle (SDLC). The SDLC provides a structured framework for developing software, guiding engineers through a series of phases including planning, analysis, design, development, testing, deployment, and maintenance. Various models of the SDLC, such as Waterfall, Agile, and Spiral, offer different approaches to managing the complexities of software development projects.

Requirements engineering is another crucial area in software engineering. It involves eliciting, analyzing, documenting, and validating the needs and constraints of stakeholders to ensure that the software system meets their expectations. Effective requirements engineering lays the foundation for successful software development by providing clear and unambiguous requirements that guide subsequent design and implementation efforts.

System design and architecture are central to creating software systems that are scalable, maintainable, and adaptable. Design principles and patterns help engineers to develop robust architectures that can accommodate future changes and integration with other systems. This book covers various design approaches, including modular design, user interface design, and data management.

The construction and implementation phase of software engineering involves translating design specifications into executable code. This phase includes coding standards, version control, debugging, and refactoring to ensure the creation of high-quality software. Effective construction practices are essential for building software that is reliable, maintainable, and performs well under various conditions.

Testing and quality assurance are indispensable components of software engineering. They encompass a range of testing types and techniques to identify defects and ensure that the software meets specified requirements. Automated testing, performance testing, security testing, and usability testing are some of the key areas covered in this book to help engineers develop software that is both functional and user-friendly.

Software maintenance and evolution address the ongoing needs of software systems after their initial deployment. This includes correcting defects, adapting the software to new environments, and improving performance. Effective maintenance practices are vital for extending the life of software systems and ensuring their continued relevance and reliability.

Project management in software engineering involves planning, organizing, and managing resources to achieve specific project goals. This includes risk management, cost management, and quality management to deliver projects on time and within budget. Agile project management and other modern methodologies are explored in this book to equip engineers with the skills needed to navigate complex software projects successfully.

The book also delves into the tools and environments used in software engineering, such as integrated development environments (IDEs), version control systems, build tools, and testing tools. Selecting the right tools is essential for streamlining the development process and enhancing productivity.

Finally, the book examines current trends and future directions in software engineering. Areas such as Agile and DevOps practices, microservices, cloud computing, artificial intelligence, blockchain technology, and cybersecurity are explored to highlight the evolving landscape of software engineering. Understanding these trends is crucial for staying relevant and adapting to the rapid advancements in technology.

In conclusion, "Mastering Software Engineering: From Basics to Expert Proficiency" aims to provide a thorough and detailed exploration of the essential concepts, methodologies, and practices in software engineering. Whether you are a beginner seeking to build a solid foundation or an experienced engineer looking to deepen your expertise, this book offers valuable insights and practical guidance to help you excel in the field of software engineering.

Chapter 1

Introduction to Software Engineering

Software engineering is a systematic and disciplined approach to developing, operating, and maintaining software systems. This chapter covers essential aspects such as the history and evolution of software engineering, its importance in modern society, core principles guiding the discipline, distinction from other fields, the roles and responsibilities of software engineers, ethical considerations, and fundamental concepts and terminologies that lay the groundwork for understanding more advanced topics.

1.1 What is Software Engineering?

Software engineering is defined as the application of engineering principles to the development of software systems in a systematic, disciplined, and quantifiable manner. The discipline encompasses a range of activities, including requirement analysis, design, coding, testing, and maintenance, aiming to produce robust, efficient, and maintainable software products.

The process begins with **requirement analysis**, where the software engineer works closely with stakeholders to gather and document the functional and non-functional requirements of the software system. This phase is critical as it lays the groundwork for all subsequent activities by defining what the system should do and any constraints on its operation. The functional requirements specify the behavior of the system, i.e., what it should do, while non-functional requirements impose constraints on the system, such as performance metrics, usability standards, and compliance with regulations.

Next, the design phase involves the formulation of the software architecture. This includes high-level design, where the system's structure and its major components are defined, and detailed design, where each component is elaborated to a level that allows for precise implementation. The high-level design typically involves the creation of **UML diagrams** like class diagrams, sequence diagrams, and activity diagrams to represent the interactions and relationships within the system. A good design balances various architectural concerns such as **modularity, scalability, maintainability, and usability**.

The implementation phase, or coding, is where the actual software is written. Developers translate design specifications into source code using appropriate programming languages and paradigms. This requires proficiency in coding standards, version control systems, and integrated development environments (IDEs). The quality of the codebase is maintained through practices like code reviews, pair programming, and **continuous integration/continuous deployment (CI/CD)** methodologies.

Testing is an integral part of the software engineering process to verify and validate that the software functions as intended and meets the requirements specified. This phase includes **unit testing**, **integration testing**, **system testing**, and **acceptance testing**. Automated testing tools are often employed to increase the efficiency and comprehensiveness of testing efforts. Testing ensures that defects are identified and resolved early, thereby reducing the cost of fixing bugs in later stages.

Once the software has been validated and verified, it is deployed in the operational environment. Software maintenance then begins, which covers activities such as bug fixing, updates, performance tuning, and adapting the software to new platforms or integration with other systems. The maintenance phase is often the longest phase in the software life cycle, demanding rigorous change management and version control practices.

```
$ git commit -m "Fixed user authentication bug"
```

```
Output:
[main 1a2b3c4d] Fixed user authentication bug
 1 file changed, 5 insertions(+), 2 deletions(-)
```

Apart from technical activities, software engineering emphasizes the importance of documentation and rigorous project management. Documentation, which may include requirement specifications, design documents, user manuals, and maintenance guides, ensures that all stakeholders have a clear understanding of the system. Effective project management methodologies like **Agile, Scrum, and Waterfall** models guide the planning, execution, and monitoring of software projects.

One key distinction of software engineering from traditional computer programming is its focus on large-scale, team-based, and long-term projects. Software engineering projects typically involve multiple developers, require a mix of specialized skills such as project management and quality assurance, and have timelines that span months or years.

Software engineering also involves dealing with complexities related to software reliability, security, and performance. Practices such as **formal methods** for specification and verification, **design patterns**, and **software metrics** are employed to manage these complexities. For example, formal methods use mathematical techniques to specify and verify systems, providing a high level of assurance of correctness, especially in critical systems such as aerospace or medical software.

```
public class Singleton {
    private static Singleton instance;

    private Singleton() {
        // private constructor
    }

    public static Singleton getInstance() {
        if (instance == null) {
            instance = new Singleton();
        }
        return instance;
    }
}
```

```
Output:
Singleton instance created.
```

Software engineering, as a discipline, ensures that software systems are built to a high standard, addressing issues of quality, reliability, and user satisfaction. It is the cornerstone of modern software development, providing the tools, techniques, and processes necessary to build and maintain complex software systems in an efficient and effective manner.

1.2 History and Evolution of Software Engineering

The history and evolution of software engineering have fostered the development of advanced methodologies and tools that underpin modern computing. This historical progression can be traced back to the mid-20th century and characterizes several pivotal milestones and evolving paradigms that shaped the discipline.

The term *software engineering* was formally introduced in 1968 at the NATO Software Engineering Conference held in Garmisch, Germany. This conference recognized the *software crisis*—a term that reflected the widespread issues of the time, including cost overruns, missed deadlines, and unreliable software systems. The software crisis underscored the need for a more structured and scientific approach to software development, inspiring research and innovation in the burgeoning field of software engineering.

The 1950s and 1960s saw the establishment of fundamental concepts such as structured programming and modular design. During this period, software development was primarily the domain of computer scientists and mathematicians who leveraged assembly languages and early high-level languages like FORTRAN and COBOL. Programs were relatively small in scale, and individual programmers were responsible for entire projects.

As software complexity grew, it became evident that systematic methodologies were necessary to manage development more effectively. In the 1970s, the advent of the **Waterfall Model**, proposed by Winston W. Royce, provided a sequential approach to software development. The Waterfall Model, characterized by its linear phases—requirements, design, implementation, verification, and maintenance—emphasized meticulous documentation and upfront planning. Despite its structured approach, the Waterfall Model exhibited limitations, particularly in accommodating changing requirements and iterative development.

The 1980s introduced more versatile methodologies, such as the **Spiral Model** developed by Barry Boehm. The Spiral Model integrated iterative processes and risk management practices, acknowledging the evolving nature of software projects. Each iteration, or spiral, encompassed planning, risk analysis, engineering, and evaluation, thereby facilitating more adaptive and incremental development.

In the 1990s, as software applications grew in complexity and scale, the industry witnessed the emergence of **Agile methodologies**. Agile development, epitomized by the *Agile Manifesto* articulated in 2001, prioritized individuals and interactions, working software, customer collaboration, and responsiveness to change. Agile methodologies, including Scrum, Kanban, and Extreme Programming (XP), emphasized iterative development, continuous integration, and frequent delivery of functional software components. These methodologies fostered more adaptive and collaborative workflows, addressing many shortcomings of traditional linear models.

Concurrent with the rise of Agile, the field of **Object-Oriented Programming (OOP)** gained widespread adoption. Pioneered by Alan Kay and popularized by programming languages like Smalltalk, C++, and later, Java, OOP emphasized the concept of *objects*—encapsulated entities containing data and behavior. OOP facilitated modular, reusable, and scalable codebases, aligning closely with software engineering principles such as abstraction, encapsulation, inheritance, and polymorphism.

Advancements in software engineering have been further catalyzed by the proliferation of **Open Source Software (OSS)**. Initiatives like the GNU Project and communities hosted by platforms such as GitHub have democratized access to powerful software tools and libraries. Open source contributions have driven significant innovation in areas ranging from operating systems (e.g., Linux) to web development frameworks (e.g., Django, Ruby on Rails).

Technology evolution continued into the 21st century with the advent of **DevOps**, a paradigm unifying software development (Dev) and IT operations (Ops). DevOps practices emphasize continuous integration, continuous deployment (CI/CD), automation, and monitoring, aiming to enhance collaboration and accelerate software delivery cycles. Tools such as Jenkins, Docker, and Kubernetes have become vital in implementing DevOps pipelines, reinforcing infrastructure as code and microservices architectures.

Emerging fields such as **Artificial Intelligence (AI)** and **Machine Learning (ML)** have also integrated into software engineering paradigms. AI/ML systems necessitate specialized methodologies for developing, training, and deploying models, often involving data-intensive processes and iterative refinement. The integration of AI/ML further propels the demand for sophisticated engineering practices, robust infrastructure, and a nuanced understanding of ethical considerations.

To encapsulate, the historical trajectory of software engineering encapsulates a rich tapestry of evolving methodologies and technological advancements. From the recognition of the software crisis and the inaugural NATO conference to contemporary frameworks like Agile, DevOps, and AI/ML integration, software engineering continues to adapt and thrive in an ever-evolving technological landscape. The discipline's evolution underscores the importance of systematic approaches, continual learning, and innovation in crafting reliable and effective software systems.

1.3 Importance of Software Engineering

Software engineering plays a critical role in the development and maintenance of reliable, efficient, and scalable software systems. In our current technological era, software powers an immense variety of applications and systems that are central to both everyday life and numerous industries, from healthcare to finance and beyond. The importance of software engineering lies in several key areas, each of which contributes to the creation of high-quality software products that meet complex specifications and user needs.

First, software engineering provides a structured methodology for software development. This structured approach, often encapsulated in software development life cycle (SDLC) models such as Waterfall, Agile, and DevOps, ensures that all stages of software creation – from requirement gathering and system design to implementation, testing, deployment, and maintenance – are systematically executed. The structured methodologies help in managing the complexities associated with large-scale software projects, thereby reducing the risk of errors, defects, and project overruns.

Consider the following simple pseudocode that illustrates the initial phases within a Waterfall model:

```
Requirements_Gathering() {
    // Collect requirements from stakeholders
    document requirements;
    validate requirements;
}

System_Design() {
    // Create system architecture
    design system modules;
    prepare design documentation;
```

```
}

Implementation() {
    // Code the system based on design
    write code;
    integrate modules;
}

Testing() {
    // Test the system for defects and issues
    perform unit testing;
    perform system testing;
}
```

The sequential nature of the Waterfall model, as portrayed in the pseudocode above, exemplifies the importance of adhering to a defined process to ensure completeness and correctness at each phase before proceeding to the next.

Another critical aspect of software engineering's importance is ensuring software quality. Quality in software is multi-faceted, encompassing various attributes such as functionality, reliability, usability, efficiency, maintainability, and portability. Software engineering practices incorporate standard quality assurance (QA) processes, automated testing tools, review techniques, and more to ensure that the final product meets the specified quality standards. High-quality software not only satisfies user requirements but also ensures safety, security, and performance, which are particularly vital in critical systems such as medical devices and financial systems.

Effective quality assurance might involve practices such as code review and the use of automated testing frameworks, as shown in the example below:

```
Perform_Code_Review() {
    // Review code for defects
    check for coding standards adherence;
    identify potential bugs;
}

Automated_Testing() {
    // Automated test cases to validate functionality
    run unit tests;
    run integration tests;
    report test outcomes;
}
```

In the scenario above, performing code reviews and automated testing collectively ensures a higher standard of software quality before the deployment phase.

Moreover, software engineering promotes software project management and risk mitigation. Good project management practices – such as scheduling, resource allocation, cost estimation, and risk management – are integral to successful software projects. The engineer's role includes anticipating potential issues, adhering to timelines, and managing human and technical resources effectively. Methods like critical path analysis and risk assessment tools facilitate proactive management, drastically reducing the likelihood of project failures.

The importance of software engineering can also be seen in enhancing collaboration among multidisciplinary teams. Software projects often require collaboration between developers, designers, testers, business analysts, and stakeholders. Software engineering methodologies like Agile introduce mechanisms for frequent communication, continuous feedback, and iterative development. These practices help align the team's efforts with user needs and project objectives, ensuring a cohesive and collaborative working environment.

For example, a typical Agile approach might include the following routine:

```
Sprint_Planning() {
    // Plan work for the next sprint
    define sprint goals;
    select user stories;
    estimate effort;
}

Daily_Standup() {
    // Daily team sync-up
    discuss progress;
    identify roadblocks;
    adjust tasks;
}

Sprint_Review() {
    // Review sprint outcomes with stakeholders
    demonstrate completed work;
    gather feedback;
}
```

These routines underscore the proactive involvement of all team members, fostering improved communication and collaboration, ultimately leading to a successful project outcome.

Furthermore, software engineering principles drive innovation and adaptability. Engineers are constantly experimenting with new tools, languages, frameworks, and methodologies to meet the evolving demands of technology. Whether it is adopting microservices architecture for scalability or implementing machine learning algorithms for enhanced functionality, the practice of software engineering is foundational to technological advancement.

Software engineering also plays a pivotal role in maintaining systems post-deployment. Effective maintenance requires ongoing adjustments to accommodate new features, performance improvements, and bug fixes. Without systematic maintenance practices, software can become obsolete or fail to adapt to changing user requirements and technological environments. Engineering standards ensure that software remains maintainable, scalable, and robust through its lifecycle.

Overall, software engineering's structured methodologies, quality assurance techniques, project management strategies, collaborative frameworks, innovative practices, and maintenance protocols collectively underscore its profound importance in the context of modern software development.

1.4 Principles of Software Engineering

Software engineering is governed by a set of principles that guide practitioners in creating high-quality, maintainable, and robust software. These principles are derived from both theoretical frameworks and practical experience, ensuring that software projects can be executed efficiently and effectively.

The following core principles encapsulate the essence of software engineering:

- **1. Abstraction:** Abstraction involves removing or suppressing the irrelevant details to focus on the relevant aspects of a problem or a system. It enables software engineers to manage complexity by hiding the lower-level details and providing a clear structure. This principle ensures that software design and implementation remain manageable and aligned with user requirements.
- **2. Modularity:** Modularity entails dividing a software system into distinct components or modules that can be developed, tested, and maintained independently. Each module should encapsulate a single aspect of the system's functionality. This separation of concerns facilitates parallel development and simplifies debugging and maintenance efforts.
- **3. Encapsulation:** Encapsulation is the practice of bundling the data and the methods that operate on the data into a single unit or

class, restricting the access to some of the object's components. This principle enforces a clean boundary between the internal representation of data and the external interface, enhancing data security and reducing the impact of changes in one part of the software on other parts.

- **4. Information Hiding:** A direct consequence of encapsulation, information hiding, implies that only the necessary aspects of a module are visible and accessible from outside the module, while the internal workings remain hidden. This minimizes interdependencies between different parts of the software, promoting flexibility and robustness.

- **5. Separation of Concerns:** This principle dictates that a software system should be organized so that distinct concerns or functionalities are addressed by separate modules. By segregating different aspects of the system, such as user interfaces, business logic, and data management, this principle helps isolate changes and faults, simplifying development and maintenance.

- **6. Single Responsibility Principle:** The single responsibility principle asserts that a class or module should have only one reason to change, essentially meaning it should have one and only one job or responsibility. This reduces the complexity and increases the cohesion within the module, leading to cleaner, more understandable, and more maintainable code.

- **7. Open/Closed Principle:** The open/closed principle posits that software entities (such as classes, modules, functions) should be open for extension but closed for modification. This encourages developers to extend an existing system's functionality without altering its existing code, thereby reducing the risk of introducing bugs and maintaining the integrity of the system.

- **8. Dependency Inversion Principle:** According to the dependency inversion principle, high-level modules should not depend on low-level modules. Instead, both should depend on abstractions. Furthermore, abstractions should not depend on details; details should depend on abstractions. This principle promotes loose coupling and ensures that high-level policies are not affected by low-level implementation details.

- **9. Interface Segregation Principle:** The interface segregation principle asserts that no client should be forced to depend on methods it does not use. This principle encourages the design of specific and refined interfaces tailored to the needs of distinct client classes, thereby reducing the interface's overall dependency and complexity.

- **10. Continuous Integration:** Continuous integration (CI) is a practice where developers integrate code into a shared repository frequently, ideally multiple times a day. Each integration is verified by an automated build and automated tests, allowing teams to detect problems early. CI promotes a healthy codebase, reduces integration risks, and enhances overall software quality.

```
public class Example {
    private int data; // Encapsulated data

    // Encapsulated method
    public int getData() {
        return data;
    }

    // Another encapsulated method
    public void setData(int value) {
        data = value;
    }
}

interface Printable {
    void print();
}

class Report implements Printable {
    public void print() {
        // Implementation of print method
    }
}

public class Application {
    private Printable printable;

    public Application(Printable printable) {
        this.printable = printable; // Dependency Injection
    }

    public void generateReport() {
        printable.print(); // Abstraction and Dependency Inversion
    }
}
```

- **11. Version Control:** Version control systems are tools used to track changes in the codebase over time. They facilitate collaboration among team members, allow for the recovery of previous versions, and help in managing parallel development efforts. Popular tools include Git, Subversion, and Mercurial.

```
// Example Git commands
git init
git add .
git commit -m "Initial commit"
git remote add origin <repository-URL>
git push -u origin master
```

- **12. Code Review:** Code review is the systematic examination of source code by other developers. It aims to identify bugs, improve code quality, and ensure adherence to coding standards. Conducting code reviews helps in sharing knowledge among team members and enhances the overall maintainability of the codebase.

- **13. Testing:** Effective testing practices are crucial for delivering reliable software. Different types of testing, including unit testing, integration testing, system testing, and acceptance testing, are employed to verify that the software functions correctly at various levels. Automation of tests can greatly enhance efficiency and coverage.

```
import unittest

class TestExample(unittest.TestCase):
    def test_add(self):
        self.assertEqual(add(2, 3), 5)

if __name__ == '__main__':
    unittest.main()
```

- **14. Documentation:** Thorough documentation, including code comments, design documents, user manuals, and API references, is vital for understanding and maintaining software systems. Good documentation ensures that knowledge is preserved and can be efficiently transferred within and between development teams.

- **15. Maintainability:** Maintainability reflects how easily software can be modified to correct faults, improve performance, or adapt to a changed environment. It encompasses readable code, clear documentation, test coverage, and the use of conventions and standards.

- **16. Scalability:** Scalability is the ability of the software to handle growth, whether by accommodating more users, larger datasets, or more complex transactions. Software should be designed with scalability in mind to ensure it can evolve with increasing demands.

These principles collectively ensure the development of software that is robust, flexible, and maintainable, supporting the ever-evolving landscape of technological needs.

1.5 Software Engineering vs. Other Disciplines

Software engineering is distinct from other disciplines due to its focus on the systematic development, operation, and maintenance of software systems. This section will compare software engineering with related fields such as computer science, systems engineering, and information technology to highlight the unique characteristics and scope of software engineering.

Software engineering involves the application of engineering principles to software development. This encompasses a wide array of activities including requirements analysis, design, coding, testing, and maintenance. The main objective is to produce reliable, efficient, and maintainable software within the constraints of time, cost, and available resources.

Computer science, on the other hand, is more theoretical and focuses on the foundations of computation, algorithms, and programming languages. It delves deeply into mathematical principles of computation, the theory behind algorithms, and the architecture of computer systems. While a computer scientist might explore new algorithms, data structures, or computational theories, a software engineer applies these theories to solve practical problems and to build real-world software systems.

Example: Sorting Algorithms

To illustrate, a computer scientist may be interested in the theoretical efficiency of various sorting algorithms. They might analyze and compare algorithms such as quicksort, mergesort, and heapsort based on their time complexity and space complexity. In contrast, a software engineer might use this analysis to decide which sorting algorithm to implement in a particular application, considering factors such as the size of the input data, memory constraints, and the overall impact on the system's performance.

```
def quicksort(arr):
    if len(arr) <= 1:
        return arr
    pivot = arr[len(arr) // 2]
    left = [x for x in arr if x < pivot]
    middle = [x for x in arr if x == pivot]
    right = [x for x in arr if x > pivot]
    return quicksort(left) + middle + quicksort(right)

# Example usage
array = [3,6,8,10,1,2,1]
print(quicksort(array))
```

Comparatively, systems engineering is broader in scope than software engineering and focuses on the integration of various system components—hardware, software, people, processes—to form a complete, functioning system. Systems engineers tend to work on the high-level design and integration of complex systems, ensuring that all the components—mechanical, electrical, software—work together seamlessly. Software engineering, in this context, can be seen as a subset of systems engineering, specifically addressing the software components of a larger system.

Example: Autonomous Vehicles

Consider the development of autonomous vehicles. A systems engineer would be responsible for designing the overall architecture of the vehicle, integrating sensors, control systems, and software algorithms to ensure the vehicle's safe and efficient operation. A software engineer, working within this broader context, would focus on the development of the software responsible for path planning, obstacle avoidance, and vehicle control.

Information Technology (IT) encompasses a wide range of activities related to the use and management of computing technology within organizations. IT professionals manage infrastructure such as networks, servers, databases, and enterprise applications. Software engineering differs from IT in that it specifically addresses the creation and maintenance of software products. While IT professionals might deploy and manage software systems, software engineers are involved in the actual design and development of these systems.

Example: Enterprise Resource Planning (ERP) Systems

In the context of ERP systems, an IT professional might be responsible for the installation, configuration, and maintenance of the ERP software across the organization. They ensure that the software is running smoothly, that data is backed up, and that users have access to the functionalities they need. A software engineer, however, would be responsible for the development of ERP modules, working on code to implement functionalities such as inventory management, human resources, and financial accounting.

To further clarify the distinctions, we can visually represent the relationship between these disciplines using the following Venn diagram:

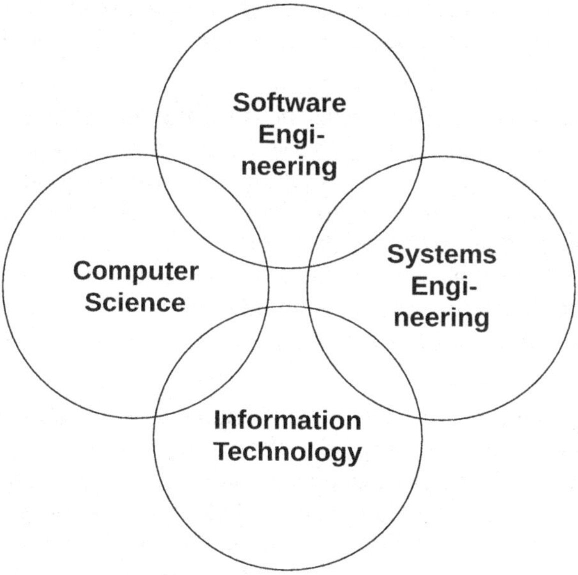

From this comparison, it is evident that while software engineering shares common ground with other disciplines, it maintains a unique focus on the practical aspects of developing and maintaining software systems. Understanding these distinctions is crucial for anyone involved in the field, ensuring clarity of roles, responsibilities, and professional expectations.

1.6 Roles and Responsibilities of a Software Engineer

Software engineers play a multifaceted role in the development and maintenance of software systems. Their responsibilities encompass a diverse range of tasks, all of which are vital for the successful delivery of reliable, efficient, and high-quality software. Understanding these roles and responsibilities is crucial to appreciating the complexity and significance of the work performed by software engineers.

Initially, software engineers are involved in the gathering and analysis of requirements. This stage necessitates close collaboration with stakeholders, including clients, end-users, and business analysts to ascertain the desired functionalities and constraints of the software system. Precision in capturing these requirements is critical, as any misinterpretations or omissions can lead to significant issues later in the development cycle.

Once the requirements are clear and documented, software engineers engage in the design phase. This is where they utilize their technical expertise to architect software solutions that are both efficient and scalable. The design phase often includes the creation of various models and diagrams, such as UML diagrams, which illustrate the system's components and their interactions. These artifacts serve not only as blueprints for development but also as communication tools to ensure all team members have a consistent understanding of the system architecture.

Following the design phase, software engineers transition to implementation, which involves coding the software according to the specified design. This task requires proficiency in multiple programming languages and frameworks, detailed knowledge of algorithms and data structures, and the ability to write clean, maintainable code. Engineers must also adhere to best practices such as version control, code reviews, and unit testing to ensure code quality and facilitate collaboration within the development team. Below is an example of a simple class implementation in Python:

```python
class ExampleClass:
    def __init__(self, value):
        self.value = value

    def increment(self):
        self.value += 1

    def get_value(self):
        return self.value
```

Throughout the implementation phase, software engineers continuously integrate and test their code. Integration testing ensures that individual modules function correctly when combined, while unit testing verifies that each module behaves as expected in isolation. Below is an example of unit tests for the above class using the unittest framework in Python:

```
import unittest
from example import ExampleClass

class TestExampleClass(unittest.TestCase):
    def test_increment(self):
        instance = ExampleClass(0)
        instance.increment()
        self.assertEqual(instance.get_value(), 1)

    def test_initial_value(self):
        instance = ExampleClass(10)
        self.assertEqual(instance.get_value(), 10)

if __name__ == '__main__':
    unittest.main()
```

Upon coding completion, the software must undergo rigorous testing to identify and rectify defects. This includes not only functional testing to ensure the software meets its requirements but also non-functional testing that evaluates aspects such as performance, security, and usability. Software engineers might employ automated testing tools and continuous integration systems to streamline this process:

```
$ pytest test_example.py
================================ test session starts =================================
platform linux -- Python 3.8.5, pytest-6.2.4, py-1.10.0, pluggy-0.13.1
collected 2 items

test_example.py ..                                   [100%]

================================= 2 passed in 0.01s ==================================
```

In addition to technical responsibilities, software engineers are often involved in the deployment and maintenance of software systems. This includes configuring environments for deployment, monitoring system performance, and ensuring the software remains functional and up-to-date post-release. Engineers may use tools such as Docker for containerization and Jenkins for continuous deployment to maintain software reliability and scalability.

Furthermore, software engineers play a crucial role in project management. They contribute to the planning, estimation, and scheduling of tasks to ensure timely delivery of software products. Their technical insight is invaluable for making informed decisions about project scope, risk management, and resource allocation. Effective communication and teamwork are paramount, as software projects typically involve cross-disciplinary collaboration.

Finally, software engineers must remain committed to continuous learning and professional development. The rapid pace of technological advancement mandates that engineers keep abreast of new programming languages, frameworks, tools, and industry best practices. Participation in conferences, professional organizations, and ongoing education enables software engineers to enhance their skills and stay competitive in the field. Additionally, they often mentor junior engineers, fostering the next generation of talent in the software engineering discipline.

Overall, the roles and responsibilities of a software engineer are diverse and demanding, requiring a balance of technical skill, analytical thinking, and interpersonal abilities. Understanding these facets is fundamental to appreciating the vital contributions of software engineers to the ever-evolving landscape of software development.

1.7 Ethics in Software Engineering

The field of software engineering is not only about technical prowess but also about adhering to ethical principles that guide the behavior and decision-making processes of professionals. Understanding these principles is crucial for developing software that is reliable, secure, and beneficial to society. Ethical considerations in software engineering encompass various aspects including privacy, security, intellectual property, and professional conduct.

Privacy is paramount in a world where data is continuously being generated and processed. Software engineers often handle sensitive information such as personal identification details, financial records, and health data. It is their responsibility to ensure that this data is collected, stored, and processed in a manner that respects privacy. Implementing strong encryption methods, ensuring data anonymization, and adhering to data protection regulations such as the General Data Protection Regulation (GDPR) are necessary practices. For instance, consider the following pseudocode for encrypting user data:

```
from cryptography.fernet import Fernet

# Generate a key for encryption
key = Fernet.generate_key()
cipher_suite = Fernet(key)

# Example user data
user_data = "User's sensitive information"

# Encrypting the user data
encrypted_data = cipher_suite.encrypt(user_data.encode())

print(encrypted_data)
```

When executed, this code produces encrypted output, safeguarding the user's sensitive information:

b'gAAAAABf2Vz6vW8GQ894vV8ohdQxV2gvgz2-4JkUBMDnzMys4IbjUy5y5YSpVAzTlKnFEOAKAOgZVpfVER1yeIWkgdfHt5lPG==

Security considerations are closely linked to privacy. Security breaches can lead to significant harm, including financial loss and compromised personal safety. Software engineers must be vigilant about potential vulnerabilities in their systems and should adopt best practices in software development such as regular security audits, code reviews, and testing for vulnerabilities. One common approach to testing for vulnerabilities is using automated security testing tools like OWASP ZAP or Burp Suite.

Intellectual property (IP) ethics involve the rightful ownership and proper use of software and digital content. Engineers must respect the IP rights of others by not engaging in software piracy, plagiarism, or unauthorized duplication of code. Understanding and complying with software licenses, whether they are open-source or proprietary, is essential. For example, the GNU General Public License (GPL) mandates that derivative works must also be open-source and under the same license.

Professional conduct in software engineering means adhering to a set of ethical standards and practices that govern how engineers interact with colleagues, clients, and the public. Professional bodies such as the Association for Computing Machinery (ACM) and the Institute of Electrical and Electronics Engineers (IEEE) have established codes of ethics that professionals are encouraged to follow. These codes emphasize principles like honesty, integrity, and respect for the public interest.

One of the notable ethical codes is the ACM Code of Ethics and Professional Conduct, which consists of several essential principles including:

- **Contributing to society and human well-being:** Software engineers should advance the societal good by ensuring the software they create improves the quality of life.
- **Avoiding harm:** Engineers should mitigate risks and avoid unjustified harm, ensuring that software is safe to use and free from defects.
- **Being honest and trustworthy:** Integrity and transparency in communication and actions are vital. Engineers should be clear about the limitations and potential risks of their software.

- **Respecting privacy:** The privacy of stakeholders and users must be respected, especially regarding data protection and usage.
- **Continuous improvement:** Engineers should commit to lifelong learning and skill advancement to maintain proficiency and adapt to new challenges.

The application of these principles often requires engineers to make difficult decisions. For example, a software engineer may encounter a situation where the client requests the implementation of a feature that may compromise user privacy. In such cases, it is the ethical duty of the engineer to inform the client about the potential risks and suggest alternative approaches, if feasible.

Ethical dilemmas in software engineering can be complex, with no clear right or wrong answers. Engineers must weigh the consequences of their actions, considering both immediate and long-term impacts on all stakeholders. Ethical training and a strong organizational culture that promotes ethical behavior are critical in navigating these challenges.

Ethics in software engineering is an integral part of the profession, guiding engineers to make decisions that respect privacy, ensure security, honor intellectual property, and embody professional conduct. By adhering to these principles, engineers contribute positively to society and uphold the trust placed in them by users, clients, and colleagues.

1.8 Fundamental Concepts and Terminologies

In software engineering, a solid grasp of fundamental concepts and associated terminologies is imperative. This section delves into the pivotal concepts and terms that lay the groundwork for deeper understanding and proficiency in software engineering practices. The discussion spans various dimensions including software development methodologies, design principles, and key paradigms, making it a comprehensive resource for both novice and experienced practitioners.

The term **software engineering** refers to the application of engineering principles to the development of software. Positioned at the intersection of computer science and engineering, it encompasses a systematic, disciplined, and quantifiable approach to the creation, operation, and maintenance of software.

Software Development Life Cycle (SDLC) is a crucial concept that represents the phases through which software progresses from inception to deployment and maintenance. The primary stages in the SDLC include:

- **Requirement Analysis**: This phase involves gathering and analyzing the requirements from stakeholders to ensure the project's objectives are clearly understood and achievable. Functional and non-functional requirements are documented in detail.
- **Design**: In this stage, architects and designers create the system architecture and design elements that encapsulate the functional requirements. It includes both high-level design (HLD) and low-level design (LLD).
- **Implementation (Coding)**: Here, the design is translated into source code using appropriate programming languages and tools.
- **Testing**: This phase involves verifying that the software meets the specified requirements by identifying and fixing defects. It includes unit testing, integration testing, system testing, and user acceptance testing (UAT).
- **Deployment**: The software is deployed to the production environment where it will be used by the end users.
- **Maintenance**: Post-deployment, the software undergoes maintenance to correct issues, improve performance, or adapt to changes in the requirements.

Agile Methodology represents a group of software development methodologies based on iterative development, wherein requirements and solutions evolve through collaboration between self-organizing cross-functional teams. Key practices in Agile include:

- **Scrum**: A framework within Agile that uses fixed-length iterations called sprints, typically two weeks long, to deliver increments of potentially shippable product.

- **Kanban**: A visual process management method that shows what to produce, when to produce it, and how much to produce. It emphasizes continuous delivery without overburdening the team.

Waterfall Model is a traditional software development methodology characterized by a linear and sequential design approach. Each phase must be completed before moving to the next, with little interaction between them. This approach is often contrasted with iterative methodologies like Agile.

Object-Oriented Design (OOD) focuses on designing software by defining data as objects with associated behaviors. Core concepts include:

- **Class and Object**: A class is a blueprint for creating objects (instances of the class). An object is an instance that contains data and methods to manipulate this data.
- **Inheritance**: This principle allows a new class to inherit properties and behaviors from an existing class, promoting code reuse.
- **Encapsulation**: Bundling the data (attributes) and methods (functions) that operate on the data into a single unit or class. This restricts direct access to some of the object's components.
- **Polymorphism**: The ability of different classes to respond to the same message (method call) in different ways. It enables one interface to be used for a general class of actions.
- **Abstraction**: Simplifying complex systems by modeling classes appropriate to the problem, and working at the most relevant level of inheritance for a particular aspect of the problem.

Design Patterns are standard solutions to common problems in software design. They represent best practices that can be used to solve recurring problems. Important design patterns include:

- **Singleton**: Ensures a class has only one instance and provides a global point of access to it.
- **Factory Method**: Defines an interface for creating an object but lets subclasses alter the type of objects that will be created.

- **Observer**: A behavioral design pattern where an object maintains a list of dependents (observers) and notifies them of any state changes, usually by calling one of their methods.
- **Decorator**: A structural pattern that allows behavior to be added to an individual object, dynamically, without affecting the behavior of other objects from the same class.

Version Control Systems (VCS), such as Git, play a critical role in collaborative software development. They facilitate tracking changes to the source code over time, enabling multiple developers to work concurrently without conflict. Key terminologies include:

- **Repository (Repo)**: A database storing all versions of files in a project.
- **Commit**: A snapshot of changes made to the files in the repo.
- **Branch**: A parallel version of the repository, allowing for feature development or bug fixing without affecting the main codebase.
- **Merge**: The process of integrating changes from one branch into another.
- **Pull Request**: A method of submitting contributions to a project. It includes a request for maintainers to review and merge the changes.

Integrated Development Environment (IDE) is a robust software application offering comprehensive facilities to programmers for software development. Examples include Visual Studio, IntelliJ IDEA, and Eclipse. IDEs typically consist of:

- **Code Editor**: Supports syntax highlighting, autocompletion, and code formatting.
- **Debugger**: Facilitates bug detection and resolution.
- **Compiler/Interpreter**: Translates and executes code.
- **Build Automation Tools**: Automates the process of software compilation and packaging.

In software engineering, testing is indispensable, with various levels and types ensuring thorough evaluation of the software:

- **Unit Testing**: Verifying the functionality of individual components or units of code. Tools like JUnit (for Java) are often used.

```
@Test
public void testAdd() {
  assertEquals(5, calculator.add(2, 3));
}
```

- **Integration Testing**: Combining individual units and testing them as a group.
- **System Testing**: Evaluating the complete system as a whole.
- **Acceptance Testing**: Validating the end-to-end business flow.

Overall, mastering these fundamental concepts and terminologies is crucial for any software engineering professional. A strong foundation will facilitate understanding of more advanced topics, leading to the efficient and effective development of robust software systems.

Chapter 2

Software Development Life Cycle (SDLC)

The software development life cycle (SDLC) provides a structured framework for the systematic development of software systems, encompassing various phases such as requirements gathering, system design, implementation, testing, deployment, and maintenance. This chapter explores each phase in detail, introduces different SDLC models like Waterfall and Agile, and examines their respective advantages and disadvantages. Additionally, it discusses the tools and techniques that support the SDLC, underscoring the importance of each step in delivering high-quality software.

2.1 Overview of the Software Development Life Cycle

The Software Development Life Cycle (SDLC) is a well-defined, structured sequence of stages in software engineering to develop intended software applications. The SDLC framework ensures that the software product meets the specified requirements while optimizing resources and performance. The key stages involved are requirements gathering, system design, implementation, testing, deployment, and maintenance.

The initial phase, requirements gathering, focuses on understanding the needs and objectives of the stakeholders. During this stage, detailed discussions are conducted to elicit, analyze, and document the required functionalities and constraints. This phase establishes a clear understanding of what the software application should achieve and serves as the foundation for subsequent stages.

System design is the next critical phase. Here, the documented requirements from the prior stage are translated into a blueprint for building the software. This involves creating architectural diagrams, data flow diagrams, and defining the overall system architecture. The design phase also includes selecting technologies, specifying hardware and software resources, and establishing the overall system structure and interfaces.

The implementation phase, also known as coding or development, converts the design into an executable form. Software developers write code using programming languages based on the design documents. This phase is characterized by the application of coding standards, code reviews, and version control mechanisms. The development team ensures that the code is modular, reusable, and adheres to the predefined specifications.

Testing and integration immediately follow implementation. This phase is crucial to ensure the correctness, completeness, and quality of the developed software. Various testing methodologies, such as unit testing, integration testing, system testing, and acceptance testing, are employed to identify and rectify defects. Testing also involves verifying that different modules work together as intended and that the software performs efficiently under various conditions.

Deployment is the process of transferring the software from a development environment to a production environment. This phase includes installation, configuration, and data migration tasks necessary to make the software operational for end users. Detailed planning and execution are pivotal to ensure a smooth transition and to minimize downtime.

Operations and maintenance is an ongoing phase that commences after the software is deployed. This involves monitoring the software for any issues, providing user support, and making necessary updates to keep the software up-to-date and running smoothly. Corrective, adaptive, and perfective maintenance tasks are performed to fix bugs, adapt to new environments, and enhance functionality respectively.

In the context of evolving industry practices, various SDLC models have emerged, such as Waterfall, Agile, Spiral, and more. These models have specific characteristics and are chosen based on project requirements, complexity, and stakeholder needs. For instance, the Waterfall model follows a linear and sequential approach, whereas the Agile model emphasizes iterative development and customer collaboration.

The advantages and disadvantages of each model vary, influencing their suitability for different types of projects. For example, the Waterfall model is straightforward and easy to manage but lacks flexibility, while Agile is highly adaptive but requires a significant level of expertise and coordination among teams.

To assist in the efficient execution of SDLC, numerous tools and techniques are employed. These range from requirement analysis tools, design modeling tools, integrated development environments (IDEs), version control systems, testing frameworks, to deployment automation tools. Each tool plays a vital role in streamlining tasks and enhancing productivity throughout the software development life cycle.

A thorough understanding of the SDLC and proper implementation of its stages is indispensable for the success of software projects. The structured approach provided by SDLC ensures that the developed software is robust, scalable, and meets the predefined requirements, resulting in high-quality deliverables and satisfied stakeholders.

2.2 Requirements Gathering and Analysis

Requirements gathering and analysis is the initial and arguably one of the most critical phases in the Software Development Life Cycle (SDLC). This phase aims to articulate the user's needs and ensure a clear understanding of what the software system should accomplish. Successful requirements gathering and analysis create a solid foundation for subsequent phases like design, implementation, and testing.

The requirements phase can be broadly divided into two key activities: requirements elicitation and requirements analysis. Each of these activities involves a systematic approach to capturing and refining user needs.

Requirements Elicitation

Requirements elicitation is the process of identifying and documenting what users require from the software system. Various techniques are employed to gather requirements, ensuring that the collected information is comprehensive and accurate. These techniques include:

- **Interviews**: Conducting structured or unstructured interviews with stakeholders to gather detailed insights into their needs and expectations.
- **Surveys and Questionnaires**: Distributing surveys with specific questions to a broader audience to obtain a diverse set of requirements.
- **Workshops**: Facilitating workshops where stakeholders collaborate to identify requirements and prioritize them.
- **Observation**: Observing users as they interact with existing systems or processes to identify pain points and areas for improvement.
- **Document Analysis**: Reviewing existing documentation such as business process documents, user manuals, and regulations to extract pertinent requirements.
- **Use Cases and Scenarios**: Developing use cases and scenarios that illustrate how users will interact with the system and what outcomes they expect.

Regardless of the technique used, effective communication with stakeholders is paramount. Miscommunication or ambiguous requirements can lead to costly errors down the line.

Requirements Analysis

Once the requirements have been gathered, the next step is to analyze and refine them. This involves several key activities:

- **Classification**: Categorizing requirements into functional and non-functional. Functional requirements define specific behavior or functions of the system, while non-functional requirements specify operational constraints such as performance, usability, and reliability.
- **Prioritization**: Assigning a priority level to each requirement based on its importance and urgency. Prioritization helps in focusing on critical requirements during the design and implementation phases.
- **Conflict Resolution**: Identifying and resolving conflicts among requirements. Conflicts can arise when different stakeholders

have competing needs or when technical constraints limit certain functionalities.

- **Feasibility Study**: Assessing the feasibility of each requirement in terms of technical capability, cost, and time. Requirements that are deemed infeasible may need to be modified or rejected.
- **Modeling**: Creating models such as data flow diagrams (DFDs), entity-relationship diagrams (ERDs), and state-transition diagrams to visualize and understand the system's requirements more clearly.

Requirements analysis ensures that the final set of requirements is clear, consistent, and achievable. Consistency checks and validations are integral to this process.

Documenting Requirements

The final output of the requirements gathering and analysis phase is the Software Requirements Specification (SRS) document. This document serves as a formal agreement between stakeholders and developers. It typically includes:

- **Introduction**: An overview of the project, including its purpose and scope.
- **Overall Description**: A high-level description of the system, its users, and its dependencies.
- **Functional Requirements**: Detailed descriptions of the system's functionalities, often organized by use cases.
- **Non-functional Requirements**: Specifications of performance metrics, security requirements, and other operational criteria.
- **Appendices**: Additional information such as glossary, acronyms, and supporting documents.

The SRS document must be reviewed and approved by all stakeholders to ensure alignment and commitment. It serves as a guiding document for all subsequent phases of the SDLC.

Tools and Techniques

Several tools and techniques aid in requirements gathering and analysis, including:

- **Requirement Management Tools**: Software like IBM Rational DOORS, Jama Connect, and Jira help in managing, tracing, and prioritizing requirements.
- **Prototyping**: Developing preliminary versions of the system to gather feedback and refine requirements.
- **Modeling Tools**: Tools like Microsoft Visio, Lucidchart, and Enterprise Architect help in creating visual models of the system.
- **Collaboration Platforms**: Tools such as Confluence, Slack, and Microsoft Teams facilitate communication and collaboration among stakeholders.

Using the right tools and techniques can significantly improve the efficiency and accuracy of the requirements gathering and analysis process.

```
1. The system shall allow users to log in using their email and password.
2. After successful login, users shall be redirected to their dashboard.
3. The dashboard shall display the user's recent activities and notifications.
```

Output:
- Login Page
- User Dashboard with Recent Activities and Notifications

The sample requirement illustrates how requirements are typically written in natural language and then translated into specific functionalities that the system must deliver. This process ensures that both technical and non-technical stakeholders can understand and contribute to the requirements.

Effective requirements gathering and analysis form the backbone of successful software development projects. Clear, well-documented requirements reduce ambiguity, enhance communication, and increase the likelihood of delivering a system that meets user expectations.

2.3 System Design

System design is a critical phase in the software development life cycle (SDLC) that translates the requirements gathered during the requirements analysis phase into a blueprint for constructing the software system. This phase acts as a bridge between the conceptual and physical parts of software development, focusing on creating an architecture that meets both functional and non-functional requirements.

During system design, we generate both high-level and detailed designs. High-level design (HLD) involves the overall system architecture, identifying the system components, their interactions, and the data flows between them. Conversely, detailed design focuses on the implementation specifications of each component making up the overall system.

A well-executed system design phase typically comprises the following key elements:

- **Architectural Design:** This aspect involves defining the system's architecture, which breaks down the system into various modules and components. Key architectural styles include layered architecture, client-server architecture, microservices architecture, and event-driven architecture. Each style has its strengths and is suitable for specific types of applications.
- **Data Design:** This involves designing the data structures and databases that will hold the data the system processes. It includes defining data models, schemas, entity-relationship diagrams, and normalization procedures to ensure data integrity and efficiency.
- **Interface Design:** Interfaces between system components and external entities (e.g., users, other systems) must be well-defined. This involves both user interfaces (UI) and application programming interfaces (API). The emphasis here is on usability, simplicity, and clarity.
- **Component Design:** This encompasses defining the properties and behaviors of the system's individual components. It includes specifying classes, methods, interfaces, data structures, and their interactions.
- **Performance Design:** This focuses on ensuring that the system meets performance requirements related to response time, throughput, and resource utilization. Techniques such as load balancing, caching, and concurrent processing are often employed.

Example: Architectural Design

Consider a typical e-commerce application. In high-level design, the architecture might be divided into several layers: presentation, business logic, and data access.

The presentation layer is responsible for interacting with the user. This could include web pages built with HTML, CSS, and JavaScript. The business logic layer manages the core functionality of the application, such as user authentication, product management, and order processing. It may be implemented using a programming language like Java, Python, or Node.js. The data access layer handles all interactions with the database, ensuring that data is stored, retrieved, and manipulated efficiently. This layer might use SQL queries or an ORM (Object-Relational Mapping) tool.

```
public class ProductDAO {
    private Connection connection;

    public ProductDAO(Connection connection) {
        this.connection = connection;
    }

    public Product getProductById(int productId) {
        String query = "SELECT * FROM products WHERE id = ?";
        try (PreparedStatement stmt = connection.prepareStatement(query)) {
            stmt.setInt(1, productId);
            try (ResultSet rs = stmt.executeQuery()) {
                if (rs.next()) {
                    return new Product(
                        rs.getInt("id"),
                        rs.getString("name"),
                        rs.getDouble("price")
                    );
                }
            }
        } catch (SQLException e) {
            e.printStackTrace();
        }
        return null;
    }
}
```

In this code, ProductDAO is a data access object (DAO) that follows the data access layer design in our e-commerce system.

Example: Data Design

Data design can be illustrated through an entity-relationship (ER) diagram. Suppose we need to design a database for our e-commerce application. We can identify entities such as User, Product, Order, and Category. Each entity will have attributes and relationships with other entities. For instance, a User can place multiple Orders, and each Order can include multiple Products.

An ER diagram may look like this:

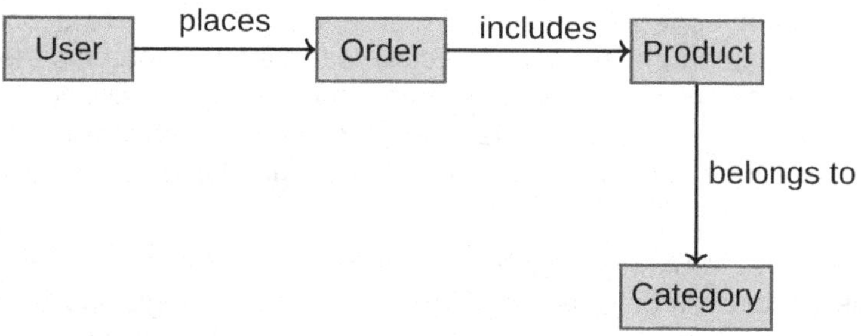

This diagram helps in visualizing the entities and their relationships, providing a clear data design framework for our database schema.

Example: Interface Design

Consider the API for managing products in our e-commerce application. The interface design involves specifying endpoints, request methods, and parameters.

An example API specification might include:

```
GET /api/products - Retrieves all products
POST /api/products - Creates a new product
GET /api/products/{id} - Retrieves a specific product
PUT /api/products/{id} - Updates a specific product
DELETE /api/products/{id} - Deletes a specific product
```

The design ensures that the API is consistent and predictable, enabling developers to efficiently interact with the system.

The system design phase also involves producing various documents and diagrams, such as class diagrams, sequence diagrams, and state diagrams, to represent different design aspects. These artifacts are vital for communicating the design to stakeholders and guiding the implementation phase effectively.

Ultimately, thorough system design lays the groundwork for a robust, maintainable, and scalable software system. Each design decision should be justified based on the project requirements, constraints, and overall objectives, ensuring the system meets its intended purpose efficiently and effectively.

2.4 Implementation and Coding

The implementation and coding phase is where the software design is translated into a functional software product. This phase involves writing the actual code for the software components that were described during the design phase. The objective is to develop source code that is operational, maintainable, and meets the project requirements and specifications. Attention to detail in this phase is critical to ensure that subsequent phases, such as testing and deployment, proceed smoothly.

Different programming languages and tools may be used depending on the software requirements. The choice of language and development environment is influenced by multiple factors, including the application's domain, performance requirements, scalability, and the development team's expertise. Commonly used programming languages include Java, Python, C++, and JavaScript, among others.

During coding, adherence to coding standards and best practices is essential to produce high-quality, maintainable code. These standards help in ensuring consistency, readability, and reducing the chances of introducing bugs. Examples of best practices include:

- Using meaningful variable names,
- Writing modular and reusable code,
- Including comments to provide context and explanations for complex sections of code.

```
class Calculator:
    def add(self, a, b):
        """Return the sum of two numbers."""
        return a + b

    def subtract(self, a, b):
        """Return the difference of two numbers."""
        return a - b

    def multiply(self, a, b):
        """Return the product of two numbers."""
        return a * b

    def divide(self, a, b):
        """Return the division of two numbers.

        Raises:
            ZeroDivisionError: If the divisor is zero.
        """
        if b == 0:
            raise ZeroDivisionError("division by zero")
        return a / b

# Example usage
calc = Calculator()
print(calc.add(10, 5))
print(calc.divide(10, 2))
```

Following coding conventions and incorporating detailed documentation is essential for facilitating code reviews and future maintenance. Automated tools and integrated development environments (IDEs) can assist in enforcing coding standards and identifying potential issues early in the development process.

Continuous integration (CI) and continuous deployment (CD) pipelines can be established to automate the testing and deployment of code. These pipelines ensure that code changes are continuously tested and deployed to a staging or production environment. This approach helps in identifying integration issues early and allows for faster delivery of features.

```
name: CI/CD Pipeline

on:
  push:
    branches:
      - main
  pull_request:
    branches:
      - main

jobs:
  build:
    runs-on: ubuntu-latest

    steps:
    - uses: actions/checkout@v2

    - name: Set up Python
      uses: actions/setup-python@v2
      with:
        python-version: '3.x'

    - name: Install Dependencies
      run: |
        python -m pip install --upgrade pip
        pip install -r requirements.txt

    - name: Test with pytest
      run: |
        pytest
```

Code management tools (e.g., Git) are crucial in this phase for version control, enabling multiple developers to collaborate on the same project without conflicts. Branching and merging strategies help in isolating code changes until they are ready to be integrated into the main codebase.

Debugging is an integral part of the coding phase. It involves identifying and fixing errors or defects in the code. Developers use various debugging tools and techniques, such as breakpoints, logging, and unit tests, to troubleshoot and resolve issues.

```
import unittest
from calculator import Calculator

class TestCalculator(unittest.TestCase):
    def setUp(self):
        self.calc = Calculator()

    def test_add(self):
        self.assertEqual(self.calc.add(1, 2), 3)

    def test_subtract(self):
        self.assertEqual(self.calc.subtract(5, 3), 2)

    def test_multiply(self):
        self.assertEqual(self.calc.multiply(3, 7), 21)

    def test_divide(self):
        self.assertEqual(self.calc.divide(10, 2), 5)
        with self.assertRaises(ZeroDivisionError):
            self.calc.divide(10, 0)

if __name__ == '__main__':
    unittest.main()
```

The importance of code reviews and peer feedback cannot be overstated. Code reviews help in identifying issues related to code quality, maintainability, and adherence to coding standards. They provide an opportunity for knowledge sharing and collective code ownership, leading to better overall software quality.

Ultimately, the implementation and coding phase is the foundation upon which the entire software product is built. Successful implementation ensures that the software meets its intended functionality, performs efficiently, and can be easily maintained and extended in the future. The practices and tools utilized during this phase have a direct impact on the quality of the final software product.

2.5 Testing and Integration

Testing and Integration are critical phases in the Software Development Life Cycle (SDLC) responsible for ensuring the reliability, functionality, and performance of the software. These phases involve systematic activities designed to identify and rectify defects before the software is deployed to the end-users. Effective testing and integration require a structured approach and the application of various techniques and tools.

Testing is an evaluative process that encompasses different levels, types, and techniques. It aims to verify and validate the software against its requirements and specifications. Testing can be broadly categorized into static and dynamic testing. Static testing involves the examination of the software products without executing the code, including code reviews, inspections, and walkthroughs. Dynamic testing involves executing the software and can be further divided into various types such as unit testing, integration testing, system testing, and acceptance testing.

Unit Testing is the first level of dynamic testing, where individual components or units of the software are tested in isolation. The primary objective of unit testing is to validate that each unit performs as expected. It is typically conducted by developers using specific unit testing frameworks. A common example using the Python ‘unittest‘ framework is as follows:

```
import unittest

def add(a, b):
    return a + b

class TestMathOperations(unittest.TestCase):
    def test_add(self):
        self.assertEqual(add(2, 3), 5)
        self.assertEqual(add(-1, 1), 0)
        self.assertEqual(add(-1, -1), -2)

if __name__ == '__main__':
    unittest.main()
```

Integration Testing follows unit testing and involves combining individual units and testing them as a group. The objective is to detect interface defects between interacting modules. Integration testing can be conducted using various approaches such as top-down, bottom-up, and sandwich (or hybrid) integration. Consider the following Java example demonstrating a simple integration test:

```
public class Service {
    private Repository repository;

    public Service(Repository repository) {
        this.repository = repository;
    }

    public String fetchData() {
        return repository.getData();
    }
}

public class Repository {
    public String getData() {
        return "data";
    }
```

```
}

// Integration Test
public class IntegrationTest {
    public static void main(String[] args) {
        Repository repository = new Repository();
        Service service = new Service(repository);
        if ("data".equals(service.fetchData())) {
            System.out.println("Integration Test Passed");
        } else {
            System.out.println("Integration Test Failed");
        }
    }
}
```

```
Integration Test Passed
```

System Testing is a high-level testing phase where the complete and integrated software is tested as a whole. The goal is to ensure that the system complies with the specified requirements. System testing includes a myriad of tests such as functionality testing, performance testing, security testing, and usability testing. This phase demands extensive test planning and execution.

Acceptance Testing, the final level, is conducted to determine whether the software is ready for release. It is typically performed by the end-users or clients to validate the end-to-end business flow. User Acceptance Testing (UAT) and Beta Testing are common forms of acceptance testing.

Integration refers to the process of combining and linking together different modules or components of a software system to function as a cohesive whole. Integration ensures that the individual components work together without issues and meet the overall system requirements.

Integration strategies are pivotal to seamless software assembly:

- **Big Bang Integration** involves integrating all components once all unit tests are complete. It is simple but can be problematic due to the difficulty in isolating errors.
- **Incremental Integration** involves integrating modules incrementally using iterative cycles. It allows for easier detection and isolation of defects.
- **Top-Down Integration** starts with the highest-level modules and progresses to lower-level modules. This approach aids in early prototype demonstration.
- **Bottom-Up Integration** begins with lower-level modules and

works upwards. It ensures thorough testing of foundational modules early on.

- **Sandwich Integration** combines both top-down and bottom-up approaches, addressing the limitations of each.

Tools play a crucial role in facilitating testing and integration activities. Popular testing tools include:

- **JUnit** for unit testing in Java.
- **Selenium** for automated web application testing.
- **Apache JMeter** for performance testing.
- **Postman** for API testing.
- **Jenkins** for Continuous Integration (CI).

Continuous Integration (CI) is an essential practice in modern software development, integrating code changes frequently and automatically testing them. CI tools build and test the software whenever code changes are committed to the repository, ensuring early detection and resolution of defects.

Challenges in testing and integration include handling complex system dependencies, ensuring comprehensive test coverage, managing dynamic system configurations, and maintaining test environments. Adopting a test automation strategy, selecting the right set of tools, and employing best practices in CI can significantly mitigate these challenges.

Effective testing and integration are indispensable for delivering high-quality software that meets user expectations. The systematic approach, combined with the use of appropriate tools and practices, ensures that the software is reliable, functional, and performant, ready to be deployed into the production environment.

2.6 Deployment

Deployment is the phase of the Software Development Life Cycle (SDLC) where the developed and tested software is moved into the production environment, making it available for end-users. This phase involves a series of steps to ensure that the software is properly configured, optimally integrated with existing systems, and functions as expected in the live environment.

Deployment Steps:

- **Planning:** Deployment requires thorough planning. This includes selecting the deployment approach (e.g., big bang vs. phased), defining the deployment environment, identifying dependencies, outlining rollback plans, and determining the timing of deployment to minimize disruption.

- **Preparation:** Preparation involves setting up the production environment. This can include provisioning hardware, configuring network settings, installing necessary software dependencies, and performing security audits to ensure a safe deployment process.

- **Data Migration:** Often, deployment requires migrating data from previous systems to the new one. This step needs careful execution to prevent data loss or corruption. Data migration scripts and tools must be tested in a staging environment before proceeding to production.

- **Application Deployment:** This involves the actual installation or update of the software application in the production environment. It includes uploading binaries, setting environment variables, configuring databases, and setting up other required services.

- **Configuration:** Application-specific configurations are applied, such as updating configuration files, initializing databases with required data, and setting up logging and monitoring tools.

- **Verification:** Post-deployment, it is crucial to verify that the application is functioning correctly. This includes performing smoke tests, checking system logs, and ensuring all services are running as expected.

- **Post-Deployment Monitoring:** Continuous monitoring post-deployment helps in identifying potential issues early. Performance monitoring, error tracking, and user feedback collection play a vital role in maintaining the application's health.

Deployment Approaches:

- **Big Bang Deployment:** The entire application is deployed in a single instance. While simple, this approach carries the risk of significant issues, as all changes are introduced at once.
- **Phased Deployment:** The application is deployed in phases. For example, starting with a limited release to a subset of users to identify and fix issues before a full-scale launch.
- **Blue-Green Deployment:** Two identical production environments, blue and green, are maintained. At any moment, only one (e.g., blue) is live, while the new version is deployed to the other (e.g., green). Once verified, traffic is switched to the green environment.
- **Canary Deployment:** A risk-averse strategy where new changes are first released to a small group of users. Monitoring this group for issues allows developers to mitigate risk before a widespread rollout.
- **Rolling Deployment:** Gradual replacement of old versions with new ones, usually initiated through an orchestrated sequence to ensure continuous availability.

Deployment Tools:

- **Configuration Management Tools:** Tools like Ansible, Puppet, and Chef automate the setup and management of deployment environments.
- **Continuous Integration/Continuous Deployment (CI/CD) Tools:** Jenkins, Travis CI, and CircleCI facilitate automatic build, test, and deployment processes.
- **Containerization Tools:** Docker and Kubernetes can encapsulate applications and their dependencies, simplifying deployment across different environments.
- **Monitoring Tools:** Systems like Nagios, Prometheus, and New Relic help in real-time monitoring and performance tracking, crucial for post-deployment analysis.

Code Example: Basic Deployment Script

```
#!/bin/bash

# Define environment variables
```

```
export APP_ENV=production
export APP_DIR=/var/www/myapp

# Update codebase from repository
cd $APP_DIR
git pull origin master

# Install dependencies
npm install

# Run database migrations
npm run migrate

# Restart application
pm2 restart myapp

echo "Deployment complete. Monitoring application..."

# Initiate monitoring
pm2 monit
```

```
Deployment complete. Monitoring application...
```

Deployment is a critical phase that requires thorough attention to detail to minimize risks and ensure a smooth transition to the production environment. Proper planning, execution, and monitoring are essential to successful deployment.

2.7 Operations and Maintenance

Operations and Maintenance (O&M) is an essential phase in the Software Development Life Cycle (SDLC). This phase commences post-deployment and extends until the software is decommissioned. Proper management of operations and maintenance ensures the software remains functional, relevant, and secure while continuing to meet user needs. This section delves into the various activities and best practices associated with O&M, emphasizing the role of continuous monitoring, updates, and user support.

Operations involve the tasks required to keep the software running seamlessly in the production environment. Key activities include monitoring the system's performance, managing server resources, and ensuring the software's availability and reliability. Utilizing automated monitoring tools helps detect anomalies or potential issues early.

Several monitoring tools are available, such as Nagios, Prometheus, and New Relic, which provide real-time insights into system health. An illustrative configuration of a monitoring server using Nagios is provided below:

```
# Install Nagios on a Debian-based system
sudo apt-get update
sudo apt-get install nagios-nrpe-server nagios-plugins

# Configure the NRPE server
sudo vi /etc/nagios/nrpe.cfg

# Add the IP address of the Nagios server
allowed_hosts=127.0.0.1,192.168.1.10

# Enable and start the NRPE service
sudo systemctl enable nagios-nrpe-server
sudo systemctl start nagios-nrpe-server

# Add services to be monitored
sudo vi /etc/nagios/nrpe_local.cfg
command[check_disk]=/usr/lib/nagios/plugins/check_disk -w 20% -c 10% -p /dev/
    sda1
command[check_load]=/usr/lib/nagios/plugins/check_load -w 15,10,5 -c 30,25,20
```

Maintenance encompasses corrective, adaptive, perfective, and preventive activities. Corrective maintenance addresses identified bugs or faults within the software. For instance, suppose a user encounters a bug where the application crashes upon submitting a form. The immediate corrective action would be to replicate the issue in the testing environment, diagnose the root cause, and implement a fix. Below is an example fix for a null pointer exception in Java:

```
// Original buggy code
public void submitForm(UserForm form) {
    if (form.isValid()) {
        database.save(form.getData());
    }
    // Bug: null pointer exception if form is null
}

// Corrected code
public void submitForm(UserForm form) {
    if (form != null && form.isValid()) {
        database.save(form.getData());
    } else {
        throw new IllegalArgumentException("Form is null or invalid");
    }
}
```

Adaptive maintenance ensures the software remains compatible with evolving environments, such as new operating system versions or hardware changes. It may involve reconfiguring dependencies or modifying code to leverage new features available in updated systems.

Perfective maintenance enhances software performance or adds new features to meet evolving user requirements. This might include refactoring code for better performance or integrating additional functionalities based on user feedback.

Preventive maintenance focuses on proactive measures to avoid future issues. This includes activities like code refactoring, documentation updates, and implementing security patches. Regular vulnerability assessments are critical, using tools like OWASP ZAP (Zed Attack Proxy) which assists in identifying and rectifying various security vulnerabilities.

Below is a sample script using OWASP ZAP to scan a web application for vulnerabilities:

```
# Python script to run OWASP ZAP scan
from zapv2 import ZAPv2

api_key = 'your_api_key'
target = 'http://example.com'
zap = ZAPv2(apikey=api_key)

# Start the spidering process
print('Spidering target %s' % target)
zap.spider.scan(target)
while int(zap.spider.status()) < 100:
    print('Spider progress %: ' + zap.spider.status())
    time.sleep(2)

# Run the active scan
print('Running active scan on target %s' % target)
zap.ascan.scan(target)
while int(zap.ascan.status()) < 100:
    print('Scan progress %: ' + zap.ascan.status())
    time.sleep(2)

# Print vulnerabilities found
print('Alerts:')
alerts = zap.core.alerts()
for alert in alerts:
    print(alert)
```

Effective O&M also relies heavily on documentation. Comprehensive documentation supports efficient problem diagnosis and resolution, aiding current and future team members. This includes maintaining detailed records of system configurations, architectural designs, user guides, and incident logs.

Communication and coordination with users are also critical elements. Efficient support processes should be in place to manage user inquiries, issues, and feature requests. Utilizing a robust ticketing system like Jira or Zendesk ensures organized and transparent tracking of issues.

Finally, continuous improvement through regular audits and reviews of O&M practices is vital. Incorporating lessons learned, feedback, and industry best practices into the O&M processes can lead to better system reliability, security, and user satisfaction.

2.8 Models of SDLC: Waterfall, Agile, Spiral, and More

Understanding various models of the Software Development Life Cycle (SDLC) is crucial to choosing an approach that best fits the project's needs. Each model employs a unique structure, workflow, and philosophy, impacting project management, team collaboration, and final software quality. This section will delve into the notable SDLC models: Waterfall, Agile, Spiral, and others, highlighting their characteristics, strengths, and limitations.

The **Waterfall Model** is one of the earliest and most straightforward SDLC approaches. It follows a linear sequential workflow, depicting software development as flowing steadily downwards through phases like a waterfall. Each phase must be completed before the next one begins. The major phases include:

- **Requirements Analysis**: This stage involves gathering and documenting all system requirements, which should be clearly understood and agreed upon by all stakeholders.
- **System Design**: Based on the requirements, the system's overall architecture and design specifications are created.
- **Implementation**: The actual development and coding of the software project occur in this phase.
- **Testing**: Once the code is developed, it undergoes rigorous testing to identify and rectify defects.
- **Deployment**: The finished product is deployed to the end-user environment.
- **Maintenance**: Post-deployment, the software is maintained and updated based on user feedback and operational issues.

The Waterfall Model's linear nature implies that it's often suitable for small projects with well-defined requirements. However, its rigidity can be a drawback; any requirement changes during the later stages can be challenging and costly to implement.

The **Agile Model** represents a significant departure from the Waterfall's structured approach, emphasizing flexibility, collaboration, and customer satisfaction through iterative development. It groups tasks into small, manageable increments known as sprints, typically lasting 2-4 weeks, allowing for frequent reassessments and adjustments. Key Agile practices include:

- **Customer Collaboration**: Continuous involvement of customers throughout the development process to ensure the project aligns with user needs.
- **Iterative Development**: Rather than delivering a complete product at the end, Agile delivers functional increments regularly.
- **Adaptability to Change**: Flexibility to accommodate changes even late in the development process.
- **Cross-Functional Teams**: Teams consisting of members with various skills collaborate closely, improving productivity and innovation.

Agile's primary advantage is its responsiveness to change and continuous delivery of value. Nevertheless, it requires high customer involvement and can sometimes lead to scope creep if not managed carefully.

The **Spiral Model** combines elements of both iterative and Waterfall models, integrating risk assessment throughout the development process. It's defined by its unique spiral structure, consisting of repeated cycles or "spirals" each consisting of four main activities:

- **Planning**: Determining objectives, alternatives, and constraints.
- **Risk Analysis**: Identifying and resolving risks through prototyping and simulations.
- **Engineering**: Actual development and testing of the software product.
- **Evaluation**: Customer evaluation of the developed software and planning for the next iteration.

By addressing risks early and revisiting plans continuously, the Spiral Model is particularly suited for large, complex, and high-risk projects.

However, it can be more costly and less straightforward to manage due to the need for extensive documentation and rigorous risk analysis.

Other Models worth noting also add value to the SDLC landscape:

- **V-Model (Verification and Validation Model)**: An extension of the Waterfall Model, emphasizing validation and verification at each development stage. Every phase includes corresponding testing activities.

- **Incremental Model**: Combines aspects of iterative and Waterfall models, breaking the project into smaller increments that are developed, tested, and delivered independently. This allows for partial implementations and quicker customer feedback.

- **Kanban**: Similar to Agile but more visual, utilizing boards to represent work stages. It emphasizes continuous delivery, workflow visualization, and WIP (Work In Progress) limits to optimize efficiency.

The choice of SDLC model has broad implications for software quality, project timeline, and team dynamics. Therefore, selecting the appropriate model involves careful consideration of project requirements, team expertise, risk factors, and stakeholder expectations. Here is an example to illustrate how a simple program can differ in the implementation across varied SDLC models. We will consider a basic program written in Python for illustrative purposes.

```
def greet_user(user_name):
    return f"Hello, {user_name}!"

if __name__ == "__main__":
    name = input("Enter your name: ")
    print(greet_user(name))
```

```
Enter your name: Alice
Hello, Alice!
```

In the Waterfall Model, changes to this program after implementation would necessitate revisiting earlier stages, while in Agile, this program would be part of a larger sprint, allowing for iterative improvement based on immediate user feedback. Different SDLC models offer distinct approaches but aim towards the unified goal of delivering high-quality software products efficiently and effectively.

2.9 Advantages and Disadvantages of Different SDLC Models

The selection of an appropriate Software Development Life Cycle (SDLC) model is critical to the success of any software project. Different models offer varying approaches to achieving the same goal: delivering high-quality software that meets user requirements within constraints like time, budget, and resources. This section evaluates the most prevalent SDLC models, focusing on their advantages and disadvantages to equip practitioners with the knowledge necessary for informed decision-making.

Waterfall Model

The Waterfall Model is one of the oldest and most well-established SDLC models. It is a linear and sequential approach where each phase must be completed before the next begins.

- **Advantages:**
  - **Simplicity and Clarity:** The model is straightforward, with well-defined stages that facilitate easy understanding and implementation.
  - **Control:** The rigid structure allows for comprehensive documentation and clear milestones, aiding in project management and progress tracking.
  - **Validation and Verification (V&V):** Given the sequential nature, each phase undergoes a review before moving to the next stage, ensuring issues are resolved early.
- **Disadvantages:**
  - **Inflexibility:** Once a phase is completed, returning to it is challenging, making it unsuitable for projects where requirements are likely to change.
  - **Late Testing:** Testing is conducted late in the development process, making early error detection difficult, often leading to higher costs of fixing defects.
  - **Assumption of Requirements:** It assumes that all requirements can be gathered at the beginning, which is rarely feasible for complex and dynamic projects.

Agile Model

The Agile Model emphasizes incremental development and iterative releases. Software is developed in small, manageable segments called iterations, each delivering a functional portion of the software.

- **Advantages:**
  - **Flexibility and Adaptability:** Agile is highly adaptive to changes, allowing requirements to evolve and be incorporated throughout the development process.
  - **Customer Collaboration:** Continuous involvement of the customer ensures that the end product aligns closely with user needs and expectations.
  - **Frequent Deliveries:** Regular iterations mean that functional software is delivered early and frequently, providing immediate value and opportunities for feedback.
- **Disadvantages:**
  - **Scope Creep:** Flexibility can lead to scope expansion due to continuous changes and additions, potentially affecting timelines and budgets.
  - **Less Predictability:** The iterative nature can make it hard to predict the final cost, time, and effort at the project's outset.
  - **Requires Skilled Teams:** Success with Agile requires experienced and well-coordinated teams adept at managing flexible development practices.

Spiral Model

The Spiral Model combines aspects of both iterative and Waterfall models. It emphasizes risk management through repeated cycles (spirals) of planning, risk analysis, engineering, and evaluation.

- **Advantages:**
  - **Risk Management:** Continuous risk assessment and mitigation are integral, making it suitable for large, complex, and high-risk projects.
  - **Iterative Development:** Incorporates iterative development, allowing for user feedback and refinements throughout the project lifecycle.

  - **Flexibility:** Can accommodate changes at various stages, including enhancements and feature modifications.

- **Disadvantages:**
  - **Complexity:** The model's complexity and dependency on risk analysis can make it challenging to manage and execute.
  - **Resource Intensive:** Typically more expensive and time-consuming due to the continuous risk evaluation and multiple iterations of development.
  - **Expertise Requirement:** Effective implementation requires skilled personnel in both risk assessment and iterative methodologies.

V-Model (Validation and Verification Model)

The V-Model is an extension of the Waterfall Model, emphasizing concurrent testing and development processes. Each development stage is associated with a corresponding testing phase.

- **Advantages:**
  - **Enhanced Testing:** Parallel development and testing help in early detection and fixing of defects, thus improving product quality.
  - **Clarity and Organization:** Like the Waterfall Model, it has clear stages and deliverables, which foster structured project management.
  - **Ensured Compliance:** Suitable for projects with stringent regulatory requirements, where documentation and compliance are critical.

- **Disadvantages:**
  - **Inflexibility:** Similar to its Waterfall roots, it is less accommodating to changes once the development has started.
  - **Dependency on Initial Requirements:** Assumes that all requirements can be gathered at the beginning, which might be impractical for some projects.
  - **High Initial Investment:** Upfront investment in comprehensive planning and design can be substantial.

Incremental Model

The Incremental Model involves developing a system through multiple increments, where each increment builds on the previous additions until the full system is implemented.

- **Advantages:**
  - **Reduced Initial Costs:** Increments can be developed and delivered early, reducing initial development costs and risks.
  - **Flexibility:** The model allows partial implementation and provides flexibility to respond to changing user requirements.
  - **Easy Testing and Debugging:** Smaller increments simplify testing and debugging processes.
- **Disadvantages:**
  - **Integration Challenges:** Integrating increments can become complicated if the architecture is not well-defined and maintained throughout the development process.
  - **Dependency Management:** Extensive dependency management is required to ensure each increment aligns correctly with the others.
  - **Incomplete Version Delivery:** Early increments may not always be full systems, potentially causing user dissatisfaction or misinterpreted progress.

RAD Model (Rapid Application Development)

The RAD Model emphasizes rapid prototyping over rigorous planning, allowing for quick development cycles and user feedback.

- **Advantages:**
  - **Speed:** RAD facilitates faster development and quick release of prototypes for user feedback.
  - **User Involvement:** Continuous user involvement ensures the final product closely aligns with user needs and reduces the risk of user rejection.
  - **Flexibility:** Prototyping and iterative improvements allow for flexible requirement changes.

- **Disadvantages:**
  - **Sustainability:** The focus on rapid development can compromise long-term maintainability and scalability of the product.
  - **Resource Intensive:** Requires significant user involvement and commitment, which may not always be feasible.
  - **Scope Limitation:** More effective for smaller projects as scaling RAD for larger projects can introduce complexity and resource constraints.

Each SDLC model exhibits distinct characteristics that render it suitable for particular types of projects and organizational environments. The careful selection, informed by these advantages and disadvantages, is crucial for optimizing project success and delivering high-quality software aligned with user expectations.

2.10 Tools and Techniques for SDLC

The successful execution of the Software Development Life Cycle (SDLC) requires the application of various tools and techniques that assist in automating processes, managing tasks, ensuring quality, and facilitating communication among team members. These tools and techniques span all phases of the SDLC, contributing significantly to efficient, consistent, and high-quality software development. Below, we categorize and describe essential tools and techniques used throughout each SDLC phase.

Requirements Gathering and Analysis: Prior to the initiation of the actual development process, it is crucial to gather and analyze requirements effectively. Tools like IBM Rational DOORS, JIRA, and Confluence play an instrumental role during this phase.

- **IBM Rational DOORS**: This tool helps in capturing, tracing, analyzing, and managing changes to requirements. Its capabilities ensure that all stakeholders have a clear understanding of what is to be built.

- **JIRA**: JIRA, although widely used for project tracking, is also employed to document and manage requirements. Integrations with other Atlassian products like Confluence allow for comprehensive requirements documentation.

- **Confluence**: A collaborative workspace, Confluence enables teams to create, share, and discuss requirements. It integrates well with JIRA, facilitating seamless transition and traceability.

System Design: During the design phase, tools that support modeling and architectural design are indispensable. Examples include Enterprise Architect, Microsoft Visio, and Lucidchart.

- **Enterprise Architect**: A comprehensive UML modeling tool, Enterprise Architect supports the creation of various system models like use case diagrams, class diagrams, and sequence diagrams. It allows for detailed architectural modeling.
- **Microsoft Visio**: This diagramming tool is used to create flowcharts, process diagrams, and other visual representations of systems. Its extensive library of stencils assists in building detailed designs.
- **Lucidchart**: An online diagramming tool that provides a collaborative platform for designing system architectures. It supports UML diagrams and integrates with various cloud services.

Implementation and Coding: In the coding phase, integrated development environments (IDEs) and version control systems (VCS) are critical. Popular tools include Visual Studio, Eclipse, Git, and GitHub.

- **Visual Studio**: This IDE supports multiple programming languages and provides features like code editing, debugging, and deployment. Extensions available in Visual Studio Marketplace further enhance its capabilities.
- **Eclipse**: A widely used open-source IDE, Eclipse caters to a variety of programming languages and provides robust support for plugins, which enhance its functionality for different development needs.
- **Git and GitHub**: Git, a distributed VCS, allows for version control and collaboration. GitHub hosts Git repositories and provides a web-based interface for code management, collaboration through pull requests, and continuous integration pipelines.

Testing and Integration: Ensuring the quality of the software is paramount, and tools designed for automated testing, continuous integration, and deployment are essential.

- **Selenium**: A framework for testing web applications, Selenium supports browser automation and can integrate with other testing tools like JUnit to create robust test suites.

```
// Import WebDriver
import org.openqa.selenium.WebDriver;
import org.openqa.selenium.chrome.ChromeDriver;

public class SeleniumTest {
    public static void main(String[] args) {
        // Initialize WebDriver
        WebDriver driver = new ChromeDriver();

        // Open webpage
        driver.get("http://www.example.com");

        // Close browser
        driver.quit();
    }
}
```

- **JUnit**: A testing framework for Java applications, JUnit enables the creation and execution of repeatable tests. It serves as a foundation for developing test-driven development (TDD) practices.

- **Jenkins**: An open-source automation server, Jenkins facilitates continuous integration and continuous deployment (CI/CD). It automates testing and deployment, ensuring quicker and more reliable software releases.

```
- Jenkins Deployment Log -
Started by user Jenkins Admin
Building in workspace /var/lib/jenkins/workspace/MyProject
[Git] Fetching changes from the remote Git repository
[Gradle] - Launching build.
[Gradle] - Executing build.
Build succeeded.
Finished: SUCCESS
```

Deployment: Effective deployment tools ensure that software is correctly delivered and configured in different environments.

- **Docker**: A containerization platform, Docker packages applications and their dependencies into containers, ensuring consistent across different environments.

- **Kubernetes**: An orchestration tool for automating the deployment, scaling, and management of containerized applications. Kubernetes works well with Docker and other container systems.

Operations and Maintenance: Tools for monitoring, logging, and incident management are vital during the operations and maintenance phase.

- **Prometheus**: A monitoring system and time series database that collects metrics from various sources. Combined with Grafana, it provides powerful visualization and alerting capabilities.
- **Splunk**: A platform for searching, monitoring, and analyzing machine-generated data. Splunk helps in log analysis, security monitoring, and operational efficiency.

Communication and Collaboration: Throughout the SDLC, seamless communication and collaboration among team members are facilitated by various tools.

- **Slack**: A messaging platform that provides channels for different projects and topics, enabling real-time communication. Integrations with various tools like JIRA and GitHub enhance collaboration.
- **Microsoft Teams**: Another robust collaboration tool that offers chat, video conferencing, and file sharing. Integration with Office 365 tools helps in streamlined document management and collaboration.

Effective utilization of these tools and techniques across the various phases of the SDLC ensures that development processes are efficient, streamlined, and capable of producing high-quality software products. These tools not only facilitate individual phases but also promote an integrated approach that aligns with the overarching goals of software engineering.

Chapter 3

Requirements Engineering

Requirements engineering is the process of defining, documenting, and maintaining the requirements for software systems. This chapter covers the different types of requirements, including functional and non-functional, and introduces techniques for eliciting, analyzing, and negotiating requirements with stakeholders. It also addresses the importance of proper documentation, validation, verification, and managing changes to requirements, as well as requirements traceability. The chapter concludes with the use of tools and real-life case studies to illustrate practical application.

3.1 Introduction to Requirements Engineering

Requirements engineering is a critical phase in the software development lifecycle that encompasses various systematic steps and methodologies aimed at understanding, documenting, and maintaining the needs and expectations of stakeholders for a software system. It is both a technical and socio-economic domain, engaging software engineers, product managers, end-users, and other stakeholders. The importance of requirements engineering stems from its potential to significantly influence the quality, cost, and duration of the software development process.

The primary objective of requirements engineering is to ensure that the software being developed aligns with the intended purpose and is feasible within the given constraints. This process is iterative and encompasses several key activities:

- **Elicitation**: Gathering requirements from stakeholders through various techniques such as interviews, questionnaires, observations, and facilitated workshops.
- **Analysis**: Processing and interpreting the gathered requirements to identify conflicts, ambiguities, and redundancies, ensuring that they are well-understood and agreed upon by all stakeholders.
- **Documentation**: Precisely writing down the requirements in a structured format to serve as a reference point for both development and validation teams.
- **Validation and Verification**: Confirming that the documented requirements accurately capture the stakeholder needs and are unambiguous, consistent, and complete.
- **Management**: Handling changes to requirements over time, ensuring traceability, and maintaining an organized repository of requirements.

Requirement Elicitation: The process begins with elicitation, a crucial step that involves engaging with stakeholders to uncover their needs, wishes, and constraints. Elicitation techniques include:

- **Interviews**: Conducting structured, semi-structured, or unstructured interviews with stakeholders to understand their expectations and requirements.
- **Questionnaires and Surveys**: Using written sets of questions to gather information from a large group of stakeholders, particularly useful for distributed teams.
- **Observation**: Studying stakeholders' interactions with existing systems to identify pain points and areas for improvement.
- **Workshops**: Facilitated sessions designed to foster collaboration among stakeholders to collectively generate and refine requirements.

- **Document Analysis**: Reviewing existing documentation such as business plans and technical specifications to derive requirements.

Requirement Analysis and Negotiation: After elicitation, the collected requirements are analyzed to detect inconsistencies, ambiguities, and conflicts. This activity involves evaluating the feasibility of the requirements in terms of technical and business constraints. Techniques used in this phase include:

- **Prioritization**: Ranking requirements based on their importance, urgency, and impact on the overall system.
- **Modeling**: Creating abstract representations of the requirements using models such as use cases, data flow diagrams, and entity-relationship diagrams.
- **Prototyping**: Building preliminary versions of the system to help stakeholders visualize and validate their requirements.

Negotiation is often required to reconcile conflicting requirements and ensure that all stakeholders have a shared understanding of the requirements. This may involve trade-offs, compromises, and setting realistic expectations.

Requirement Documentation: Documenting requirements is critical for maintaining a clear and comprehensive reference throughout the software development process. Common formats for requirement documentation include:

- **Natural Language Specifications**: Detailed descriptions of requirements written in plain language.
- **Models and Diagrams**: Visual representations such as UML diagrams, which provide a structured view of the system requirements.
- **User Stories**: Short descriptions of a feature from the perspective of an end-user.

Requirement Validation and Verification: This phase ensures that the documented requirements accurately represent the stakeholders' needs and that they are feasible. Validation techniques include reviews, inspections, and walkthroughs, while verification ensures that the requirements are correctly implemented through testing activities.

Managing Requirements: Effective management practices are vital to accommodate changes in requirements as the project evolves. Change management processes and tools provide mechanisms to track modifications, ensuring that any changes are controlled and communicated to all stakeholders. Proper traceability practices link requirements to their origins and track their status throughout the development lifecycle.

These activities form the backbone of requirements engineering, ensuring that software products are developed in alignment with stakeholder needs and project constraints. Through rigorous and systematic approaches, requirements engineering strives to minimize ambiguities, reducing the risk of costly errors and rework further down the development pipeline.

3.2 Types of Requirements: Functional and Non-Functional

Understanding the different types of requirements is crucial in ensuring that a software system meets the needs of its users and stakeholders. Requirements are generally categorized into functional and non-functional requirements, each serving distinct purposes.

Functional requirements describe the specific behavior or functions of a system—what the system should do. These requirements are typically written from the perspective of the user, focusing on the tasks the software must be able to perform. They are characterized by defining input to be provided to the system, its operations, and the expected outcome. Functional requirements are crucial for determining the functionality of the system and guiding the development process.

Examples of functional requirements include:

- User authentication
- Data entry and retrieval
- Generation of reports
- Performing calculations

- Handling user interactions

Consider the following example of a functional requirement specification for a user authentication system:

```
1.1.1 User Authentication
   a. The system shall allow users to log in using a username and password.
   b. The system shall verify the username and password against stored credentials.
   c. The system shall lock the user account after five unsuccessful login attempts.
   d. The system shall allow users to request a password reset via email.
```

Non-functional requirements, on the other hand, specify criteria that judge the operation of a system, rather than specific behaviors. These requirements often refer to the quality attributes of the system, including performance, usability, reliability, and security. Non-functional requirements ensure that the user experience and operational environment are adequately addressed.

Examples of non-functional requirements include:

- Performance such as response time, throughput, and scalability
- Usability including user interface design and ease of use
- Reliability encompassing availability, error rates, and mean time to failure
- Security encompassing data protection, user privacy, and threat prevention

Here is an example of non-functional requirements for the same user authentication system:

```
1.2.1 Performance
   a. The system shall respond to login requests within 2 seconds under normal load
        conditions.
   b. The system shall support a minimum of 100 concurrent users without
        performance degradation.

1.2.2 Security
   a. The system shall encrypt user passwords using a secure hashing algorithm.
   b. The system shall log all unsuccessful login attempts and notify the security team
        of potential breaches.
```

Functional and non-functional requirements form the backbone of requirements engineering. They complement each other by ensuring not only that the system performs the desired tasks but also that it meets certain standards of quality. It is essential for these requirements to be diligently gathered, analyzed, and specified to build a software system that is both functional and efficient.

Addressing non-functional requirements poses unique challenges due to their qualitative nature. For instance, while a functional requirement can be verified through direct testing—such as confirming a user can log in—non-functional requirements often require empirical analysis and extensive testing under various conditions. Effective ways to validate non-functional requirements include performance testing, usability testing, security assessments, and reliability testing.

Tools such as requirement management systems often categorize and trace both functional and non-functional requirements, providing facilities to visualize, verify, and validate them throughout the project lifecycle. This ensures that every requirement is accounted for and that their interdependencies are properly managed. Proper classification and documentation of both types of requirements are pivotal in navigating the complexity of software development, ultimately contributing to the success of the project.

3.3 Requirement Elicitation Techniques

Requirement elicitation is a critical phase in the requirements engineering process, aiming to gather detailed and precise requirements from stakeholders. This phase ensures that the development team has a comprehensive understanding of what the stakeholders need and expect from the software system. Various techniques can be applied to elicit requirements, each with its strengths and weaknesses. Employing a combination of techniques can often yield the best results. Below, we discuss several prevalent requirement elicitation techniques:

- **Interviews:** Conducting interviews is one of the most common methods to gather requirements. Interviews can be structured (with a predefined set of questions), semi-structured (with some prepared questions and room for discussion), or unstructured (more like a free-form conversation). The goal is to encourage stakeholders to share their needs, constraints, and expectations. A structured interview provides consistency across multiple stakeholders, while an unstructured interview can reveal unexpected insights.
- **Surveys and Questionnaires:** These tools are effective for collecting information from a large group of stakeholders within a short period. Surveys and questionnaires typically consist of

open-ended questions, closed-ended questions, or a mixture of both. Open-ended questions allow stakeholders to express their thoughts in detail, while closed-ended questions can be used for quantitative analysis.

- **Workshops:** Requirement workshops involve bringing together various stakeholders to collaboratively discuss and define requirements. Facilitated workshops can foster a shared understanding among stakeholders and help resolve conflicts or ambiguities in requirements. Techniques such as brainstorming and nominal group technique (NGT) can be used within workshops to encourage participation and idea generation.

- **Focus Groups:** Similar to workshops, focus groups involve discussions with a selected group of stakeholders. Unlike workshops, focus groups usually concentrate on specific topics or issues. This technique is particularly useful for exploring stakeholders' attitudes, perceptions, and needs in-depth.

- **Ethnographic Studies:** This technique involves observing stakeholders in their natural work environment to understand how they interact with existing systems and processes. By immersing themselves in the stakeholders' context, analysts can uncover implicit requirements that may not surface during interviews or surveys.

- **Prototyping:** Prototyping involves creating an early version of the system, which can be a throwaway prototype, evolutionary prototype, or incremental prototype. Stakeholders can interact with the prototype, providing feedback that helps refine and validate requirements. Prototyping is particularly useful for uncovering usability requirements and verifying the feasibility of specific features.

- **Document Analysis:** Reviewing existing documentation, such as business process descriptions, regulations, and previous project materials, can provide valuable insights into the requirements. Document analysis helps identify constraints, standards, and historical context that are critical for the new system.

- **Interface Analysis:** This technique focuses on understanding and defining the interactions between the system being developed and external systems, users, devices, or other interfaces.

By analyzing these interactions, requirements engineers can identify dependencies, integration needs, and data exchange requirements.

- **JAD (Joint Application Development) Sessions:** JAD sessions involve intensive collaborative meetings where stakeholders and developers come together to rapidly gather and refine requirements. The sessions are highly structured and facilitated, aiming for a consensus on requirements through real-time discussion and decision-making.
- **Use Case Modeling:** This technique involves creating use cases that describe how users will interact with the system to achieve specific goals. Use cases capture both functional and non-functional requirements and help identify user roles, system boundaries, and interactions.

When selecting elicitation techniques, it is crucial to consider factors such as the project scope, stakeholder availability, and the type of information needed. Combining different techniques can mitigate the limitations of individual methods and provide a comprehensive understanding of the requirements. The choice of techniques should align with the project's context and the stakeholders' preferences to ensure effective and efficient elicitation.

A balanced and systematic application of these elicitation techniques can lead to a robust set of requirements that accurately reflect stakeholder needs, paving the way for successful system development.

3.4 Requirement Analysis and Negotiation

Requirement analysis and negotiation is a pivotal phase in the requirements engineering process. During this phase, the gathered requirements are carefully examined for consistency, completeness, feasibility, and clarity. Additionally, any conflicts among stakeholders' requirements are resolved to form a consolidated set of requirements. This section provides a comprehensive exploration of the techniques and methodologies employed in requirement analysis and negotiation, emphasizing the critical aspects that contribute to the development of robust software systems.

Requirement analysis involves various activities including classification, organization, prioritization, and formal modeling. Initial analysis starts by categorizing the requirements based on their types, such as functional or non-functional requirements, supplementary constraints, domain requirements, and so on. It is essential to distinguish between these different types to apply the appropriate analysis techniques to each category.

Requirement classification often utilizes taxonomies to systematically account for all requirement types and subtypes. For instance, functional requirements can be subdivided into data-related, control, and domain-specific functionality, while non-functional requirements might be categorized into performance, security, usability, and reliability requirements. This classification aids in the comprehensive analysis of requirements.

```
# Sample script for basic requirement analysis
requires = {
    "functional": ["authentication", "data storage", "report generation"],
    "non-functional": ["response time", "scalability", "usability"]
}

for category, reqs in requires.items():
    print(f"Category: {category}")
    for req in reqs:
        print(f" - {req}")
```

```
Category: functional
 - authentication
 - data storage
 - report generation
Category: non-functional
 - response time
 - scalability
 - usability
```

After classification, requirements are organized to highlight their relationships and dependencies. This organization might involve creating conceptual models or diagrams, such as use case diagrams, data flow diagrams, or entity-relationship diagrams. These models assist in visualizing the interactions and dependencies between different system components and user interactions, further enhancing the comprehensibility of the analyzed requirements.

The next step in requirement analysis is prioritizing requirements. Not all requirements hold equal importance or contribute equally to the perceived value of the software system. Techniques such as the MoSCoW method (Must have, Should have, Could have, Won't have this time) and numerical assignment can be used to determine the priority of each requirement based on stakeholder input, feasibility studies, and resource availability.

- **Must have:** Essential for system operation.
- **Should have:** Important but not critical; high-priority setting.
- **Could have:** Desirable but not necessary; added if resources permit.
- **Won't have:** Unnecessary for current iteration; potentially revisited later.

Formal modeling is another critical aspect of requirement analysis that involves creating precise and unambiguous models representing the requirements. These models can include mathematical models, state machines, formal specifications, or other algorithmic approaches. The clarity provided by formal models aids in detecting ambiguities and inconsistencies early in the development process.

Negotiation is an ongoing process that complements analysis by addressing instances where stakeholder requirements conflict or where practical limitations (such as budget or technical constraints) necessitate compromise. Effective negotiation ensures that the most critical requirements are given precedence while balancing the diverse interests of different stakeholders. The goal is to achieve a mutually agreeable set of requirements without sacrificing the overall quality or viability of the software project.

A common approach in negotiation is to arrange collaborative workshops or Joint Application Development (JAD) sessions where stakeholders and developers meet to discuss and reconcile conflicting requirements. The facilitation of open communication and the use of structured methods, such as the Weighted Scoring Model, contribute significantly to arriving at consensus.

```
public class Requirement {
    private String name;
    private int importance; // From 1 to 10
    private int feasibility; // From 1 to 10

    public Requirement(String name, int importance, int feasibility) {
        this.name = name;
        this.importance = importance;
        this.feasibility = feasibility;
    }

    public int weightedScore() {
        return importance * feasibility;
    }

    public String toString() {
        return name + " (Score: " + weightedScore() + ")";
```

```
    }
}
```

```
// Example Output
Requirement: Authentication (Score: 70)
Requirement: Data Storage (Score: 50)
Requirement: Report Generation (Score: 40)
```

Effective negotiation also emphasizes the need for flexibility and iterative refinement. As new information emerges or stakeholders reconsider their priorities, requirements may need to be renegotiated and adjusted. Using iterative development methodologies such as Agile can naturally incorporate ongoing negotiation and adaptation of requirements throughout the project lifecycle.

Requirement analysis and negotiation form the backbone of a successful requirements engineering process. Analyzing requirements systematically and addressing conflicts effectively ensures that the final set of requirements is feasible, comprehensive, and reflects the stakeholders' true needs. Enhanced by collaborative techniques and formal methodologies, these processes contribute to the development of quality software systems that are aligned with user expectations and operational constraints.

3.5 Requirement Documentation

Requirement documentation is a fundamental aspect of software engineering that encompasses the process of capturing, recording, and maintaining all requirements that a software system must satisfy. This phase serves as the cornerstone for subsequent development activities, ensuring that all stakeholders have a consistent and clear understanding of system requirements. Proper documentation is vital for effective communication, precise specification, and systematic validation and verification.

Characteristics of Good Requirement Documentation

To ensure high-quality requirement documentation, certain characteristics should be maintained:

- **Clarity**: Requirements should be clearly and unambiguously stated to avoid any misinterpretation.
- **Completeness**: All necessary requirements must be documented to prevent gaps that could lead to additional costs

or project delays.

- **Consistency**: There should be no conflicting requirements within the documentation. If any inconsistencies are found, they must be resolved before proceeding.
- **Verifiability**: Each requirement should be testable; that is, there should be a way to verify that the system meets the requirement.
- **Modifiability**: The documentation should be structured in a way that allows easy updates and modifications.
- **Traceability**: Each requirement should be traceable back to its origin, as well as to the system design and implementation that satisfy it.

Standard Types of Requirement Documents

The most common types of requirement documents include:

- **Software Requirements Specification (SRS)**: This detailed document encompasses all functional and non-functional requirements of a system. It serves as a contractual blueprint between stakeholders and developers.
- **System Requirements Document (SRD)**: Often more extensive than the SRS, this document includes a broader scope covering hardware, software, and interfaces.
- **User Requirements Document (URD)**: This document focuses primarily on the user's perspective and includes all the functionalities the end-users expect from the system.
- **Business Requirements Document (BRD)**: Emphasizes the business perspective, detailing high-level business objectives that the system must achieve.

Structure of a Software Requirements Specification (SRS)

An SRS should have a well-defined structure to ensure all aspects of requirements are comprehensively covered. A typical SRS includes the following sections:

- **Introduction**

  - **Purpose**: Describes the purpose of the document.
  - **Scope**: Outlines the scope of the system to be developed, including benefits, objectives, and goals.
  - **Definitions, Acronyms, and Abbreviations**: Provides a glossary of terms to ensure common understanding.
  - **References**: Lists all documents referenced in the SRS.
  - **Overview**: Gives a brief overview of the contents of the SRS.

- **Overall Description**
  - **Product Perspective**: Describes the system's context and interface with other systems.
  - **Product Functions**: Overview of system functions.
  - **User Characteristics**: Detailing the characteristics of the intended user base.
  - **Constraints**: Enumerates constraints such as regulatory policies, hardware limitations, etc.
  - **Assumptions and Dependencies**: Lists assumptions and potential dependencies affecting the system.

- **Specific Requirements**
  - **Functional Requirements**: Detailed, numbered requirements specifying the functionalities.
  - **External Interface Requirements**: Describes interfaces to other systems or hardware.
  - **Performance Requirements**: Specifies performance-related criteria like speed, reliability, etc.
  - **Design Constraints**: Restrictions affecting design considerations.
  - **Quality Attributes**: Pertains to aspects like maintainability, portability, usability, etc.
  - **Other Requirements**: Any additional requirements not covered in the above sections.

Best Practices for Requirement Documentation

- **Utilize Requirement Management Tools**: Tools such as IBM Rational DOORS, JIRA, and others facilitate the documentation and traceability of requirements.
- **Involve Stakeholders**: Regularly review requirement documents with stakeholders to ensure accuracy and validity.
- **Versioning and Change Control**: Implement version control to manage changes and maintain a history of document revisions.
- **Template Utilization**: Use standardized templates to maintain consistency and completeness.
- **Continuous Review and Refinement**: Periodically review requirements to accommodate evolving needs and rectify any discrepancies.

Example of a Functional Requirement Document

Below is an example of a segment from an SRS document addressing functional requirements:

```
1.0 Functional Requirements
1.1 User Authentication
    1.1.1 The system shall allow users to create an account using a valid email address
          and password.
    1.1.2 The system shall support password recovery through the user's registered
          email.
    1.1.3 The system shall lock the user account after five unsuccessful login attempts.

1.2 Data Management
    1.2.1 The system shall allow users to create, read, update, and delete (CRUD) their
          data entries.
    1.2.2 The system shall validate all data entries before saving to ensure data
          integrity.
    1.2.3 The system shall maintain a history of all modifications to the user's data.
```

Example Output of a Requirement Verification

Consider functional requirement 1.1.3: "The system shall lock the user account after five unsuccessful login attempts." A verification test might be:

```
Input:
User1 attempts to login with incorrect password five times.

Expected Output:
Account locked message displayed to User1.
```

The actual test execution would produce:

```
Attempt 1: Incorrect password, try again.
Attempt 2: Incorrect password, try again.
Attempt 3: Incorrect password, try again.
Attempt 4: Incorrect password, try again.
Attempt 5: Incorrect password, account locked.
```

This demonstrates the practical applicability of the documented requirements and their subsequent verification.

Maintaining robust, clear, and modifiable requirement documentation is essential for ensuring that software development proceeds on a solid foundation, aligning stakeholder expectations with implemented functionalities. Through meticulous documentation and continuous stakeholder engagement, the integrity and success of the software development process are upheld.

3.6 Requirement Validation and Verification

Requirement validation and verification are critical activities within requirements engineering. These processes ensure that the requirements are both correct and complete, as well as conformant to user needs and expectations.

Validation verifies that the documented requirements accurately reflect the desires and needs of stakeholders, while verification ensures that the requirements are well-formed, feasible, and testable. Both activities are essential to the development of high-quality software systems and help reduce the costs associated with late defect detection.

Validation

Validation is a process that evaluates the requirements to ensure they truly meet the business goals and stakeholder expectations. Techniques used for validation include reviews, prototyping, model validation, and acceptance tests.

- **Requirements Review**: A systematic manual analysis where stakeholders and project team members examine the requirements document. Reviews can be structured or semi-structured and often follow a checklist to ensure completeness and accuracy.
- **Prototyping**: Building an executable model of some aspect of the final software product. It assists stakeholders in articulating their needs by providing a tangible form to ambiguous or poorly understood requirements.

- **Model Validation**: Using models like data flow diagrams, entity-relationship diagrams, and state machines to illustrate and validate the requirements. This technique ensures that the requirements are not only valid but also consistent across various levels of abstraction.
- **Acceptance Tests**: Developing and executing test cases derived from the requirements. Acceptance tests involve stakeholders and are performed to ensure the system will meet their needs when completed.

Verification

Verification, in contrast, ensures that requirements are documented correctly, clearly, and are feasible for implementation. Verification techniques include inspections, formal methods, tool support, and consistency checking.

- **Inspections**: Formal, rigorous process that involves detailed examination of the requirements document by a team of reviewers. Inspections focus on finding defects such as ambiguities, incomplete requirements, and inconsistencies.
- **Formal Methods**: Mathematically-based techniques for specification, development, and verification. Formal methods provide frameworks for proving the correctness of requirements and can be used to verify properties of systems using tools like theorem provers.
- **Tool Support**: Automated tools facilitate verification by checking for syntactic and semantic correctness, completeness, and consistency of the requirements. Examples include requirements management tools like IBM Rational DOORS and ReqIF Studio, which interoperate with other development tools.
- **Consistency Checking**: Ensuring that all documented requirements are consistent with each other and with external documents such as standards and regulations. This may involve cross-referencing requirements to identify logical inconsistencies.

Joint Validation and Verification Techniques

Many techniques serve both validation and verification purposes, providing a holistic approach to assessing requirements.

- **Walkthroughs**: Semi-formal process where the author of a requirements document leads stakeholders and project team members through the document to obtain constructive feedback.
- **Scenario Analysis**: Developing and analyzing detailed scenarios that describe specific interactions with the system. Scenarios help in both validating stakeholder needs and verifying the logical coherence of requirement statements.
- **Simulations**: Creating dynamic models that simulate the behavior of the system under different conditions. Simulations help in understanding the operational aspects and validating user expectations and needs while verifying feasibility.

These combined methods increase the confidence that the requirements are both valid and verifiable, bridging the gap between stakeholder needs and technical implementation constraints.

Common Issues and Mitigation

Validation and verification can be challenging due to ambiguous requirements, stakeholder miscommunications, and evolving business needs. Some common issues include requirement creep, conflicting requirements, and gaps between elicited requirements and stakeholder intent.

- **Requirement Creep**: The progressive expansion of requirements without corresponding adjustments in project scope or timeline. Mitigation strategies include rigorous change management processes and maintaining a well-documented requirements baseline.
- **Conflicting Requirements**: Stakeholders may have differing priorities or contradicting needs. Conflict resolution techniques, such as negotiation and prioritization, help reconcile these differences.
- **Ambiguity and Miscommunications**: Vague requirements lead to misinterpretations. Clear, concise, and unambiguous documentation, coupled with frequent stakeholder reviews and feedback loops, mitigate these risks.

Ultimately, effective requirement validation and verification contribute significantly to the success of software projects by ensuring that the final product aligns with stakeholder expectations and is free of defects that would otherwise surface later in the development lifecycle. The integration of systematic techniques for both validation and verification helps in gaining stakeholder trust and fostering a shared understanding of the system's goals and functionalities.

Example: Using Tools for Validation and Verification

Consider a scenario where a team uses IBM Rational DOORS for requirements management. They incorporate a variety of validation and verification activities, leveraging the tool's extensibility and integration capabilities.

```
# Example: Configuration in IBM Rational DOORS
Configure requirement baselines and establish traceability links:
1. Establish Baselines: Capture a snapshot of requirements at a given point.
2. Traceability: Link requirements to their respective test cases and design artifacts.
3. Consistency Checking: Automated checks for inconsistencies and missing linkages.
4. Review Process: Schedule and document review comments directly within the tool.
5. Reporting: Generate compliance and progress reports to facilitate stakeholder
    communication.

# Verification Example Using Formal Methods
Formal Specification of a System Requirement in Z Notation

SCHEMA BankingSystem
[AccountID, Balance]
Withdraw(AccountID, Amount) == schema
    balance[AccountID] >= Amount ==> balance[AccountID] -= Amount
```

```
Output:
Formal proof validates that the Withdraw operation preserves the system invariants.
```

These configurations, combined with a robust toolchain and formal methods, enhance both the validation and the verification process, thereby ensuring a high-quality and reliable requirements set.

By meticulously applying these techniques and addressing common challenges, teams can ensure the development of software that meets user needs and upholds high standards of quality and performance.

3.7 Managing Requirements Changes

Managing requirements changes is a crucial aspect of requirements engineering, as software projects often encounter modifications in requirements due to evolving stakeholder needs, market dynamics, regulatory updates, or technological advancements. Efficient management ensures that these changes are systematically addressed without compromising the project's objectives, timeline, or budget.

Requirements change management involves three primary activities:

identification and initiation, analysis and evaluation, and implementation and verification. The process begins with detecting the need for a change, followed by assessing the impact and feasibility, and concluding with the controlled implementation and validation of the update.

Change requests can originate from various sources, including stakeholders, project team members, regulatory bodies, or market trends. Each request should be documented meticulously using a standardized Change Request Form (CRF). The CRF typically includes the change description, rationale, affected requirements, proposed solution, potential impacts, and the originator's details. Here is an example of a simplified Change Request Form definition in a structured format:

```
<changeRequest>
  <id>CR001</id>
  <date>2023-10-01</date>
  <originator>Jane Doe</originator>
  <description>Update user authentication to include two-factor authentication (2FA)
       .</description>
  <rationale>Enhanced security measure as per new compliance regulations.</
       rationale>
  <affectedRequirements>FR102, FR103</affectedRequirements>
  <proposedSolution>Implement 2FA using phone number verification.</
       proposedSolution>
  <impact>Moderate - will require changes to login module and user database schema
       .</impact>
</changeRequest>
```

Following the initiation of a change request, the subsequent step is a comprehensive analysis and evaluation. This phase involves assessing the technical feasibility, cost implications, schedule adjustments, and potential risks associated with the proposed change. A Change Control Board (CCB), usually comprised of project managers, requirements engineers, developers, quality assurance, and stakeholders, is responsible for reviewing, approving, or rejecting change requests. The decision-making process incorporates various factors such as:

- **Impact Analysis:** Determining the effect on the current system, including dependencies and interactions with other requirements or components.
- **Cost-Benefit Analysis:** Evaluating the financial implications versus the benefits gained from the change.
- **Risk Assessment:** Identifying and mitigating potential risks introduced by the change.
- **Schedule Analysis:** Assessing the impact on project timelines and deliverables.

For effective impact analysis, traceability matrices play a crucial role. These matrices help map requirements to corresponding components, test cases, and documentation, enabling thorough evaluations. An excerpt of a traceability matrix linking requirements to software modules and test cases is shown below:

Requirement ID	Software Module	Test Case ID
FR102	Authentication Module	TC101, TC102
FR103	User Database	TC103, TC104
FR201	Payment Processing	TC201, TC202

Table 3.1: Traceability Matrix

Once a change is approved by the CCB, implementation planning begins. This involves updating the relevant requirement specifications, design documents, codebase, and test plans. Version control systems (VCS) such as Git play a vital role in managing changes to these artifacts by maintaining historical versions and enabling collaborative updates. The following Git commands illustrate a basic workflow for handling changes:

```
# Clone the repository
git clone https://github.com/example/project.git

# Create a new branch for the change
git checkout -b feature/update-authentication

# Implement the changes in the local repository
# (Edit files, commit changes)
git commit -am "Implement 2FA for user authentication."

# Push the changes to the remote repository
git push origin feature/update-authentication

# Create a Pull Request (PR) for team review
```

Verification of the implemented changes is essential to ensure that the updates fulfill the requirements without introducing defects. This involves regression testing, system integration testing, and user acceptance testing (UAT). The outputs of these tests help validate that the changes are correctly integrated and perform as intended. Sample test results can be captured as follows:

```
Test Case: TC101 - Verify 2FA Implementation
--------------------------------------------------
Result: PASSED
Execution Date: 2023-10-15
Performed By: QA_Team
Comments: 2FA functions correctly; code reviewed and approved.
--------------------------------------------------

Test Case: TC102 - Validate Login Without 2FA
--------------------------------------------------
Result: FAILED
Execution Date: 2023-10-15
Performed By: QA_Team
Comments: System allows login without 2FA; requires fix.
--------------------------------------------------
```

Change management in requirements engineering also necessitates continuous communication with stakeholders to keep them informed about the status, impacts, and benefits of changes. Maintaining an updated change log provides transparency and traceability throughout the project lifecycle.

Incorporating these practices facilitates controlled evolution of requirements, enabling software projects to adapt efficiently to changing contexts while ensuring alignment with stakeholder expectations and project goals.

3.8 Requirements Traceability

Requirements traceability is a critical aspect of requirements engineering, representing the ability to describe and follow the life of a requirement, in both a forwards and backwards direction (i.e., from its origin, through its specification and development, to its subsequent deployment and use, and through periods of ongoing refinement and iteration in any of these phases). This concept ensures that each requirement is properly evaluated in all stages of its lifecycle, and that its relationships are understood and managed.

Traceability links can exist between different types of requirements as well as between requirements and other artifacts. For instance, functional requirements might be traced to user stories, test cases, design documents, and source code implementations, while non-functional requirements might be traced to performance benchmarks, compliance documents, and quality assurance reports.

Types of Traceability

- **Forward Traceability:** Ensures that each requirement is developed into a deliverable. It helps in verifying that the project is proceeding in the correct direction with respect to the functionality and strategic goals laid out in the initial requirements.

- **Backward Traceability:** Ensures that the deliverables can be traced back to the corresponding requirements. It helps verify changes to requirements and ensures that the relevant parts of the project are modified accordingly.

- **Bidirectional Traceability:** Combines both forward and backward traceability to ensure a comprehensive trace across the project's lifecycle. This provides a robust framework to validate that requirements are being met by the deliverables and conversely that all deliverables can be tied to specific requirements.

Creating Traceability Matrices

Requirement ID	Description	Design Specification	Test Case
R1	User login functionality	DS1	TC1, TC2
R2	Password recovery process	DS2	TC3, TC4
R3	User profile management	DS3	TC5, TC6

Traceability matrices are valuable tools that provide a visual representation of the bi-directional relationship between requirements, design specifications, and test cases. Each matrix cell ensures that specific requirements, design elements, and test cases are explicitly linked, thus confirming consistency and coverage throughout the project lifecycle.

Benefits of Requirements Traceability

- **Impact Analysis:** Helps in understanding the impact of changes to requirements on project components, ensuring informed decision-making when modifications are necessary.

- **Validation and Verification:** Assures that the requirements are correctly implemented by providing a structured method to trace requirements to test cases.

- **Compliance and Auditability:** Facilitates proving compliance with standards or regulations by illustrating clear relationships between requirements and deliverables.

- **Project Tracking and Oversight:** Enhances the ability to track project progress and manage scope, ensuring that all defined requirements are addressed.

Challenges in Requirements Traceability

- **Complexity:** Maintaining traceability in large-scale systems can lead to complex networks of relationships that require robust tools and processes for effective management.
- **Tool Integration:** Integrating traceability tools with other systems (such as version control systems, test management, and issue tracking) can be complicated and requires careful planning.
- **Consistency:** Ensuring consistency across multiple phases and artifacts can be challenging, particularly in agile environments where requirements constantly evolve.
- **Resource Intensive:** Establishing and maintaining traceability links can be resource-intensive, demanding both time and effort.

Tools for Traceability Various requirements management tools facilitate traceability by providing functionalities to create and manage traceability links. Examples include IBM Rational DOORS, Jama Connect, and Microsoft Azure DevOps. These tools enable the entire lifecycle management of requirements, ensuring that traceability links are maintained dynamically as the project evolves.

In practice, establishing end-to-end traceability necessitates a combination of tool support and disciplined processes. Whether through automated matching in requirements management systems, or manual updates in traceability matrices, effective traceability ensures requirements integrity, verifies completeness, and supports compliance — ultimately contributing to a well-managed and successful software engineering project.

3.9 Tools for Requirements Engineering

Requirements engineering tools are essential for systematically managing the various aspects of requirements development, from elicitation to validation and maintenance. These tools provide a structured environment for capturing, managing, and tracking requirements, ensuring consistency and traceability throughout the software development life cycle. This section explores the prominent tools used in the industry, their features, and their applications in facilitating effective requirements engineering.

Requirement Management Tools:

- **IBM Engineering Requirements Management DOORS Next:** This is a powerful tool that supports requirement capture, tracing, analysis, and management. DOORS Next integrates with other tools in the IBM ecosystem, facilitating comprehensive lifecycle management. Key features include collaborative capabilities, impact analysis, and customizable templates.
- **Jama Connect:** Jama Connect facilitates team collaboration and traceability. It provides a centralized repository for storing requirements, supporting real-time collaboration among team members. Features include requirement versioning, impact analysis, and test management integration.
- **RequirementsHub:** RequirementsHub focuses on simplifying requirement management with a user-friendly interface. It supports elicitation, documentation, prioritization, and traceability of requirements. The tool's modular design allows flexibility in adapting to various project needs.
- **Visure Requirements:** This tool supports the entire requirements lifecycle with features for elicitation, analysis, verification, and validation. Visure Requirements integrates with other development tools and supports standards like ISO 26262 for safety-critical systems. It offers robust traceability features and customizable reporting.

Requirement Elicitation Tools:

- **JIRA:** Originally designed for issue tracking, JIRA by Atlassian has evolved to support requirements management through add-ons like JIRA Align and Confluence. These extensions enable comprehensive requirement elicitation, documentation, and integration within the broader development framework.
- **MindManager:** This is a mind-mapping tool that supports brainstorming and visualization of requirements. It helps in capturing ideas, organizing thoughts, and structuring information in a hierarchical manner, which is crucial for requirement elicitation sessions.

- **ReqChecker:** As a straightforward tool, ReqChecker emphasizes documentation consistency and completeness. It helps ensure that all aspects of a requirement are covered, minimizing the risk of missing details during the elicitation process.

Requirement Analysis and Modeling Tools:

- **Enterprise Architect:** Developed by Sparx Systems, Enterprise Architect is an extensive modeling tool supporting UML, SysML, BPMN, and other modeling standards. It facilitates requirement analysis through detailed modeling, ensuring robust understanding and validation of requirements.
- **MagicDraw:** MagicDraw, by No Magic, offers powerful modeling capabilities to analyze and visualize requirements. It supports UML, SysML, and BPMN, providing a platform for in-depth requirement analysis and design.
- **Rational Software Architect:** This tool by IBM integrates with DOORS Next and other IBM tools, supporting comprehensive analysis and design through UML modeling. It helps bridge the gap between requirement definition and software architecture.

Validation and Verification Tools:

- **Helix RM by Perforce:** Helix RM supports requirement validation through cross-referencing with test cases and defect tracking. It ensures requirements are met and validated through continuous verification processes.
- **TestRail:** While primarily a test management tool, TestRail integrates with requirement tools like JIRA, enabling validation of requirements against test cases. It supports traceability from requirement specification to test execution results.
- **SpiraTest:** This tool integrates requirements management with test management and bug tracking. It provides end-to-end traceability from requirements to test cases and defect resolution.

Traceability Tools:

- **TraceCloud:** TraceCloud focuses on requirement traceability, offering features for managing complex requirement relationships.

It supports compliance tracking, impact analysis, and comprehensive traceability matrix generation.

- **codeBeamer ALM:** An Application Lifecycle Management (ALM) tool, codeBeamer supports requirement traceability through its various lifecycle phases. It provides bi-directional traceability links, ensuring requirement compliance and impact analysis.

- **ReqView:** ReqView emphasizes simple and effective requirement traceability. It offers a clear view of requirement relationships, change impact analysis, and ensures alignment between requirements and project deliverables.

Integrated Requirements Engineering Environments:

Several tools provide integrated environments covering multiple aspects of requirements engineering, offering a holistic approach to managing requirements throughout their lifecycle.

- **Polarion ALM:** By Siemens, Polarion ALM provides a unified platform covering requirement elicitation, modeling, validation, and traceability. It supports collaborative work and integrates with various development tools, ensuring seamless requirement management.

- **Azure DevOps:** Microsoft's Azure DevOps offers integrated services for requirement management, version control, CI/CD, and project tracking. It facilitates continuous requirement management within an agile development framework.

- **IBM Engineering Lifecycle Management (ELM):** ELM integrates requirements management, quality management, and workflow. It supports comprehensive lifecycle management with robust traceability, ensuring requirements are effectively managed and validated across all development phases.

The selection of tools depends on factors including project size, complexity, compliance requirements, and the development methodology employed. By leveraging these tools, teams can enhance the accuracy, consistency, and traceability of requirements, leading to improved project outcomes and higher-quality software systems.

3.10 Case Studies in Requirements Engineering

Examining real-world instances where requirements engineering was pivotal can provide invaluable insights that deepen our understanding of theoretical concepts. This section discusses three case studies: an e-commerce platform, a healthcare management system, and an autonomous vehicle control system. Each case illustrates how requirements engineering techniques were applied to address specific challenges and achieve successful project outcomes.

E-commerce Platform Case Study

In this case study, a leading retail company decided to develop an in-house e-commerce platform to replace a third-party solution. The main goals were to improve performance, increase flexibility in feature integration, and reduce long-term costs. The requirements engineering process began with stakeholder identification, involving retail managers, IT staff, customer service representatives, and end-users.

- **Elicitation Techniques:** An array of elicitation techniques was employed to gather comprehensive requirements. Interviews provided detailed insights into managerial and operational needs. Surveys were distributed to end-users to understand their preferences and pain points. Additionally, focus groups facilitated in-depth discussions and uncovered latent requirements.
- **Functional Requirements:** The functional requirements outlined essential features such as user account management, product catalog browsing, shopping cart functionalities, payment processing, and order tracking. System performance metrics were specified, aiming for transaction processing within two seconds under peak load conditions.
- **Non-Functional Requirements:** The platform needed to maintain high availability (99.99%) and be scalable to handle seasonal traffic surges. Security requirements included compliance with PCI DSS standards and robust user data protection measures.
- **Requirement Documentation:** The requirements were documented using UML diagrams, user stories, and use cases, which were stored in a requirements management tool for ease of traceability.

- **Validation and Verification:** Prototyping was used to validate user interface requirements with stakeholders, ensuring the design met user expectations. Verification was conducted through continuous integration and automated testing frameworks to ensure all specified requirements were implemented correctly.

Challenges such as evolving customer expectations and integration with legacy systems were managed through iterative feedback loops and a flexible architecture that supported ongoing enhancements.

Healthcare Management System Case Study

A hospital sought to develop a comprehensive healthcare management system to improve patient care coordination and streamline administrative tasks. This project involved multiple stakeholders, including healthcare professionals, administrative staff, patients, and regulatory bodies.

- **Elicitation Techniques:** Workshops and brainstorming sessions were crucial in gathering requirements from diverse healthcare teams. Ethnographic studies, including shadowing doctors and nurses, provided insights into daily workflows and pain points.
- **Functional Requirements:** The system needed to support patient record management, appointment scheduling, billing, pharmacy management, and integration with diagnostic devices. Interoperability with existing healthcare information systems was essential.
- **Non-Functional Requirements:** System usability was a priority, ensuring minimal training requirements for hospital staff. Data security and patient privacy were addressed through HIPAA compliance and secure access controls.
- **Requirement Documentation:** Detailed requirements were captured using data flow diagrams and entity-relationship models. These artifacts were continually updated to reflect changing regulatory requirements and stakeholder feedback.
- **Validation and Verification:** Pilot testing in selected hospital departments validated the system's effectiveness in real-world scenarios. Verification included rigorous compliance checks and performance testing, ensuring the system could handle high volumes of patient data without performance degradation.

Managing scope changes due to evolving healthcare regulations was a significant challenge, effectively addressed through adaptive planning and frequent stakeholder reviews.

Autonomous Vehicle Control System Case Study

An automobile manufacturer embarked on developing an autonomous vehicle control system (AVCS). This complex project required integrating various subsystems, including sensors, decision-making algorithms, and vehicle control actuators.

- **Elicitation Techniques:** Expert panel discussions and iterative prototyping with functionality reviews played a crucial role. Scenario-based elicitation helped in identifying requirements for diverse driving conditions and edge cases.
- **Functional Requirements:** Key functionalities included obstacle detection, path planning, adaptive cruise control, emergency braking, and traffic sign recognition. The system needed to process sensory data in real-time and make split-second decisions.
- **Non-Functional Requirements:** Real-time processing capabilities and system reliability were paramount, with stringent safety standards. The AVCS had to operate fault-tolerantly and provide fail-safe mechanisms.
- **Requirement Documentation:** Functional requirements were detailed using SysML diagrams to capture the interplay between various subsystems. Scenario-based tests and simulation models supported documentation efforts.
- **Validation and Verification:** Extensive simulation testing validated system behavior in thousands of virtual driving scenarios. Verification involved hardware-in-the-loop (HIL) testing to ensure real-time response correctness, meeting automotive safety integrity levels (ASIL).

Addressing the uncertainties of real-world driving environments required robust requirement change management practices and continuous validation against evolving safety standards.

```
#include <iostream>
#include <vector>

class Sensor {
public:
    virtual std::vector<float> getData() = 0;
```

```
};

class LidarSensor : public Sensor {
public:
    std::vector<float> getData() override {
        // Implementation code for data retrieval
        return std::vector<float>{/* sensor data */};
    }
};

class ObstacleDetection {
public:
    void processSensorData(Sensor& sensor) {
        std::vector<float> data = sensor.getData();
        // Process data for obstacles
    }
};

int main() {
    LidarSensor lidar;
    ObstacleDetection detection;
    detection.processSensorData(lidar);
    std::cout << "Obstacle processing complete." << std::endl;
    return 0;
}
```

```
Obstacle processing complete.
```

Through these case studies, the application of requirements engineering principles in varied contexts underscores the importance of tailored approaches to address specific project needs. Each case demonstrates the necessity of thorough elicitation, precise documentation, and rigorous validation and verification processes to ensure successful project outcomes.

Chapter 4

System Design and Architecture

System design and architecture are critical phases in software engineering that focus on creating a blueprint for the software system. This chapter introduces design principles and patterns, explores various architectural styles, and emphasizes modular design and decomposition. It covers user interface design, data design, and component-level design, explaining how to effectively represent and document designs. The chapter also discusses methods for evaluating and reviewing design choices to ensure they meet the required standards for scalability, maintainability, and adaptability.

4.1 Introduction to System Design and Architecture

System design and architecture are the foundational phases in the development of a robust software system. These stages transform the initial user requirements and specifications into a structured and coherent blueprint, guiding the subsequent phases of development. Understanding the principles of system design and architecture is crucial for creating software that is scalable, maintainable, and adaptable to changing requirements.

At its core, system design involves defining the system's overall structure. This includes specifying its components, their interactions, and the technologies to be utilized. The architecture of a system serves as a blueprint for both the system and the project developing it. It encompasses a set of structures needed to reason about the system, which comprise software elements, relations among them, and properties of both elements and relations.

One of the fundamental concepts in system design is the separation of concerns. This principle states that a system should be divided into distinct features that overlap in functionality as little as possible. By decomposing a system into various components or modules with distinct responsibilities, it becomes easier to manage and evolve.

Modular design is integral to system architecture. Each module should be an encapsulated unit with a well-defined interface, allowing for independent development and testing. This approach is beneficial not only for system complexity management but also for enhancing collaboration among development teams. Each team can work on different modules simultaneously without causing significant disruptions to the overall system.

Another key element of system architecture is the choice of design patterns. Design patterns are general reusable solutions to common problems. They represent best practices that can be applied to recurring design problems within a given context. For instance, the Model-View-Controller (MVC) pattern is frequently deployed in web applications to separate the data model (Model), the user interface (View), and the control logic (Controller). This separation facilitates modularization and improves code maintainability.

Architectural styles play a critical role in defining the system's high-level structure. Some common architectural styles include layered architecture, microservices architecture, and event-driven architecture. Each style has its own set of principles and benefits, tailored to different types of applications and business needs.

Layered Architecture is one of the most prevalent. It organizes the system into layers, each of which has a specific role. Typically, these layers include the presentation layer, business logic layer, data access layer, and sometimes an integration layer. This separation helps in isolating changes, improving code manageability and allowing layers to be developed and updated independently.

Microservices Architecture involves decomposing the system into small, loosely coupled services, each implementing a specific business capability. This approach enhances scalability and flexibility but requires managing communication between services, ensuring fault tolerance, and maintaining data consistency.

Event-Driven Architecture is centered around producing and handling events. An event signals a significant change in state, and other components react accordingly. This architecture is particularly useful in systems where high decoupling and asynchronous communication are necessary.

Ensuring that a system design adheres to essential quality attributes is a fundamental aspect of architecture. These attributes include performance, security, reliability, maintainability, and usability. Incorporating these attributes from the early stages of design ensures the system meets its intended use case effectively and efficiently.

Consideration of scalability and performance is paramount, especially for systems expected to handle a large number of users or transactions. Scalability can be achieved through vertical or horizontal scaling. Vertical scaling (scaling-up) involves adding more resources to a single node, whereas horizontal scaling (scaling-out) involves adding more nodes to a system.

Security is another critical quality attribute. It encompasses various aspects such as authentication, authorization, confidentiality, integrity, and availability. A good architectural design will incorporate security measures from the outset, following principles such as least privilege, defense in depth, and secure defaults.

Reliability ensures that the system remains operational over time, handling expected and unexpected failures gracefully. Techniques such as redundancy, replication, and failover mechanisms are often employed to enhance reliability.

Maintainability relates to how easy it is to update the system to correct faults, improve performance, or adapt to a changed environment. Modular design, use of design patterns, documentation, and coding standards are some practices that enhance maintainability.

Ultimately, usability focuses on the user experience. It ensures that the system is easy to use, understand, and navigate. Design decisions related to the user interface (UI) and user experience (UX) directly impact usability.

Design principles provide the bedrock for creating well-structured and high-quality systems. Principles such as simplicity, flexibility, reusability, and robustness should guide the design process. Simplicity aids in reducing complexity, flexibility allows for future enhancements, reusability fosters the use of existing components in new ways, and robustness ensures the system can handle edge cases and unexpected inputs gracefully.

Successful system design and architecture require thorough documentation and communication. Design artifacts such as architectural diagrams, interface specifications, and design rationale documents are essential. They convey the architect's vision to the development team, facilitate alignment, and serve as reference points throughout the project's lifecycle.

```
public class UserService {

    private UserRepository userRepository;

    public UserService(UserRepository userRepository) {
        this.userRepository = userRepository;
    }

    public User getUserDetails(int userId) {
        return userRepository.findById(userId);
    }
}

public class UserRepository {

    private DatabaseConnection dbConnection;

    public UserRepository(DatabaseConnection dbConnection) {
        this.dbConnection = dbConnection;
    }

    public User findById(int userId) {
        // Query database and return user details
    }
}

public class DatabaseConnection {

    public Connection getConnection() {
        // Return a database connection
    }
}
```

```
Output:
User Details: {Name: 'John Doe', ID: 12345, Email: 'john.doe@example.com'}
```

This example illustrates how a layered architecture separates different responsibilities into distinct classes, promoting better organization and easing future modifications.

As we continue to delve deeper into the realm of system design and architecture, the succeeding sections will build upon these fundamental concepts, exploring design patterns, architectural styles, modularity, user interfaces, and data management in greater detail.

4.2 Design Principles and Patterns

In software engineering, design principles function as a guide to ensure consistency, accuracy, and robustness within the system architecture. They act as fundamental axioms that foster quality attributes such as maintainability, scalability, and reliability. Patterns, on the other hand, provide reusable solutions to common design problems, encapsulating best practices that have been refined through experience. This section delves into key design principles and elucidates several essential design patterns.

Design principles define the guidelines that should be adhered to throughout the software development process. A few critical principles include:

- **Single Responsibility Principle (SRP)**: This principle asserts that a class should have only one reason to change, meaning it should only have one job or responsibility. Adhering to SRP reduces the risk of code fragility and promotes cohesion within a class.

- **Open/Closed Principle (OCP)**: OCP posits that software entities such as classes, modules, and functions should be open for extension but closed for modification. This principle facilitates the addition of new features without altering existing code, thus ensuring backward compatibility.

- **Liskov Substitution Principle (LSP)**: LSP advocates that objects of a superclass should be replaceable with objects of a subclass without affecting the correctness of the program. This ensures that a subclass can stand in for its superclass without introducing errors.

- **Interface Segregation Principle (ISP)**: ISP contends that clients should not be forced to depend on interfaces they do not use. It promotes the creation of smaller, more specific interfaces instead of large, monolithic ones.

- **Dependency Inversion Principle (DIP)**: DIP suggests that high-level modules should not depend on low-level modules, but both should depend on abstractions. Furthermore, abstractions should not depend on details, whereas details should depend on abstractions. This principle reduces the coupling between components and enhances module interchangeability.

Alongside these principles, design patterns are categorized into three main types: creational, structural, and behavioral patterns. Each category addresses a specific aspect of object creation, composition, or interaction.

Creational Patterns focus on object creation mechanisms, aiming to create objects in a manner suitable to the situation. Key patterns include:

- **Singleton** ensures that a class has only one instance and provides a global point of access to it.

```
public class Singleton {
    private static Singleton instance;

    private Singleton() {}

    public static Singleton getInstance() {
        if (instance == null) {
            instance = new Singleton();
        }
        return instance;
    }
}
```

- **Factory Method** defines an interface for creating an object but allows subclasses to alter the type of objects that will be created.

```
abstract class Creator {
    public abstract Product createProduct();
}

class ConcreteCreator extends Creator {
    public Product createProduct() {
        return new ConcreteProduct();
    }
}
```

- **Abstract Factory** provides an interface for creating families of related or dependent objects without specifying their concrete classes.

```
interface AbstractFactory {
    ProductA createProductA();
```

```
    ProductB createProductB();
}

class ConcreteFactory1 implements AbstractFactory {
    public ProductA createProductA() {
        return new ProductA1();
    }

    public ProductB createProductB() {
        return new ProductB1();
    }
}
```

Structural Patterns deal with object composition, forming larger structures from individual objects. Key patterns include:

- **Adapter** allows otherwise incompatible classes to work together by converting an interface of a class into another interface a client expects.

```
interface Target {
    void request();
}

class Adaptee {
    public void specificRequest() {
        // Specific implementation
    }
}

class Adapter implements Target {
    private Adaptee adaptee;

    public Adapter(Adaptee adaptee) {
        this.adaptee = adaptee;
    }

    public void request() {
        adaptee.specificRequest();
    }
}
```

- **Composite** allows you to compose objects into tree structures to represent part-whole hierarchies. It enables clients to treat individual objects and compositions uniformly.

```
interface Component {
    void operation();
}

class Leaf implements Component {
    public void operation() {
        // Leaf specific operation
    }
}
```

```
class Composite implements Component {
    private List<Component> children = new ArrayList<>();

    public void add(Component component) {
        children.add(component);
    }

    public void operation() {
        for (Component child : children) {
            child.operation();
        }
    }
}
```

Behavioral Patterns are concerned with algorithms and the assignment of responsibilities between objects. Key patterns include:

- **Observer** defines a one-to-many dependency between objects so that when one object changes state, all its dependents are notified and updated automatically.

```
interface Observer {
    void update();
}

class ConcreteObserver implements Observer {
    public void update() {
        // Update observer state
    }
}

class Subject {
    private List<Observer> observers = new ArrayList<>();

    public void attach(Observer observer) {
        observers.add(observer);
    }

    public void notifyObservers() {
        for (Observer observer : observers) {
            observer.update();
        }
    }
}
```

- **Strategy** defines a family of algorithms, encapsulates each one, and makes them interchangeable. This pattern lets the algorithm vary independently from the clients that use it.

```
interface Strategy {
    void execute();
}

class ConcreteStrategyA implements Strategy {
    public void execute() {
        // Implementation of Strategy A
```

```
    }
}

class Context {
    private Strategy strategy;

    public Context(Strategy strategy) {
        this.strategy = strategy;
    }

    public void executeStrategy() {
        strategy.execute();
    }
}
```

Both design principles and patterns are pivotal in crafting resilient software architectures. They promote the establishment of well-structured, scalable, and maintainable systems, achieving a balance between theory and practical application. The adherence to principles ensures disciplined development, while patterns offer concrete solutions to recurrent problems, solidifying the foundation for effective software design.

4.3 Architectural Styles and Patterns

Architectural styles and patterns are foundational to the systemic organization and high-level structuring of software systems. They provide established frameworks and templates for constructing robust, scalable, and maintainable systems. In this section, we shall delve into the core architectural styles, elucidate their characteristics, and examine the applicable scenarios for each style. Furthermore, we will explore some fundamental architectural patterns that guide the interactions and data flow within these structures.

Heralding a comprehensive understanding, we begin with a brief overview of some prominent architectural styles: layered architecture, client-server, event-driven, microservices, and service-oriented architecture (SOA). Each style will be dissected to reveal its inherent advantages and potential drawbacks.

Layered Architecture: The layered architecture style organizes the system into a hierarchy of layers, each layer providing services to the layer above it and consuming services from the layer below. This promotes separation of concerns, facilitating manageability and scalability.

- **Presentation Layer:** Responsible for user interface and user interactions.

- **Business Logic Layer:** Contains business rules and logic.
- **Application Layer:** Manages application-specific functionality.
- **Data Layer:** Manages data storage and retrieval.

Benefits of layered architecture include ease of maintenance, the ability to modify layers independently, and enhanced scalability. However, it can introduce latency due to inter-layer communication and may not be suitable for performance-critical applications.

Client-Server Architecture: The client-server architecture delineates the system into two principal components: clients and servers. Clients request services and resources, while servers process these requests and provide the necessary services.

- **Scalability:** Servers can be scaled horizontally to manage increased load.
- **Manageability:** Centralized server management is simplified.
- **Flexibility:** Clients can be of varied types (e.g., desktop, web, mobile).

Challenges include potential server bottlenecks, maintaining server robustness, and ensuring high availability and fault tolerance.

Event-Driven Architecture: In event-driven architecture, the system components interact through the production and consumption of events. Components are decoupled, promoting a highly modular and asynchronous system. This style is particularly suitable for applications requiring real-time processing and responsiveness.

- **Event Producers:** Generate events based on changes or actions.
- **Event Consumers:** React to events, initiating appropriate responses.
- **Event Channels and Queues:** Facilitate the transmission of events.

Advantages include increased responsiveness and flexibility. However, complexity in managing events and ensuring consistency can be a downside.

Microservices Architecture: Microservices architecture breaks down the system into a suite of small, independently deployable services. Each service focuses on a specific business function, promoting high cohesion and low coupling among services.

- **Independence:** Services can be developed, deployed, and scaled independently.
- **Resilience:** Faults in one service do not necessarily impact the entire system.
- **Technology Diversity:** Different services can leverage different technologies.

Challenges involve managing inter-service communication, ensuring transactional consistency, and handling deployment complexity.

Service-Oriented Architecture (SOA): SOA defines a structure where services are the fundamental units of application logic. Services communicate over a network, following standard protocols and data formats. This style underscores interoperability and reusability of services.

- **Service Composition:** Services can be composed to solve complex business problems.
- **Interoperability:** Services interact using standardized protocols.
- **Reusability:** Services are designed for reuse across multiple applications.

Potential downsides include the overhead of service orchestration and the need for robust security measures given that services typically communicate over a network.

Architectural styles are typically implemented via specific patterns which provide concrete solutions to recurring design problems. Some widely adopted architectural patterns include:

Model-View-Controller (MVC): MVC segregates an application into three interconnected components: Model, View, and Controller. This separation of concerns enhances modularity and facilitates parallel development.

- **Model:** Manages the data and business logic.

- **View:** Handles the display and user interface.
- **Controller:** Manages the flow of data to and from the model and the view.

```
// Simplified example of MVC pattern in Java
public class Model {
    private String data;
    public String getData() { return data; }
    public void setData(String data) { this.data = data; }
}

public class View {
    public void displayData(String data) { System.out.println("Data: " + data); }
}

public class Controller {
    private Model model;
    private View view;
    public Controller(Model model, View view) { this.model = model; this.view = view;
        }
    public void updateView() { view.displayData(model.getData()); }
}
```

```
Data: Example Data
```

Observer Pattern: The observer pattern facilitates a one-to-many dependency between objects, allowing the state change in one object to notify all dependent objects. This pattern is extensively used in event-driven systems.

```
// Example of Observer pattern in Java
public interface Observer {
    void update(String eventData);
}

public class Subject {
    private List<Observer> observers = new ArrayList<>();
    public void addObserver(Observer observer) { observers.add(observer); }
    public void notifyObservers(String eventData) {
        for (Observer observer : observers) {
            observer.update(eventData);
        }
    }
}

public class ConcreteObserver implements Observer {
    public void update(String eventData) { System.out.println("Received event data: "
        + eventData); }
}

public static void main(String[] args) {
    Subject subject = new Subject();
    ConcreteObserver observer = new ConcreteObserver();
    subject.addObserver(observer);
    subject.notifyObservers("Sample Event");
}
```

Received event data: Sample Event

Singleton Pattern: The singleton pattern ensures that a class has only one instance and provides a global access point to this instance. This is beneficial when exactly one object is needed to coordinate actions across a system.

```
// Example of Singleton pattern in Java
public class Singleton {
    private static Singleton instance;
    private Singleton() {}
    public static Singleton getInstance() {
        if (instance == null) {
            instance = new Singleton();
        }
        return instance;
    }
}
```

When employing these architectural patterns, consider the specific requirements and constraints of the system being designed. The patterns not only provide a structured approach to solving common issues but also significantly impact the maintainability, scalability, and performance of the application. Combining architectural styles with well-chosen patterns fosters the creation of software systems that are resilient, flexible, and aligned with the business objectives.

4.4 Modular Design and Decomposition

Modular design and decomposition are fundamental concepts in software engineering that aim to divide a software system into distinct, manageable modules. These modules can be developed, tested, and maintained independently, contributing to the overall system's scalability, maintainability, and adaptability. The following discussion focuses on the primary objectives, benefits, and techniques of modular design and decomposition.

Objectives of Modular Design and Decomposition

The primary objective of modular design is to break down a complex system into smaller, more manageable parts. Each module should encapsulate a specific aspect of the system's functionality. Key objectives include:

- **Simplicity:** Reducing the complexity of the system by handling smaller, more understandable parts.

- **Reusability:** Developing modules that can be reused in different parts of the system or even in different projects.
- **Maintenability:** Facilitating easier updates and modifications by isolating changes to individual modules.
- **Parallel Development:** Enabling multiple developers or teams to work concurrently on different modules.

Benefits of Modular Design

The modular approach to system design offers several significant benefits:

- **Enhanced Understandability:** Smaller modules are easier to understand, which helps developers and stakeholders comprehend the system.
- **Improved Testability:** Modules can be tested independently, ensuring that each part functions correctly before integrating it into the larger system.
- **Reduced Risk:** Isolating changes to individual modules minimizes the risk of introducing bugs into the entire system.
- **Parallel Development:** Multiple teams can work on different modules simultaneously, speeding up the development process.

Techniques for Modular Decomposition

Effective modular design and decomposition require systematic techniques to identify and create modules. The following are some well-known methods:

High Cohesion and Low Coupling

A fundamental principle in modular decomposition is to ensure high cohesion within modules and low coupling between modules. Cohesion refers to how closely related the responsibilities and functions within a module are. A highly cohesive module performs a single, well-defined task. Coupling, on the other hand, refers to the dependencies between modules. Low coupling implies that changes to one module will have minimal impact on others.

Consider the following pseudocode for a tightly coupled system:

```
class OrderProcessor:
    def processOrder(order):
        paymentGateway = PaymentGateway()
        paymentGateway.processPayment(order.paymentInfo)

        inventory = Inventory()
        inventory.updateStock(order.items)

        shipment = Shipment()
        shipment.scheduleDelivery(order.address)
```

In this example, the OrderProcessor class tightly couples the payment, inventory, and shipment processes. A more modular approach would involve separating these concerns into individual modules:

```
class PaymentService:
    def processPayment(paymentInfo):
        # Code to process payment

class InventoryService:
    def updateStock(items):
        # Code to update inventory

class ShipmentService:
    def scheduleDelivery(address):
        # Code to schedule shipment

class OrderProcessor:
    def processOrder(order):
        paymentService = PaymentService()
        paymentService.processPayment(order.paymentInfo)

        inventoryService = InventoryService()
        inventoryService.updateStock(order.items)

        shipmentService = ShipmentService()
        shipmentService.scheduleDelivery(order.address)
```

This decomposition reduces coupling and increases cohesion, making the system easier to maintain and extend.

Layered Architecture

Layered architecture is a design pattern that organizes the system into layers with specific responsibilities. Each layer relies on the layers directly below it and provides services to the layers above. Common layers include:

- **Presentation Layer:** Handles user interface and user interaction.
- **Business Logic Layer:** Contains business rules and logic.
- **Data Access Layer:** Manages data retrieval and storage.

The following diagram illustrates a simple layered architecture:

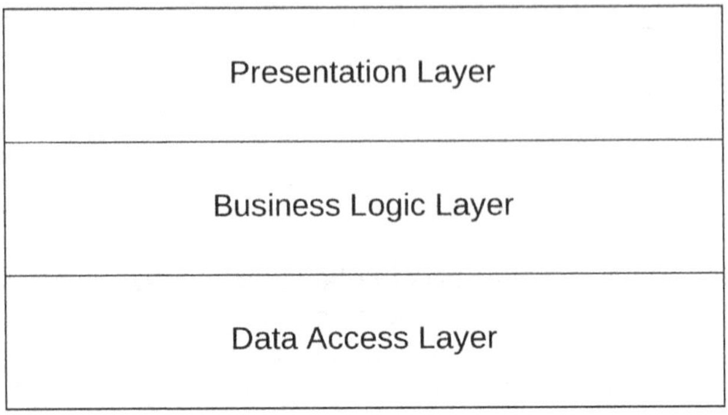

Component-Based Development

Component-based development (CBD) promotes building software systems from pre-existing components. Each component encapsulates specific functionality and communicates with other components through well-defined interfaces. Components can be developed and updated independently, promoting reusability and modularity.

For instance, consider a web application with distinct components for authentication, user management, and data reporting. Each component is self-contained and interacts with others through APIs or messaging systems.

Domain-Driven Design

Domain-Driven Design (DDD) is an approach to design complex software systems by focusing on the core domain logic. It involves identifying the core domain and subdomains, then creating modules (or bounded contexts) that represent these domains. Each module is responsible for a specific domain concept, minimizing dependencies and enhancing cohesion.

Consider a retail application where the core domain involves order processing, and subdomains include inventory management and customer relationship management (CRM). In DDD, you would create separate modules for each subdomain, such as OrderProcessing, InventoryManagement, and CRM, each encapsulating relevant domain logic.

```
class OrderProcessingService:
    def validateOrder(order):
        # Validation logic specific to order processing

class InventoryManagementService:
    def checkStock(items):
```

```
        # Stock checking logic specific to inventory management

class CRMService:
    def updateCustomerDetails(customer):
        # Customer details update logic specific to CRM
```

By organizing the application into domain-specific modules, DDD helps manage complexity and aligns the system with business requirements.

Design Patterns for Modular Design

Several design patterns support modular design and decomposition:

- **Facade Pattern:** Provides a simplified interface to a complex subsystem, reducing dependencies between client code and the subsystem.
- **Adapter Pattern:** Allows incompatible interfaces to work together by converting one interface to another expected by the client.
- **Factory Pattern:** Encapsulates object creation logic, promoting loose coupling and flexibility.
- **Observer Pattern:** Defines a one-to-many relationship between objects, facilitating communication between modules without tight coupling.

These patterns promote modularity by ensuring that modules interact through well-defined interfaces and encapsulate their internal details.

Modular design and decomposition are essential practices in software engineering, enabling the creation of scalable, maintainable, and adaptable systems. By adhering to principles of high cohesion and low coupling, leveraging design patterns, and employing techniques such as layered architecture, component-based development, and domain-driven design, developers can effectively manage complexity and enhance the quality of their software systems.

4.5 User Interface Design

User Interface (UI) Design is a central element of system design, providing a direct channel through which users interact with the software. Good UI design ensures that the system is easy to use, facilitates user task completion, and enhances overall user satisfaction. This section delves into the principles, processes, and techniques involved in the creation of effective user interfaces.

Principles of User Interface Design

Adhering to established UI design principles ensures consistency and usability across different parts of the system. These principles include:

- **Consistency:** Similar elements should look and behave similarly. This includes using consistent color schemes, fonts, and layout styles throughout the application.
- **Feedback:** The system should provide users with feedback on their actions, such as acknowledging when an action has been performed successfully or alerting them to errors.
- **Visibility:** Important information should be visible without overwhelming the user. Critical features and actions should be easily accessible.
- **Affordance:** UI elements should visually suggest their functionality. For example, buttons should look clickable, and sliders should look adjustable.
- **Simplicity:** Interfaces should be as simple as possible, removing unnecessary elements that do not add value to the user.
- **Error Prevention and Recovery:** The design should minimize the possibility of user error and provide clear instructions on how to recover from mistakes.

User-Centered Design Process

The user-centered design (UCD) approach places the user at the forefront of the design process. It involves the following stages:

- **Research:** Understanding the users, tasks, and environments by conducting user interviews, surveys, observations, or contextual inquiries.
- **Design:** Creating wireframes, mockups, and prototypes to visualize the UI. Tools like Sketch, Figma, and Adobe XD are commonly used for this purpose.

- **Evaluation:** Conducting usability testing with real users to identify issues and areas for improvement. Based on the feedback, iterative refinements are made to the design.
- **Implementation:** Translating the finalized design into code. HTML, CSS, and JavaScript are fundamental technologies for web-based UI, while languages like Swift and Kotlin are used for mobile applications.

Wireframing and Prototyping

Wireframes serve as blueprints of the UI, providing a skeletal view of the layout and interaction flow without delving into visual design details. Prototypes, on the other hand, are more refined and interactive models that closely mimic the final product.

Using wireframes:

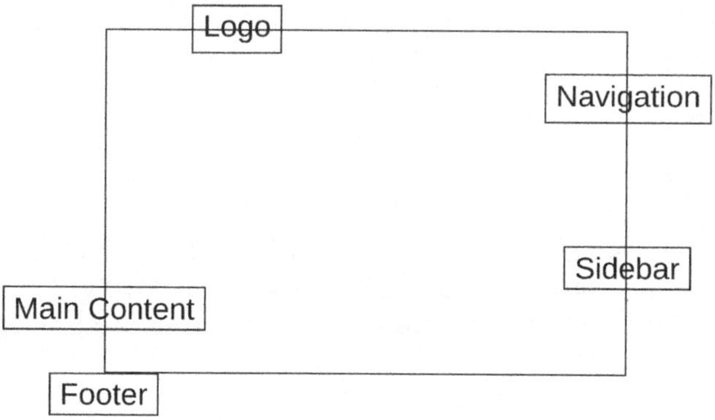

Prototypes are often developed using software tools that allow for dynamic, interactive models. User feedback on prototypes can be used to make data-driven design decisions.

Usability Testing

Usability testing is critical to gauge how real users interact with the system. There are various methods for conducting usability tests:

- **Moderated vs Unmoderated:** In moderated testing, a facilitator guides the user through tasks, while in unmoderated testing, users navigate the interface independently.
- **Remote vs In-Person:** Remote testing allows users to perform tasks in their typical environment using their own devices. In-person testing provides more controlled conditions.

- **A/B Testing:** Users are shown different versions of the UI to determine which design performs better based on predefined metrics like task completion rate and time.

Developing a usability test script:

- **Introduction**
  - Brief the participants about the purpose of the test.
  - Ensure participants know their feedback will be used to improve the system.
- **Tasks**
  - Task 1: Register a new account.
  - Task 2: Navigate to the dashboard.
  - Task 3: Create a new project.
- Finalize
  - Collect final thoughts and suggestions.

Accessibility

Ensuring the software is accessible to all users, including those with disabilities, is a fundamental aspect of UI design. This involves adhering to guidelines such as the Web Content Accessibility Guidelines (WCAG) which cover:

- **Perceivable:** Information and UI components must be presentable in ways that users can perceive (e.g., text alternatives for images).
- **Operable:** UI components and navigation must be operable (e.g., keyboard accessibility).
- **Understandable:** Information and operation of the user interface must be understandable (e.g., clear error messages).
- **Robust:** Content must be robust enough to be interpreted reliably by a wide variety of user agents, including assistive technologies.

User Interface Design Patterns

UI design patterns are reusable solutions to common design problems. Examples include:

- **Navigation Patterns:** Such as breadcrumbs or mega menus for helping users navigate complex websites.

- **Input Patterns:** Including dropdown menus, radio buttons, and checkboxes for user input.

- **Feedback Patterns:** Like tooltips and notifications to provide instant feedback on user actions.

Incorporating these principles and techniques in UI design leads to systems that not only function effectively but also provide an intuitive and enjoyable user experience.

4.6 Data Design and Management

Data design and management are pivotal components in the system design and architecture phase, tasked with ensuring data consistency, integrity, and availability. This section will delve into the essential aspects of designing data structures, managing data distribution, and ensuring data quality. We will discuss the importance of database management systems (DBMS), explore various data models, and highlight best practices for data security and backup strategies.

Data Structures and Data Models

Designing efficient data structures that align with the application's requirements is crucial. Core data structures include arrays, linked lists, trees, and hash tables, each suited for specific scenarios depending on their performance characteristics. Selection should be guided by considerations of time complexity, space complexity, and the specific operations (insertion, deletion, searching) that will be most frequently performed.

Data models provide an abstract representation of the database. The primary data models include:

- **Relational Model:** Based on first-order predicate logic, this model organizes data into tables (relations) comprising rows and columns. Each table contains rows (tuples) and columns (attributes). The relational model leverages Structured Query Language (SQL) for database management.

- **Entity-Relationship (ER) Model:** This model uses entities, relationships, and attributes to represent data objects and their interactions. ER diagrams visualize this model, showcasing entities as rectangles, attributes as ovals, and relationships as diamonds.
- **Object-Oriented Model:** Supporting complex data structures, this model integrates object-oriented programming principles. Data and behavior are encapsulated into objects, aligning with classes and inheritance.
- **NoSQL Model:** Adapted for unstructured data, this model includes document stores, key-value stores, column-family stores, and graph databases. NoSQL databases are optimal for horizontal scaling and handle large volumes of diverse data types such as JSON documents, wide-column stores, and graph-based data.

Normalization and Denormalization

Normalizing data structures minimizes data redundancy and dependency by organizing fields and table relations. Key forms of normalization include:

- **First Normal Form (1NF):** Eliminates duplicate columns from the same table and establishes primary keys.
- **Second Normal Form (2NF):** Ensures that all non-key attributes are fully functionally dependent on the primary key.
- **Third Normal Form (3NF):** Removes transitive dependencies, ensuring non-key attributes are dependent solely on primary keys.

However, in some cases, denormalization may be employed to enhance read performance by allowing redundancy in the data. This involves combining tables or including redundant columns, reducing the need for complex joins and improving read-heavy applications' throughput.

Data Integrity and Constraints

Data integrity ensures data accuracy and consistency throughout its lifecycle. Strategies to maintain data integrity include:

- **Entity Integrity:** Guarantees that each table has a unique primary key.

- **Referential Integrity:** Ensures that foreign keys correctly reference primary key values in related tables, preserving the logical relationships between tables.
- **Domain Integrity:** Enforces valid entries via data type constraints, default values, and validity checks.
- **User-Defined Integrity:** Customized rules that address specific business requirements.

Key constraints help enforce these types of integrity by enforcing rules on the data:

- **Primary Key Constraints:** Uniquely identifies each record in a table.
- **Foreign Key Constraints:** Links two tables, ensuring referential integrity.
- **Unique Constraints:** Ensures all values in a column are unique.
- **Check Constraints:** Validates data based on a boolean expression.

Database Management Systems (DBMS)

DBMS are software systems designed to manage databases. They provide the necessary tools for data creation, updating, retrieval, and administration. Key functionalities of a DBMS include:

- **Data Definition Language (DDL):** Enables the creation and modification of the database schema.
- **Data Manipulation Language (DML):** Handles data insertion, update, deletion, and retrieval.
- **Data Control Language (DCL):** Manages access and permissions.
- **Transaction Control Language (TCL):** Ensures data integrity by managing transactions, supporting operations such as commit and rollback.

Popular DBMS include MySQL, PostgreSQL, Oracle, and Microsoft SQL Server for relational databases, while MongoDB, Cassandra, and Amazon DynamoDB are significant for NoSQL databases.

Data Security

Ensuring data security is paramount to protect against data breaches and unauthorized access. Key practices include:

- **Encryption:** Encrypt data at rest and in transit using algorithms such as AES (Advanced Encryption Standard).
- **Access Controls:** Implement role-based access control (RBAC) to restrict data access based on user roles.
- **Auditing:** Maintain comprehensive audit logs to monitor and review data access and modifications.
- **Authentication and Authorization:** Employ multi-factor authentication (MFA) and robust authorization mechanisms.

Data Backup and Recovery

Regular data backup and a solid recovery plan are essential to mitigate data loss risk. Strategies include:

- **Full Backup:** Complete backup of the entire database at specified intervals.
- **Incremental Backup:** Backup of only the data that has changed since the last backup.
- **Differential Backup:** Backup of data changed since the last full backup.
- **Log Shipping:** Regular transfer of transaction logs to a standby server.
- **Replication:** Real-time copying of data to another server.

Automating the backup process, validating backups, and regularly testing recovery procedures ensures data availability and resilience against data loss events.

Understanding these fundamental aspects of data design and management equips software engineers with the necessary tools to create robust, secure, and efficiently managed data architecture.

4.7 Component-Level Design

Component-level design focuses on the detailed definition and implementation of the individual components that make up a software system. It emphasizes the synthesis of data structures, algorithms, and control flow to create self-contained and efficient components. The primary goal of component-level design is to ensure each component fulfills its responsibilities while maintaining a high level of cohesion and low coupling with other components.

Components can be thought of as encapsulated units of behavior and data that interact with other components through well-defined interfaces. This encapsulation promotes reusability and maintainability. Each component should have a clear responsibility and perform a specific task within the system.

Designing Components:

Designing components involves several key activities:

- **Identifying Components:** Begin by decomposing the system into smaller, manageable parts. Use modular design principles to separate concerns and identify which components are necessary based on system requirements and architectural design.

- **Defining Interfaces:** Clear and well-defined interfaces are essential for component interaction. Interfaces should specify the methods or functions provided by the component, the inputs they require, and the outputs they produce. Interfaces serve as contracts, ensuring that components interact predictably.

- **Specifying Data Structures:** Each component may require internal data structures to manage its state. Choose appropriate data structures that optimize performance and fit the component's responsibility.

- **Developing Algorithms:** Implement the logic needed to fulfill the component's responsibilities. This involves writing algorithms that manipulate the internal data structures and handle input-output operations as defined by the interface.

- **Ensuring Cohesion and Minimizing Coupling:** Strive for high cohesion within components — where all functions and data are closely related to the component's purpose. Minimize the dependency of one component on others (low coupling) to enhance modularity and agility.

Example: Banking System – Transaction Processing Component

Consider a component-based design approach for a banking system. One key component could be *TransactionProcessing*. This component would encapsulate the logic for handling various types of banking transactions like deposits, withdrawals, and transfers.

First, identify the component and its responsibilities:

- Processing user-initiated transactions.
- Updating account balances.
- Ensuring transaction validity and integrity.

Next, define the component's interface. In this example, the interface may include methods for each transaction type:

```
public interface TransactionProcessing {
    void deposit(Account account, double amount);
    void withdraw(Account account, double amount);
    void transfer(Account fromAccount, Account toAccount, double amount);
}
```

Specify the data structures needed. For instance, the *Account* class represents bank accounts and stores account details:

```
public class Account {
    private String accountNumber;
    private double balance;

    // Getters and Setters
    public String getAccountNumber() { return accountNumber; }
    public void setAccountNumber(String accountNumber) { this.accountNumber =
         accountNumber; }
    public double getBalance() { return balance; }
    public void setBalance(double balance) { this.balance = balance; }
}
```

Develop efficient algorithms to perform transactions. Below is a simple implementation of the *TransactionProcessing* interface:

```
public class TransactionProcessingImpl implements TransactionProcessing {

    @Override
    public void deposit(Account account, double amount) {
        if(amount > 0) {
            account.setBalance(account.getBalance() + amount);
```

```
        } else {
            throw new IllegalArgumentException("Amount must be greater than zero.");
        }
    }

    @Override
    public void withdraw(Account account, double amount) {
        if(amount > 0 && account.getBalance() >= amount) {
            account.setBalance(account.getBalance() - amount);
        } else {
            throw new IllegalArgumentException("Insufficient balance or invalid amount.
                ");
        }
    }

    @Override
    public void transfer(Account fromAccount, Account toAccount, double amount) {
        if(fromAccount != null && toAccount != null && amount > 0 && fromAccount.
                getBalance() >= amount) {
            fromAccount.setBalance(fromAccount.getBalance() - amount);
            toAccount.setBalance(toAccount.getBalance() + amount);
        } else {
            throw new IllegalArgumentException("Invalid accounts or amount.");
        }
    }
}
```

Cohesion and Coupling:

This design ensures high cohesion, as each method in the *TransactionProcessingImpl* class is closely related to the component's responsibility of handling transactions. It also achieves low coupling because the interaction with the *Account* class is minimal and clearly defined through interfaces, avoiding tight integration.

Component Testing:

Individual component testing is imperative to ensure each part functions correctly before integrating. Unit tests can be written for the *TransactionProcessing* component to verify its behavior under various scenarios.

```
public class TransactionProcessingTest {

    private TransactionProcessingImpl transactionProcessing;

    @Before
    public void setUp() {
        transactionProcessing = new TransactionProcessingImpl();
    }

    @Test
    public void testDeposit() {
        Account account = new Account();
        account.setAccountNumber("12345");
        account.setBalance(1000.0);

        transactionProcessing.deposit(account, 500.0);
```

```
        assertEquals(1500.0, account.getBalance(), 0.01);
    }

    @Test
    public void testWithdraw() {
        Account account = new Account();
        account.setAccountNumber("12345");
        account.setBalance(1000.0);

        transactionProcessing.withdraw(account, 400.0);
        assertEquals(600.0, account.getBalance(), 0.01);
    }

    @Test
    public void testTransfer() {
        Account fromAccount = new Account();
        fromAccount.setAccountNumber("12345");
        fromAccount.setBalance(1000.0);

        Account toAccount = new Account();
        toAccount.setAccountNumber("67890");
        toAccount.setBalance(500.0);

        transactionProcessing.transfer(fromAccount, toAccount, 300.0);

        assertEquals(700.0, fromAccount.getBalance(), 0.01);
        assertEquals(800.0, toAccount.getBalance(), 0.01);
    }
}
```

The results of the unit tests should indicate whether the *Transaction-ProcessingImpl* component behaves as expected.

```
Running TransactionProcessingTest
- testDeposit PASSED
- testWithdraw PASSED
- testTransfer PASSED
```

Component-level design is a critical step in software engineering, and proper execution ensures robust, maintainable, and scalable systems. By focusing on clear interfaces, appropriate data structures, and efficient algorithms, developers can create components that integrate seamlessly into the larger system while promoting reusability and ease of maintenance.

4.8 Design Notations and Representations

Design notations and representations are essential in conveying the system architecture and design clearly to all stakeholders, including developers, designers, and clients. Various diagrams and symbols are standardized to avoid ambiguity and ensure consistency. This section explores several commonly used design notations and representations, providing detailed descriptions and usage examples.

Unified Modeling Language (UML)

UML is a standardized modeling language that provides a set of graphical notations to represent software systems. It is widely used in the software engineering field because of its flexibility and comprehensive coverage. UML includes several types of diagrams, each serving a particular purpose:

- **Class Diagrams:** Class diagrams represent the static structure of a system by illustrating classes, their attributes, methods, and relationships among objects. Below is an example of a UML class diagram for a simple e-commerce application:

```
class Order {
    int orderID;
    Date orderDate;
    Customer customer;
    List<Product> products;
    void calculateTotal();
    void confirmOrder();
}

class Customer {
    int customerID;
    String name;
    String email;
    void register();
    void login();
}

class Product {
    int productID;
    String productName;
    float price;
    void getDetails();
}
```

- **Use Case Diagrams:** Use case diagrams provide a high-level view of user interactions with the system by depicting actors and their goals represented as use cases. They help in identifying functional requirements and scope.

  Example use case diagram for the same e-commerce application:

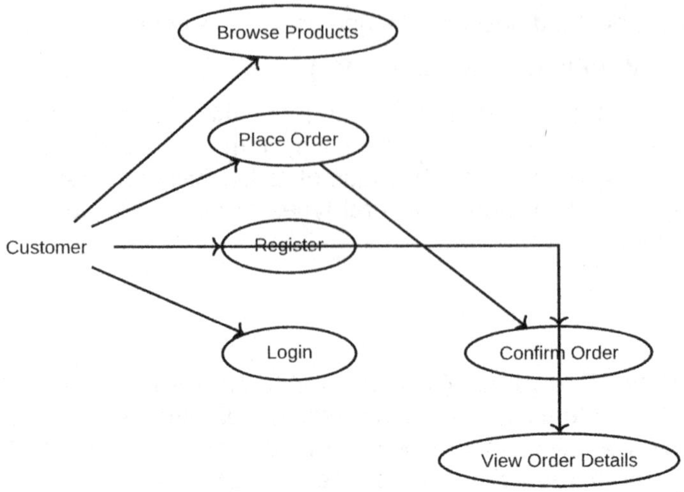

- **Sequence Diagrams:** Sequence diagrams describe the sequence of messages exchanged among different objects to carry out a specific function or a process. They are particularly useful in understanding the flow of control and identifying potential bottlenecks.

  Example sequence diagram for the order placement in the e-commerce application:

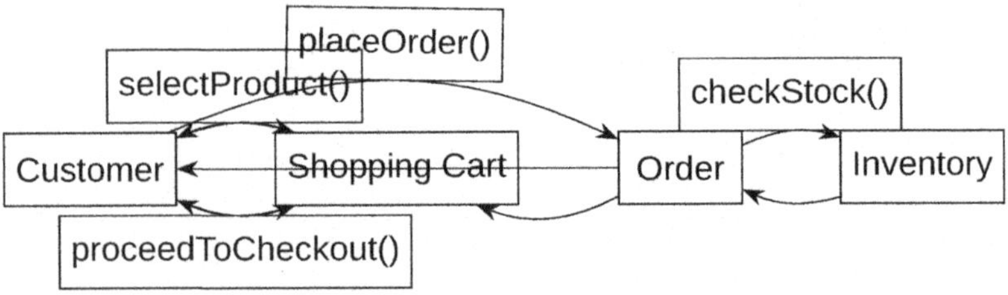

- **Activity Diagrams:** Activity diagrams model the workflow and depict the detailed logic of a business process or system function. They show the control flow from one activity to another with constructs such as decision points, concurrency, and synchronization.

  Example activity diagram for the order processing workflow:

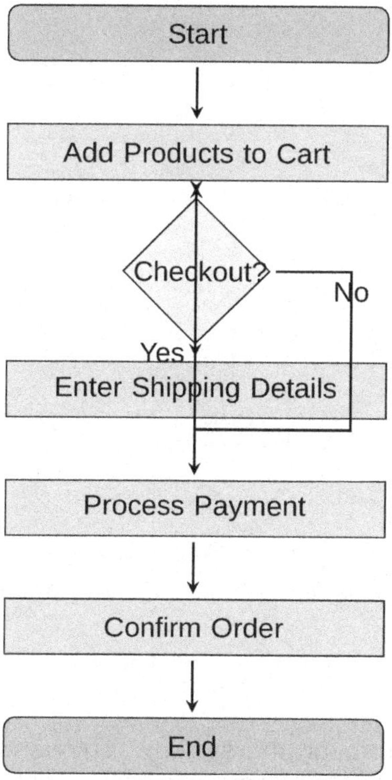

Entity-Relationship Diagrams (ERD)

ERDs represent the database schema by showing entities, their attributes, and relationships. This notation is crucial in data design and management, laying the groundwork for the system's data layer.

Example ERD for the e-commerce application:

State Machine Diagrams

State machine diagrams, also known as state charts, represent the states of an object and the transitions between these states. These diagrams are valuable for modeling dynamic behaviors within the system.

Example state machine diagram for order processing:

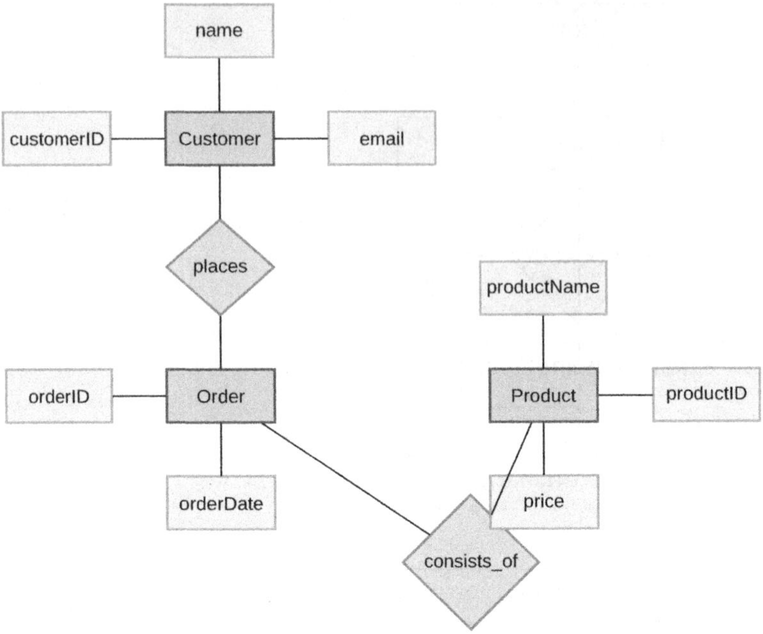

Data Flow Diagrams (DFD)

DFDs illustrate how data flows through the system. They show the sources and destinations of data and the processes that transform data. DFDs are useful in understanding the functional aspects and data dependencies.

Example DFD for order management:

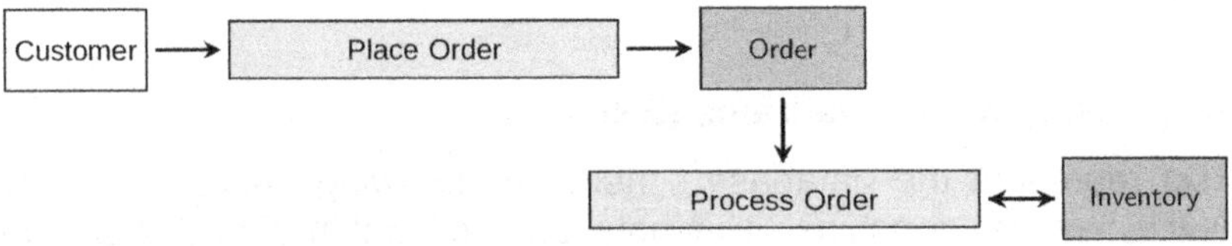

Each of these notations provides a different perspective on the system, helping to ensure comprehensive coverage of all aspects of the design. Proper use of these notations not only facilitates clear communication among team members but also contributes to effective system documentation and maintenance.

4.9 Design Documentation

Design documentation serves as a critical cornerstone in the software development lifecycle, providing a formalized account of the design decisions, methodologies, and specifications that guide the construction and future maintenance of the software system. Effective design documentation ensures that all stakeholders, including developers, testers, maintainers, and clients, are aligned with the system's architectural blueprint and implementation details.

- **Purpose of Design Documentation:** The primary objective of design documentation is to capture comprehensive details about the system's design, facilitating clear communication among team members and ensuring the system's functionality, performance, and maintainability. It acts as a reference point during the development process and throughout the system's lifecycle.
- **Components of Design Documentation:** Design documentation typically encompasses multiple components, including but not limited to:
  - *System Overview:* High-level description of the system's purpose, scope, and objectives.
  - *Architectural Views:* Representations of the system's architecture using various views such as logical, development, process, and physical views.
  - *Design Diagrams:* Visual representations like UML diagrams (class, sequence, activity, use-case diagrams) that depict the structure and behavior of the system.
  - *Component Specifications:* Detailed descriptions of each system component, including interfaces, dependencies, and interactions.
  - *Data Models:* Depictions of data structures, database schemas, and the relationships between different data entities.
  - *Algorithm Descriptions:* Specifications of the algorithms used, including pseudo-codes, data flow diagrams, and complexity analysis.
  - *User Interface Design:* Mockups, wireframes, and interaction flows that outline the user interactions with the system.

  - *Design Rationale:* Justifications for key design decisions, highlighting trade-offs and alternatives considered.

- **Tools for Design Documentation:** Various tools and software are available to aid in the creation and management of design documentation. Commonly used tools include:

  - *Integrated Development Environments (IDEs):* Many modern IDEs provide plugins for generating documentation directly from the source code.
  - *UML and Diagram Tools:* Tools like Microsoft Visio, Lucidchart, and PlantUML are used to create and manage design diagrams.
  - *Documentation Generators:* Tools like Doxygen, Sphinx, and Javadoc automatically generate documentation from annotated code.
  - *Version Control Systems:* Systems like Git and SVN are used to track changes in the documentation and collaborate among team members.
  - *Wikis and Collaborative Platforms:* Platforms like Confluence, SharePoint, and GitHub Wikis facilitate collaborative documentation efforts and ensure accessibility.

- **Best Practices for Design Documentation:** Ensuring the quality and usefulness of design documentation involves adhering to certain best practices:

  - *Consistency:* Maintain consistency in terminology, symbols, and formatting throughout the documentation.
  - *Clarity and Precision:* Ensure that the documentation is clear, precise, and accessible to audiences with varying levels of technical expertise.
  - *Completeness:* Cover all critical aspects of the system design without omitting significant details.
  - *Up-to-date Information:* Regularly update the documentation to reflect changes and modifications in the system design.
  - *Modularity:* Structure the documentation into manageable, modular sections to facilitate navigation and comprehension.

- *Accessibility:* Ensure that the documentation is easily accessible to all team members and stakeholders.

A practical example of documenting a component specification is illustrated below. Consider a hypothetical class 'User' in a user management system.

```
public class User {
    private String userId;
    private String username;
    private String password;
    private String email;

    // Constructor
    public User(String userId, String username, String password, String email) {
        this.userId = userId;
        this.username = username;
        this.password = password;
        this.email = email;
    }

    // Getters and Setters
    public String getUserId() {
        return userId;
    }

    public void setUserId(String userId) {
        this.userId = userId;
    }

    public String getUsername() {
        return username;
    }

    public void setUsername(String username) {
        this.username = username;
    }

    public String getPassword() {
        return password;
    }

    public void setPassword(String password) {
        this.password = password;
    }

    public String getEmail() {
        return email;
    }

    public void setEmail(String email) {
        this.email = email;
    }
}
```

In the context of the user management system, the 'User' class represents a basic unit encapsulating user-specific information such as user ID, username, password, and email. The above Java code snippet delineates the attributes and methods associated with the 'User' class, forming a part of the component specification section in the design documentation.

The design documentation should also include the design rationale for important decisions made during the development process. For instance, the choice of data structures, algorithms, design patterns, or third-party libraries, and their implications on performance, scalability, and maintainability, should be meticulously recorded.

Comprehensive design documentation bridges the gap between ideation and implementation, providing a roadmap for the development team and a reference for future enhancements, thereby ensuring the system's robustness and adaptability over time.

4.10 Evaluating and Reviewing Designs

Evaluating and reviewing designs are essential processes in software engineering, enabling teams to ensure that design choices meet both functional and non-functional requirements. These activities help to identify potential flaws early in the development cycle, thereby reducing the risk of costly rework later on. This section will delve into the methodologies, criteria, and tools used for evaluating and reviewing software designs.

Design evaluation aims to assess whether the design meets specified criteria, such as performance, scalability, maintainability, and usability. It involves both qualitative and quantitative assessments, typically based on standards, guidelines, and best practices.

A primary method for evaluating design is through design reviews, which can be conducted at various levels, from informal peer reviews to formal inspections. A design review aims to identify discrepancies between the design and its requirements, uncover potential issues, and ensure design consistency and completeness.

- **Peer Reviews**
- **Walkthroughs**
- **Inspections**

First, **peer reviews** involve team members examining each other's work. This method builds collective ownership and facilitates knowledge sharing. Next, **walkthroughs** are more structured, with the designer leading the review, explaining the design step-by-step to the review team. Lastly, **inspections** are formal reviews where a moderator controls the process, ensuring a systematic examination of the design documents.

Design evaluation relies heavily on metrics and checklists. Common metrics include:

- **Coupling and Cohesion:** These metrics measure the interdependencies between modules (coupling) and the internal strength of a module (cohesion). Low coupling and high cohesion are desirable for a modular and maintainable design.
- **Complexity:** Metrics such as cyclomatic complexity, which quantifies the number of linearly independent paths through a program's source code, help identify potentially problematic areas in the design.
- **Code Coverage:** This evaluates the extent to which the source code is executed during testing, helping to identify under-tested parts of the design.
- **Performance:** Performance metrics assess how well the design meets performance requirements, including response time, throughput, and resource utilization.

Checklists are valuable tools for guiding design reviews. They ensure that all critical aspects of the design are considered and help maintain consistency across different reviews. Sample checklist items might include:

- Does the design conform to the requirements specification?
- Are all design patterns applied correctly and justifiably?
- Is the design modular, with low coupling and high cohesion?
- Are the interfaces well-defined and documented?
- Has the design considered scalability, performance, and security requirements?
- Are potential failure points and recovery mechanisms identified?

```
# Sample function to evaluate design metrics
def evaluate_design(design):
    metrics = {
        'coupling': calculate_coupling(design),
        'cohesion': calculate_cohesion(design),
        'complexity': calculate_cyclomatic_complexity(design),
        'code_coverage': calculate_code_coverage(design),
        'performance': measure_performance(design)
    }
    return metrics

# Dummy implementations for illustration
def calculate_coupling(design):
    return random.uniform(1, 10)

def calculate_cohesion(design):
    return random.uniform(1, 10)

def calculate_cyclomatic_complexity(design):
    return random.randint(1, 50)

def calculate_code_coverage(design):
    return random.uniform(0.5, 1.0)

def measure_performance(design):
    return random.uniform(1, 10)
```

Design reviews can also leverage formal modeling techniques to ensure design correctness. Formal methods involve mathematically specifying design aspects which can then be rigorously analyzed. Examples include finite state machines for modeling system states and transitions, and Petri nets for concurrent systems.

Another valuable tool for evaluating designs is prototyping. By developing an early model of the system, stakeholders can interact with the design and provide feedback. Prototypes help to validate the design, uncover usability issues, and ensure alignment with user needs.

Tools like Unified Modeling Language (UML) aid in constructing, visualizing, specifying, and documenting software system artifacts. UML diagrams (e.g., class diagrams, sequence diagrams) provide a clear and standardized way of representing design structures and behaviors, facilitating better communication and understanding during reviews.

When considering design evolution, it's important to incorporate aspects such as design patterns and architectural styles. Design patterns, being well-proven solutions to common problems, ensure that the design adheres to best practices and is easier to understand and maintain. Architectural styles (e.g., layered, microservices) shape the system's high-level structure, guiding how components interact and enforce architectural principles.

```
Design Review Output:
----------------------
- Coupling: 4.5
- Cohesion: 8.2
- Complexity: 12
- Code Coverage: 0.75
- Performance: 7.3

Issues Identified:
  1. High coupling between modules A and B.
  2. Low cohesion in module C.
  3. Performance below required threshold in critical operations.
```

Incorporating automated tools and continuous integration practices can streamline the evaluation process. Tools like static code analyzers and automated testing frameworks integrate with development workflows, providing real-time feedback on design quality and adherence to coding standards.

Design reviews must be iterative. As the design evolves, continuous evaluation and feedback loops are essential for maintaining quality. Regularly revisiting design choices, especially after significant changes or new requirements, ensures that the design remains robust, scalable, and maintainable throughout the development lifecycle.

Integrating these principles and practices fosters a disciplined approach to design evaluation, promoting high-quality software systems that meet both user expectations and business goals.

Chapter 5

Software Construction and Implementation

Software construction and implementation involve translating design specifications into executable code and ensuring the reliability and maintainability of the software. This chapter covers essential practices such as adhering to coding standards, using version control systems, and following construction practices like coding and debugging. It also discusses software configuration management, the importance of code reviews and inspections, and proper documentation. The chapter concludes by exploring various implementation strategies, refactoring techniques, and best practices for writing efficient, maintainable code.

5.1 Introduction to Software Construction

Software construction is a critical phase in the software development life cycle, characterized by the implementation of design specifications into reliable, functional, and maintainable code. This section delves into the foundational aspects of software construction, examining its essential principles and methodologies, while laying the groundwork for more advanced topics covered in subsequent sections.

At its core, software construction encompasses several interrelated activities including coding, verification, unit testing, debugging, integration, and maintenance. Each activity contributes to transforming the abstract design into a working software product. This requires a thorough understanding of programming languages, development environments, and the application domain.

Coding Practices:

Effective coding practices form the backbone of software construction. These practices ensure that code is not only functional but also maintainable and understandable. Key coding practices include:

- **Code Readability:** The ease with which code can be read and understood by other developers is paramount. Use meaningful variable names, consistent indentation, and appropriate comments.
- **Consistency:** Adhering to coding standards and guidelines established by the development team or organization ensures uniformity throughout the codebase. This includes naming conventions, code structure, and documentation style.
- **Modularity:** Code should be organized into reusable modules or functions. This promotes separation of concerns, making the system easier to understand, test, and maintain.
- **Error Handling:** Robust error handling and logging mechanisms are crucial in identifying and troubleshooting issues during development and after deployment.

Verification and Unit Testing:

Verification involves ensuring that the code meets its requirements and performs as expected. Unit testing is a vital verification technique, where individual units or components of the software are tested in isolation.

```
import unittest

def add(a, b):
    return a + b

class TestMathOperations(unittest.TestCase):
    def test_add(self):
        self.assertEqual(add(1, 2), 3)
        self.assertEqual(add(-1, 1), 0)

if __name__ == '__main__':
    unittest.main()
```

In the above example, the unittest framework in Python is used to test the add function. Writing and running unit tests help developers identify defects early in the construction process, reducing the cost and effort associated with fixing bugs at later stages.

Debugging:

Debugging is the process of identifying, analyzing, and fixing defects in the code. Effective debugging requires not only technical proficiency but also logical thinking and problem-solving skills. Modern integrated development environments (IDEs) provide powerful debugging tools that aid in setting breakpoints, inspecting variables, and stepping through code execution.

Consider the following scenario in a C++ program where a segmentation fault occurs:

```
#include <iostream>

void printArray(int* arr, int size) {
    for (int i = 0; i <= size; ++i) { // Off-by-one error
        std::cout << arr[i] << " ";
    }
    std::cout << std::endl;
}

int main() {
    int arr[5] = {1, 2, 3, 4, 5};
    printArray(arr, 5); // Expected size is 5
    return 0;
}
```

When executed, this code may cause a segmentation fault due to an off-by-one error in the printArray function. Using a debugger, a developer can step through the loop and observe the value of i exceeding the bounds of the array, enabling the identification and correction of the error.

Integration:

Integration involves combining the individual software modules and ensuring they work together as a cohesive system. Continuous integration (CI) practices automate this process, incorporating frequent code commits, automated builds, and tests to identify integration issues as early as possible.

A typical CI pipeline might include the following steps:

- **Code Commit:** Developers commit code to a version control system (VCS).

- **Build:** An automated build system compiles the code and generates executables.
- **Test:** Automated tests are run to verify the functionality of the integrated code.
- **Deploy:** If all tests pass, the build is deployed to a staging or production environment.

Maintenance:

Post-deployment, software enters the maintenance phase where it undergoes continuous improvements and fixes. Maintenance activities include correcting faults, improving performance, and adapting the software to changed environments or requirements. Effective documentation and adherence to coding standards facilitate smoother maintenance, enabling developers to understand and modify the codebase effectively.

Within this chapter, the practices and principles discussed lay a solid foundation for constructing robust software. Building on these, the subsequent sections will delve deeper into specific strategies, tools, and techniques that enhance the efficiency and reliability of software construction and implementation.

5.2 Coding Standards and Guidelines

Coding standards and guidelines are essential to ensure the consistency, quality, and maintainability of software systems. Adherence to these practices allows multiple developers to work effectively on a single codebase, facilitates code reviews, simplifies debugging, and ultimately reduces the cost of software development and maintenance.

Coding standards encompass a set of rules and conventions for writing code, including naming conventions, formatting styles, and the use of comments. Guidelines offer broader recommendations and best practices that might be context-dependent but are equally critical in maintaining code quality.

To begin with, proper naming conventions enhance readability and are a crucial aspect of coding standards. Variable, function, and class names should be descriptive and meaningful. For instance, variables storing the count of items should be named $\mathrm{itemCount}$ rather than ambiguous identifiers like i or ic.

```
// Bad naming convention
int ic = 5;

// Better naming convention
int itemCount = 5;
```

Consistency in naming conventions also extends to the case style. Common styles include camelCase, PascalCase, and snake_case, among others. Choosing a case style and consistently applying it across the entire codebase is crucial for maintaining readability. For example, camelCase is often used for variables and functions in Java, whereas C++ favors snake_case for variables and camelCase for functions.

```
// Consistent camelCase in Java
int totalItemCount = 0;

void calculateItemTotal() {
    // function implementation
}
```

Proper indentation and spacing are other fundamental aspects of coding standards. They improve the visual structure of the code, making it easier to understand logical blocks and flow. While different programming languages and organizations may have specific guidelines (such as indenting by four spaces or using tabs), the key is consistent application throughout the codebase.

```
# Incorrect indentation
if a > b:
print("a is greater than b")

# Correct indentation
if a > b:
    print("a is greater than b")
```

Commenting is a practice that, when done properly, provides clarity and insight into the code's functionality. Comments should not restate the obvious, but rather explain the why behind complex logic or algorithmic decisions. Inline comments are beneficial for explaining small pieces of code, while block comments or documentation comments (docstrings) are helpful for providing an overview and usage details for functions and classes.

```
# Correct use of comments

# Function to calculate the factorial of a number
def factorial(n):
    """
    Calculate the factorial of a number n.
    :param n: Integer for which the factorial is to be computed.
```

```
    :return: Factorial of n.
    """
    # Base case: if n is 0, return 1
    if n == 0:
        return 1
    else:
        # Recursive case: n * factorial of (n-1)
        return n * factorial(n-1)
```

Guidelines on error handling are pivotal for writing robust code. Proper error handling involves anticipating potential failures and implementing strategies to handle those failures gracefully. This includes checking for null values, validating user inputs, and using try-catch blocks to manage exceptions.

```
// Example of using try-catch blocks for error handling
public void readFile(String fileName) {
    try {
        FileReader fileReader = new FileReader(fileName);
        BufferedReader bufferedReader = new BufferedReader(fileReader);
        String line;

        while ((line = bufferedReader.readLine()) != null) {
            System.out.println(line);
        }
        bufferedReader.close();
    } catch (FileNotFoundException e) {
        System.err.println("File not found: " + fileName);
    } catch (IOException e) {
        System.err.println("Error reading file: " + fileName);
    }
}
```

Another critical guideline pertains to code organization. Functions should be small and focused on a single task, adhering to the principle of single responsibility. This practice not only makes the code more readable but also facilitates easier testing and debugging.

```
// Poor code organization
public void processOrder(Order order) {
    // Validate order
    if (order == null || order.getItems().isEmpty()) {
        throw new IllegalArgumentException("Order is invalid");
    }

    // Calculate total price
    double totalPrice = 0;
    for (Item item : order.getItems()) {
        totalPrice += item.getPrice();
    }

    // Update order status
    order.setStatus("Processed");

    // Notify the customer
    notifyCustomer(order);
}
```

```
// Improved code organization with single responsibility
public void processOrder(Order order) {
    validateOrder(order);
    double totalPrice = calculateTotalPrice(order);
    updateOrderStatus(order, "Processed");
    notifyCustomer(order);
}

private void validateOrder(Order order) {
    if (order == null || order.getItems().isEmpty()) {
        throw new IllegalArgumentException("Order is invalid");
    }
}

private double calculateTotalPrice(Order order) {
    double totalPrice = 0;
    for (Item item : order.getItems()) {
        totalPrice += item.getPrice();
    }
    return totalPrice;
}

private void updateOrderStatus(Order order, String status) {
    order.setStatus(status);
}

private void notifyCustomer(Order order) {
    // Notification logic here
}
```

Testability is another key consideration. Writing code in a way that facilitates easy testing, such as using dependency injection and avoiding tight coupling between components, can significantly improve both reliability and maintainability.

```
// Code not easy to test due to tight coupling
public class OrderProcessor {
    private InventoryService inventoryService = new InventoryService();

    public void processOrder(Order order) {
        inventoryService.checkInventory(order.getItems());
        // Order processing logic
    }
}

// Improved code with dependency injection for better testability
public class OrderProcessor {
    private InventoryService inventoryService;

    public OrderProcessor(InventoryService inventoryService) {
        this.inventoryService = inventoryService;
    }

    public void processOrder(Order order) {
        inventoryService.checkInventory(order.getItems());
        // Order processing logic
    }
}
```

Maintaining a clean and consistent codebase is an ongoing process that requires discipline and collaboration from all team members. Utilizing tools such as linters and formatter plugins can help automate the enforcement of coding standards.

For example, employing a linter in a Python project can help catch stylistic errors and enforce coding standards automatically:

```
$ pylint my_project/
```

The use of formatters such as prettier for JavaScript can auto-format code on save, ensuring consistent styling across the project:

```
$ prettier --write .
```

Adopting and following coding standards and guidelines ensures that the code is not only functional but also maintainable and scalable, enabling teams to build and expand systems more effectively and with fewer errors.

5.3 Version Control Systems

Version control systems (VCS) play an indispensable role in modern software development. By managing changes to source code over time, VCS provide a systematic method for tracking revisions, collaborating with multiple developers, and maintaining the integrity of codebases. This section delves into the fundamentals of version control systems, their types, and best practices for effective usage.

Version control systems are broadly classified into two categories: centralized and distributed. Centralized version control systems (CVCS) rely on a single central repository to store all versions of the software. Developers checkout code from this central repository, make changes, and commit updates back to it. Examples include CVS (Concurrent Versions System) and Subversion (SVN). Conversely, distributed version control systems (DVCS) maintain multiple copies of the repository, thereby decentralizing the storage of code versions. Each developer has a local repository, which can be synchronized with others. Prominent examples of DVCS are Git and Mercurial.

Centralized Version Control Systems: Centralized version control systems have been pivotal in the evolution of software development. These systems store all versions of the project in a single, central repository. Developers commit their changes directly to this central point, facilitating easier management of the codebase. However, this centralization also introduces certain limitations. The dependency on a single server means that if the server becomes inaccessible, development can be severely hindered.

Distributed Version Control Systems: Distributed version control systems, such as Git and Mercurial, address some of the limitations inherent in centralized systems. In DVCS, each developer has a full copy of the entire repository, including its history. This redundancy provides robustness and flexibility. Furthermore, distributed systems excel in supporting branching and merging operations, which are crucial for modern collaborative and exploratory workflows.

Illustrating a typical workflow in Git, consider the following commands:

```
# Clone the repository
git clone https://github.com/user/repository.git

# Navigate to the repository directory
cd repository

# Create a new branch for a feature
git checkout -b feature-branch

# Add changes to the staging area
git add .

# Commit changes with a message
git commit -m "Implemented new feature"

# Push the changes to the remote repository
git push origin feature-branch

# Merge the feature branch back into the main branch
git checkout main
git merge feature-branch

# Push the updated main branch to the remote repository
git push origin main
```

Best Practices for Using Version Control Systems: To maximize the benefits of version control systems, it is essential to follow established best practices. These practices facilitate collaboration, enhance code quality, and ensure a smooth development process.

- **Commit Often:** Regularly committing changes helps track the progress of development and makes it easier to identify and isolate errors. Commits should be small, logical units of work that describe a single feature or fix.
- **Write Descriptive Commit Messages:** Commit messages should be concise yet descriptive enough to understand the

changes made. Following a structured format can enhance readability, for instance:

  - **Header:** A brief summary of the commit (50 characters or less).
  - **Body:** A detailed explanation of the changes, if necessary (wrap at 72 characters).

- **Use Branches:** Branching allows developers to work on features or fixes in isolation without affecting the main codebase. Naming conventions for branches (e.g., feature/feature-name, bugfix/bug-name) can provide clarity.

- **Merge Frequently:** Regularly merging changes from branches into the mainline codebase helps prevent integration issues and reduces the likelihood of conflicts.

- **Review Code:** Code review mechanisms, such as pull requests in Git, enable peers to inspect changes before they are merged. This practice enhances code quality and knowledge sharing among team members.

- **Tagging Releases:** Tags in VCS serve as fixed points in the repository history, often representing versions or releases of the software. This practice helps track and revert to specific versions if needed.

When utilized effectively, version control systems not only streamline the development process but also improve collaboration, accountability, and the overall quality of the software. Integrating VCS seamlessly into the software construction workflow is pivotal for ensuring the sustainment and evolution of robust, maintainable codebases.

5.4 Construction Practices: Coding and Debugging

Effective coding and debugging practices are fundamental to ensuring the quality, reliability, and maintainability of software systems. Mastering these practices involves a combination of writing clean, readable code, employing systematic debugging techniques, and using tools that facilitate the construction and testing of software components.

Adhering to Coding Standards: Implementing consistent coding standards helps in maintaining code readability and uniformity. This uniformity makes it easier for multiple developers to work on the same codebase collaboratively. Standard practices involve coherent naming conventions, consistent use of whitespace, and structured formatting. For instance, following a naming convention like camelCase for variables and PascalCase for function names can significantly enhance code clarity.

Example:

```
# Consistent naming conventions
def calculateTotalRevenue(salesData):
    totalRevenue = 0
    for entry in salesData:
        totalRevenue += entry['price'] * entry['quantity']
    return totalRevenue
```

Commenting and Documentation: In-line comments and documentation are vital for understanding the purpose and functionality of the code. Well-commented code is easier to debug and maintain. However, comments should be used judiciously; overly verbose comments can clutter the code, whereas insufficient comments can lead to confusion.

Example:

```
def calculateTotalRevenue(salesData):
    """
    Calculate the total revenue from a list of sales data.

    Args:
        salesData (list): A list of dictionaries with 'price' and 'quantity' keys.

    Returns:
        float: The total revenue.
    """
    totalRevenue = 0 # Initialize total revenue
    for entry in salesData:
        # Add to total revenue by multiplying price with quantity
        totalRevenue += entry['price'] * entry['quantity']
    return totalRevenue
```

Code Modularity and Reusability: Writing modular code improves the manageability and reusability of software components. Functions and classes should represent single responsibilities, adhering to the Single Responsibility Principle (SRP). This principle states that a class or function should have only one reason to change, leading to more robust and testable code.

Example:

```
class SalesDataProcessor:
    def __init__(self, salesData):
        self.salesData = salesData

    def calculateTotalRevenue(self):
        totalRevenue = 0
        for entry in self.salesData:
            totalRevenue += entry['price'] * entry['quantity']
        return totalRevenue

# Usage
salesData = [
    {'price': 19.99, 'quantity': 3},
    {'price': 5.99, 'quantity': 10}
]

processor = SalesDataProcessor(salesData)
print(processor.calculateTotalRevenue())
```

Systematic Debugging Techniques: Debugging is an integral part of the construction phase. Employing systematic debugging techniques can drastically shorten the time required to identify and resolve issues.

Print Statements: One of the simplest debugging techniques involves inserting print statements to output the values of variables at various points in the execution flow. This helps in understanding whether the code behaves as expected.

```
def calculateTotalRevenue(salesData):
    totalRevenue = 0
    for entry in salesData:
        print(f"Processing entry: {entry}") # Debug statement
        totalRevenue += entry['price'] * entry['quantity']
    print(f"Total Revenue: {totalRevenue}") # Debug statement
    return totalRevenue
```

Using Debuggers: Modern Integrated Development Environments (IDEs) offer robust debugging tools. Breakpoints allow the developer to pause execution at specific lines, inspect variable values, and step through code line-by-line.

Example Workflow:

- Set a breakpoint at the beginning of a function.
- Start the debugger.
- Execution will pause at the breakpoint.
- Inspect the values of variables in the IDE's debug panel.
- Step through the code line-by-line using step-over and step-into functionalities to monitor the flow.

Unit Testing: Writing unit tests for individual functions or methods ensures that each part of the codebase works as intended. Unit tests are typically automated, allowing for rapid verification of code correctness.

Example with unittest **framework:**

```
import unittest

class TestSalesDataProcessor(unittest.TestCase):
    def test_calculateTotalRevenue(self):
        salesData = [
            {'price': 19.99, 'quantity': 3},
            {'price': 5.99, 'quantity': 10}
        ]
        processor = SalesDataProcessor(salesData)
        self.assertEqual(processor.calculateTotalRevenue(), 119.87)

if __name__ == "__main__":
    unittest.main()
```

Continuous Integration and Testing: Incorporating continuous integration (CI) pipelines ensures that code changes are automatically tested, providing immediate feedback. Tools like Jenkins, Travis CI, or GitHub Actions can be configured to run a series of tests whenever code is pushed to the repository.

Process:

- Code is pushed to the repository.
- CI pipeline is triggered.
- Automated tests are executed.
- Results are reported back, highlighting any failed tests.

Example CI Configuration with GitHub Actions:

```
name: Python application

on: [push]

jobs:
  test:
    runs-on: ubuntu-latest

    steps:
    - uses: actions/checkout@v2
    - name: Set up Python
      uses: actions/setup-python@v2
      with:
        python-version: 3.8
    - name: Install dependencies
      run: |
        python -m pip install --upgrade pip
```

```
      pip install -r requirements.txt
    - name: Run tests
      run: |
        python -m unittest discover
```

Pair Programming: This collaborative technique involves two developers working together at a single workstation. One writes the code (the driver), while the other reviews each line as it is written (the observer or navigator). This practice helps catch errors early and provides instant feedback.

Deploying these construction practices ensures efficient code development, reduces the introduction of defects, and enhances the overall quality of the software product.

5.5 Software Configuration Management

Software Configuration Management (SCM) is a critical discipline in software engineering that focuses on tracking and controlling changes in the software. It ensures that the software remains consistent and reliable throughout its lifecycle. SCM encompasses a range of practices, tools, and methodologies designed to manage the evolution of software products systematically. This section delves into the various aspects of SCM, covering its importance, core activities, and the tools commonly used to implement effective configuration management.

Importance of SCM

SCM is essential for several reasons. It helps in maintaining the integrity and traceability of the software artifacts, which include source code, documentation, and configuration files. SCM ensures that changes are made systematically and can be traced back to their origins. This traceability is crucial for understanding the impact of changes and for auditing purposes.

Moreover, SCM facilitates collaboration among team members. In a multi-developer environment, it is imperative to have a system that manages concurrent access to the source code. SCM provides mechanisms to handle versioning, branching, merging, and conflict resolution, thus enabling multiple developers to work on the same project without interfering with each other's work.

Core Activities in SCM

The core activities in SCM can be categorized into the following:

- **Configuration Identification:** This involves the identification of the configuration items (CIs) that need to be managed. CIs can be any software artifact such as source code files, documentation, test scripts, and build configuration files. Each CI is uniquely identified and tracked.
- **Configuration Control:** Configuration control is the process of managing changes to the CIs. It includes the evaluation, coordination, and approval of changes before they are implemented. This activity ensures that only authorized changes are made and that the impact of changes is assessed.
- **Configuration Status Accounting:** This involves recording and reporting the status of CIs and changes. It provides information on the version history, current state, and change status of each CI. This transparency is crucial for project tracking and auditing.
- **Configuration Audits:** Configuration audits are conducted to verify that the CIs conform to their specifications and that the SCM policies are being followed. Audits can be functional, ensuring that the software performs as required, or physical, ensuring that all CIs are present and correctly configured.

Tools for SCM

Several tools are available to support the different activities of SCM. These tools can be broadly classified into Version Control Systems (VCS), Build Automation Tools, and Issue Tracking Systems.

Version Control Systems (VCS)

VCS are essential for managing changes to source code. They provide mechanisms for versioning, branching, and merging code, which are fundamental activities in collaborative development. Common VCSs include Git, Subversion (SVN), and Mercurial. Below is an example of basic Git commands used to initialize a repository, add changes, and commit those changes:

```
# Initialize a new Git repository
git init

# Add files to the staging area
git add .

# Commit the changes
git commit -m "Initial commit"
```

Build Automation Tools

Build automation tools help in automating the process of compiling source code into executable programs. They ensure that the build process is repeatable and consistent. Examples of build automation tools include Apache Maven, Gradle, and Make. An example of a Makefile for a C++ project might look like this:

```
CC=g++
CFLAGS=-I.

hellomake: hellomake.o hellofunc.o
	$(CC) -o hellomake hellomake.o hellofunc.o -I.
```

Issue Tracking Systems

Issue tracking systems, such as Jira, Bugzilla, and Trello, are used to track and manage issues, tasks, and feature requests. They provide a platform for reporting bugs, assigning tasks, and tracking the progress of development activities. These tools integrate with VCS and other SCM tools to provide a comprehensive view of the project's status.

Best Practices in SCM

Adopting best practices in SCM is vital to ensure the effectiveness of the configuration management process. Some of the best practices include:

- **Commit Often:** Frequent commits help in keeping track of changes and reduce the complexity of integrating large changes.
- **Use Descriptive Commit Messages:** Clear and descriptive commit messages help in understanding the nature of changes and facilitate easier code reviews and debugging.
- **Branching Strategy:** Adopt a branching strategy that suits the team's workflow. Common strategies include Git Flow, Feature Branching, and Trunk-Based Development.
- **Code Review:** Implement mandatory code reviews to ensure code quality and consistency. Code reviews facilitate knowledge sharing and help in identifying potential issues early in the development cycle.

SCM is fundamental to maintaining the quality and integrity of software products throughout their lifecycle. By implementing robust SCM practices and utilizing effective tools, development teams can manage changes efficiently, ensure collaboration, and maintain a high level of quality in their software projects.

5.6 Code Reviews and Inspections

Code reviews and inspections are pivotal in ensuring the quality and maintainability of software projects. These practices involve the systematic examination of source code by one or more developers, aside from the original author, to identify defects, ensure adherence to coding standards, and enhance code quality through collaborative feedback.

At the core, code reviews and inspections aim to:

- Detect and fix bugs and defects early.
- Improve code readability and maintainability.
- Ensure compliance with coding standards and guidelines.
- Facilitate knowledge sharing and team cohesion.
- Identify potential areas of improvement.

Types of Code Reviews and Inspections

Multiple types of code reviews and inspections can be integrated into the software construction process. Each type serves distinct purposes and can be applied effectively depending on the project's needs.

Formal Inspections

Formal inspections are structured processes rooted in rigorous methodologies. They typically follow a predefined checklist and involve multiple stages: planning, overview, preparation, inspection meeting, rework, and follow-up. These inspections often utilize roles such as the moderator, author, reader, and recorder, ensuring that the process is meticulous and comprehensive.

Walkthroughs

Walkthroughs are semi-formal reviews where the author guides reviewers through the code, often explaining the logic and design choices. Reviewers then question and discuss specific parts of the code to uncover potential issues. Walkthroughs are less structured than formal inspections but still provide significant value in catching defects and improving understanding.

Peer Reviews

Peer reviews, also known as teammate reviews, are informal evaluations conducted by fellow developers. These reviews are generally more casual and may take place during regular collaboration or pair programming sessions. Despite the lack of structure, peer reviews can be very effective in catching minor issues and fostering continuous feedback.

Ad-hoc Reviews

Ad-hoc reviews are the least formal type, typically involving spontaneous and impromptu examination of code changes. While they may lack the organization of formal reviews, their flexibility allows for quick feedback and immediate issue resolution.

Automated Reviews

Automated reviews leverage tools and scripts to perform static code analysis, enforce coding standards, and identify potential defects. While automated tools can significantly reduce the time spent on reviews, they should complement rather than replace human examination, as they might not fully grasp the context or intent behind the code.

Best Practices for Conducting Code Reviews

To maximize the efficacy of code reviews and inspections, adherence to best practices is crucial:

- **Define Clear Objectives:** Establish clear goals for the review process, such as ensuring code quality, identifying defects, or improving maintainability.
- **Set Ground Rules:** Specify rules for code reviews, such as the scope, frequency, and acceptable feedback methods. This ensures a standardized approach and consistency across the team.
- **Keep Reviews Focused and Manageable:** Limit the scope of each review to a manageable amount of code, typically 200-400 lines. Larger reviews can be overwhelming and less effective.
- **Foster a Constructive Atmosphere:** Encourage respectful, constructive feedback that focuses on the code rather than the developer. This helps in maintaining a positive team atmosphere and encourages openness.
- **Use Checklists:** Utilize checklists tailored to your project's specific needs to ensure that all relevant aspects of the code are examined systematically.
- **Leverage Tools:** Employ code review tools and platforms, such as GitHub, GitLab, or Bitbucket, which provide functionalities like

inline comments, approvals, and integration with version control systems.

- **Follow Up on Issues:** Ensure that identified defects and suggestions are addressed promptly. Maintain a tracking system if necessary to ensure nothing gets overlooked.
- **Continuous Improvement:** Regularly assess and refine the code review process based on team feedback and evolving project requirements.

Sample Code Review Checklist

The following is a sample checklist that can be adopted for code reviews. This checklist is not exhaustive and should be customized according to project-specific needs:

- **Code Functionality:**
  - Does the code perform the intended function?
  - Are edge cases and unexpected inputs handled appropriately?
  - Are there any logic errors or misconceptions?
- **Code Readability:**
  - Is the code easy to understand?
  - Are meaningful variable names used?
  - Are comments and documentation present where necessary?
- **Code Efficiency:**
  - Are there any performance bottlenecks?
  - Can the algorithm be optimized?
  - Are there any unnecessary computations or redundant code?
- **Code Style:**
  - Is the code consistent with the project's coding standards?
  - Are indentation and spacing properly applied?
  - Is the code free of hardcoded values?

- **Error Handling:**
  - Are errors and exceptions properly handled?
  - Are resources (e.g., memory, file handles) properly managed and released?
- **Security:**
  - Are there any potential security vulnerabilities?
  - Are user inputs properly validated and sanitized?

An Example Code Review in Practice

Consider a simple Python function designed to compute the factorial of a given number. The following listing illustrates the initial implementation:

```
def factorial(n):
    result = 1
    for i in range(2, n + 1):
        result *= i
    return result
```

During the code review, the reviewers might observe the following:

- The code correctly computes the factorial.
- The variable result is appropriately named and conveys its purpose.
- The loop construct and arithmetic operations are simple and efficient for the given task.
- There are no comments or documentation explaining the function's purpose or use cases.
- Edge cases, such as the factorial of negative numbers or large numbers, are not explicitly handled.

After the review, the revised function may look like this:

```
def factorial(n):
    """
    Computes the factorial of a non-negative integer n.

    Parameters:
    n (int): A non-negative integer whose factorial is to be computed.

    Returns:
```

```
    int: Factorial of the input integer n.

    Raises:
    ValueError: If n is negative.
    """
    if n < 0:
        raise ValueError("Input must be a non-negative integer.")

    result = 1
    for i in range(2, n + 1):
        result *= i
    return result
```

The improved implementation includes:

- A docstring that describes the function's purpose, parameters, return value, and potential exceptions.
- An explicit check for negative input values, raising a ValueError to handle this edge case.
- The rest of the code remains efficient and maintains readability.

The application of code reviews and inspections fosters a deeper understanding of code among team members and cultivates a culture of accountability and continuous improvement. Moreover, it significantly reduces the likelihood of defects making it into production, thereby enhancing the overall quality and reliability of the software project.

5.7 Documentation in Software Construction

Documentation is a fundamental aspect of software construction, serving as the cornerstone for maintainability, readability, and effective communication within the development team and beyond. Proper documentation ensures that software systems can be understood, modified, and extended over time. This section delves into the various types of documentation, best practices, tools, and methodologies for creating thorough and effective software documentation.

Types of Documentation

Documentation in software construction can be broadly categorized into several types, each serving distinct purposes and audiences:

- **Requirements Documentation**: Captures the software requirements and specifications. It is intended for stakeholders, project managers, and developers to ensure a common understanding of what the software is supposed to achieve. This includes functional requirements, non-functional requirements, use cases, and user stories.
- **Design Documentation**: Details the architecture and design decisions. This includes descriptions of the overall system architecture, design patterns used, data models, and interface design. It is primarily aimed at developers and architects.
- **Technical Documentation**: Provides in-depth details about the codebase, APIs, algorithms, and data structures. It assists developers during implementation and maintenance phases. Common formats include code comments, API documentation, and technical specifications.
- **User Documentation**: Guides end-users on how to use the software. This includes user manuals, online help, FAQs, and tutorials. The primary audience is the end-user, but developers and support staff also utilize these documents to understand end-user perspectives.
- **Process Documentation**: Records the process followed during the software development lifecycle. This encompasses project plans, test plans, meeting notes, and other documents that track the progress and methodologies used. It is essential for project managers, quality assurance teams, and for compliance purposes.

Best Practices for Documentation

Creating effective documentation requires adherence to best practices that ensure clarity, completeness, and usability:

- **Clarity and Conciseness**: Documentation should be clear and concise. Avoid jargon and ensure the content is understandable by its intended audience. Use diagrams, tables, and examples where appropriate to enhance understanding.
- **Consistency**: Maintain consistency in terminology, formatting, and structure throughout the documentation. Consistent use of naming conventions, headings, and styles helps in maintaining uniformity.

- **Up-to-Date Information**: Documentation should be regularly updated to reflect changes in the software. Outdated documentation can mislead developers and users, resulting in errors and inefficiencies.
- **Accessibility**: Ensure that documentation is easily accessible to all stakeholders. This can be achieved through organized documentation repositories, use of familiar formats, and proper indexing and navigation aids.
- **Automation**: Utilize tools that automate the generation and maintenance of documentation. For instance, tools like Doxygen, Sphinx, and Javadoc can extract comments from code to create API documentation.
- **Review and Feedback**: Regularly review documentation and incorporate feedback from users and developers. Just as code reviews are critical, documentation reviews help in identifying gaps, errors, and areas for improvement.

Tools and Technologies for Documentation

Numerous tools and technologies are available for creating and maintaining documentation:

- **Word Processors and Wiki Platforms**: Tools like Microsoft Word, Google Docs, Confluence, and MediaWiki are commonly used for requirements and design documentation.
- **Code Documentation Generators**: Tools such as Doxygen, Sphinx, and Javadoc are valuable for generating technical documentation directly from code comments.
- **Markdown and LaTeX**: These markup languages are extensively used for writing technical documents due to their simplicity and powerful formatting capabilities.
- **Integrated Development Environments (IDEs)**: Modern IDEs like Visual Studio, Eclipse, and IntelliJ IDEA often include built-in support for documentation generation and management.

Impact of Documentation on Software Quality

Effective documentation significantly impacts the quality of software:

- **Maintainability**: Comprehensive documentation helps new developers get up to speed quickly, reducing the learning curve and minimizing the risk of introducing errors during maintenance.

- **Reusability**: Well-documented components are easier to understand and reuse in different parts of the project or in other projects, promoting code reuse.

- **Collaboration**: Clear documentation serves as a common reference point for all team members, facilitating better communication and collaboration.

- **Compliance and Auditability**: Proper documentation is often required for regulatory compliance and is invaluable during audits, ensuring that software development processes follow best practices and standards.

In practice, the quality of documentation is a direct reflection of the overall quality of the software development process. Neglecting documentation can lead to misunderstandings, technical debt, and increased costs over the software lifecycle. As such, documentation should be treated as a critical element of the software construction process, receiving the same level of attention and rigor as coding and testing activities.

5.8 Implementation Strategies: Top-Down vs. Bottom-Up

In software construction, selecting the appropriate implementation strategy is crucial for ensuring that the development process is both efficient and effective. Two primary implementation strategies are frequently employed in software engineering: top-down and bottom-up. Understanding the nuances and applications of these approaches enables software engineers to make informed decisions, tailor their development process to specific project needs, and ultimately produce high-quality software.

The top-down implementation strategy, often referred to as stepwise refinement, begins with an abstract design that is progressively refined into more detailed levels of implementation. This method relies heavily on the initial specification and design phases, ensuring that the overall architecture is well-defined before coding begins. The top-down strategy emphasizes breaking down the system from the general to the specific, allowing developers to focus on high-level functionalities before delving into finer details.

Conversely, the bottom-up implementation strategy starts with developing the fundamental components or modules without necessarily having a comprehensive view of the system's overall architecture. These modules are then incrementally integrated to build higher-level functionalities. This approach emphasizes building and testing small, manageable components first, which are then combined to form larger subsystems and eventually the complete system.

Top-Down Implementation

The top-down strategy is highly effective in projects where the requirements and overall system design are well-understood from the outset. It is particularly beneficial in projects that have stringent design constraints or where high-level architectural decisions significantly impact the system's success. This approach facilitates early identification of architectural issues and enables more straightforward management of complex systems by breaking them down into hierarchical layers.

- **Benefits:**
  - Ensures a clear and consistent architectural vision.
  - Facilitates early identification of design flaws and integration issues.
  - Enhances modular design, allowing different teams to work on separate components concurrently.
- **Challenges:**
  - Requires a comprehensive initial understanding of system requirements and design.
  - Changes in high-level design can propagate and require extensive refactoring.
  - May lead to longer initial phases before any executable code is available.

The following example illustrates a simplified top-down approach using pseudocode for a library management system.

```
# High-Level Function
def manage_library():
    manage_inventory()
    manage_loans()
    manage_users()

# Breaking Down into Sub-functions
def manage_inventory():
    add_books()
    remove_books()
    update_books()

def manage_loans():
    check_out_book()
    return_book()

def manage_users():
    add_user()
    remove_user()

# Further Details in Sub-functions
def add_books():
    # Detailed implementation
    pass

def remove_books():
    # Detailed implementation
    pass

def update_books():
    # Detailed implementation
    pass

def check_out_book():
    # Detailed implementation
    pass

def return_book():
    # Detailed implementation
    pass

def add_user():
    # Detailed implementation
    pass

def remove_user():
    # Detailed implementation
    pass
```

Bottom-Up Implementation

The bottom-up strategy is suited for projects that are exploratory in nature or where the high-level requirements are not fully defined at the beginning. It is advantageous in scenarios where reusable components or libraries have already been developed, allowing for prompt integration and testing of these pre-existing components. Bottom-up development supports iterative and incremental development, facilitating frequent testing and validation of individual units.

- **Benefits:**
  - Promotes early testing and validation of system components.
  - Encourages reusability of self-contained modules.
  - Enables flexible and iterative development, which is suitable for agile methodologies.
- **Challenges:**
  - May result in integration difficulties if the overall architecture is not well-coordinated.
  - Requires careful planning to ensure all modules integrate seamlessly.

A simplified bottom-up approach is demonstrated below, where fundamental functions are developed first and then integrated.

```
# Basic Utility Functions
def add_books():
    # Detailed implementation
    pass

def remove_books():
    # Detailed implementation
    pass

def update_books():
    # Detailed implementation
    pass

# Grouping Utility Functions into Higher-Level Functions
def manage_inventory():
    add_books()
    remove_books()
    update_books()

# High-Level Function Integrating All Sub-Functions
def manage_library():
    manage_inventory()
    manage_loans() # Assuming manage_loans() and manage_users() are implemented
        similarly
    manage_users()
```

Selecting between top-down and bottom-up strategies depends on various factors such as project scope, complexity, and the specific development contexts. Top-down implementation is often preferable for large systems with a clear high-level design, ensuring that all components align with the overall architecture from the outset. Bottom-up implementation is typically more adaptable, benefiting projects that require flexible, iterative development, and early testing of individual units.

Understanding and correctly applying these strategies is essential for software engineers aiming to construct reliable, maintainable, and efficient software. By recognizing the strengths and limitations of both top-down and bottom-up approaches, developers can tailor their implementation strategy to best suit the project's unique requirements and constraints.

5.9 Refactoring Techniques

Refactoring is the process of restructuring existing computer code without changing its external behavior, aimed at improving nonfunctional attributes of the software. It is a disciplined way to clean up code that minimizes the chances of introducing bugs. Martin Fowler's catalog of code refactoring techniques serves as a seminal reference for developers seeking to improve code structure. Properly applied refactoring techniques enhance readability, reduce complexity, and make the code more maintainable and easier to extend.

Motivations for Refactoring

The primary motivations for refactoring are to improve the internal structure of a system and to facilitate further development and maintenance. The following lists some common motivations:

- **Enhanced readability**: Clearer code is easier to understand and maintain.
- **Reduced complexity**: Simplified code reduces the risk of introducing errors and improves maintainability.
- **Increased reusability**: Refactored code can be more modular and reusable.
- **Improved performance**: Although not the primary focus, refactoring can sometimes lead to performance gains.

Common Refactoring Techniques

Extract Method: This technique involves moving a fragment of code into a separate method (or function) and replacing the original code with a call to this new method. It's useful when you have a block of code that can be grouped together and given a descriptive name, enhancing readability and reusability.

```
class Order {
    void process() {
        //some code
        addBonus();
        //some code
    }

    void addBonus() {
        // Bonus calculation logic
    }
}
```

Inline Method: The inverse of extract method, this technique is used when a method's body is as clear as its name and does not warrant separate abstraction.

```
class Order {
    void process() {
        //some code
        // Bonus calculation logic directly here if the method 'addBonus()' was
              superfluous.
        //some code
    }
}
```

Rename Method: Renaming methods to better describe their purpose can greatly enhance code understanding. Method names should be descriptive and clearly indicate what the method does.

```
class Order {
    void calcOrderBonus() { // Renaming addBonus() to calcOrderBonus() for clarity
        // Bonus calculation logic
    }
}
```

Move Method: Moving a method from one class to a more appropriate class helps to reduce coupling and improve cohesion, ensuring that each class handles logically related responsibilities.

```
class BonusProcessor {
    void calcOrderBonus(Order order) {
        // Bonus calculation logic
    }
}
```

Replace Temp with Query: If you have a temporary variable holding the result of an expression, you can replace it with a method call.

```
double temp = order.basePrice() * order.discountFactor();
```

can be refactored to:

```
double basePrice = order.basePrice();
double discountFactor = order.discountFactor();
```

```
double price = basePrice * discountFactor;
```

or more compactly:

```
double price = order.calcDiscountedPrice();
```

Refactoring for Encapsulation

Encapsulation is a fundamental principle in object-oriented programming, promoting information hiding by bundling the data and the methods that operate on the data within a single unit. Techniques that aid in achieving better encapsulation include:

Encapsulate Field: Making fields private and providing access through getter and setter methods to control modifications.

```
class Order {
    private double price;

    public double getPrice() {
        return price;
    }

    public void setPrice(double price) {
        this.price = price;
    }
}
```

Encapsulate Collection: Providing methods to modify collections instead of exposing the collections directly.

```
class Order {
    private List<Item> items;

    public void addItem(Item item) {
        items.add(item);
    }

    public void removeItem(Item item) {
        items.remove(item);
    }
}
```

Refactoring for Inheritance

Inheritance enables a new class to inherit properties and behavior from an existing class. Refactoring techniques that work well with inheritance include:

Pull Up Method: Moving a method to a superclass when it is used in multiple subclasses.

```
class Employee {
    String getDetails() {
```

```
        return "Employee details";
    }
}

class Manager extends Employee {
    // Previously had its own getDetails method
}
```

Push Down Method: Moving a method from a superclass to a subclass when it is used by only one subclass.

```
class Employee {
    // General attributes and behaviors
}

class Manager extends Employee {
    String getManagerDetails() {
        return "Manager details";
    }
}
```

Refactoring Tools

Modern Integrated Development Environments (IDEs) and tools support automated refactoring. Using these tools can speed up the process and reduce the risk of human error. Popular tools include:

- IntelliJ IDEA
- Eclipse
- Visual Studio
- ReSharper
- JRefactory

Automated tools provide features such as syntax checking, dependency analysis, and previews of refactoring effects, enhancing the reliability of the refactoring process.

Refactoring is an essential practice for maintaining the quality and sustainability of software systems. By judiciously applying refactoring techniques, developers can reduce technical debt and promote more robust architectures. This discipline, when integrated into standard development processes, yields greater efficiency, improved team collaboration, and software that is resilient to change.

5.10 Best Practices for Efficient and Maintainable Code

Efficient and maintainable code is essential for the longevity and scalability of software systems. This section discusses best practices that every software engineer should adopt to ensure their code is not only efficient in execution but also easy to understand, modify, and extend.

Adhering to the DRY Principle

The DRY (Don't Repeat Yourself) principle dictates that code should not be duplicated across different parts of a program. Instead, a single, unambiguous representation should be maintained. For instance, if a specific logic is to be used in multiple places, it should be encapsulated within a function or method. This minimizes error rates and makes future modifications easier. Consider the following code snippet:

```
# Bad practice: Repeated code
def calculate_area(rectangle):
    return rectangle.width * rectangle.height

def print_area(rectangle):
    area = rectangle.width * rectangle.height
    print(f'Area: {area}')
```

A more efficient and maintainable approach would be:

```
# Good practice: DRY principle
def calculate_area(rectangle):
    return rectangle.width * rectangle.height

def print_area(rectangle):
    print(f'Area: {calculate_area(rectangle)}')
```

Consistent Coding Style

Maintaining a consistent coding style across a codebase significantly improves the readability and maintainability of the software. This includes consistent usage of indentation, naming conventions, and comment styles. Many organizations and communities adopt coding standards such as PEP 8 for Python or Google's C++ Style Guide. Tools such as linters can be integrated into the development environment to enforce these styles automatically.

Meaningful Variable and Function Names

Variables, functions, and other identifiers should have meaningful and descriptive names. This practice reduces the cognitive load on readers, allowing them to understand the code without needing extensive comments. For example:

```
# Poor naming
def f(a, b):
    return a - b

# Meaningful naming
def calculate_difference(minuend, subtrahend):
    return minuend - subtrahend
```

Commenting and Documentation

While code should be self-explanatory to the greatest extent possible, comments and documentation play a crucial role in explaining the rationale behind complex logic or decisions. High-quality comments should not restate the obvious but rather provide insights into the "why" and "how." Documentation should cover the purpose, usage, and constraints of functions, classes, and modules. Python's docstrings and tools like JSDoc for JavaScript offer structured ways of writing this documentation.

```
def calculate_difference(minuend, subtrahend):
    """
    Calculates the difference between two numbers.

    Args:
        minuend (float): The number from which another number is to be subtracted.
        subtrahend (float): The number to be subtracted.

    Returns:
        float: The difference between minuend and subtrahend.
    """
    return minuend - subtrahend
```

Modular Design

Modularity in software design involves breaking down a program into distinct components or modules that can be developed, tested, and maintained independently. This promotes reuse and minimizes the impact of changes. For instance, a monolithic function handling both database queries and UI updates should be split into separate functions encapsulating each responsibility.

Use of Design Patterns

Design patterns provide proven solutions to common software design problems. They enhance code readability and reusability while promoting best practices. Familiar patterns include the Singleton, Observer, Factory, and Strategy patterns. Implementing these patterns where appropriate can significantly improve the architecture of the code.

```
class SingletonMeta(type):
```

```
    _instances = {}

    def __call__(cls, *args, **kwargs):
        if cls not in cls._instances:
            cls._instances[cls] = super().__call__(*args, **kwargs)
        return cls._instances[cls]

class Database(metaclass=SingletonMeta):
    pass
```

Automated Testing

Unit testing, integration testing, and system testing should be automated and part of the continuous integration process. Writing tests minimizes the risk of introducing new bugs and ensures the correctness of code modifications. Frameworks like pytest for Python or JUnit for Java make it easy to write and run tests.

```
import pytest

def test_calculate_difference():
    assert calculate_difference(10, 5) == 5
    assert calculate_difference(5, 10) == -5
```

Efficient Use of Resources

Efficiency in code is not merely about speed but also about the optimal use of resources, such as memory and CPU time. Algorithms and data structures should be chosen based on the operational characteristics of the software. Profiling tools can help identify bottlenecks, enabling targeted optimizations.

Refactoring

Refactoring involves restructuring existing code without changing its external behavior. This process improves the code's internal structure and readability, making it easier to maintain and extend. Techniques include renaming variables for clarity, breaking down large functions, and eliminating dead code.

Handling Exceptions Gracefully

Proper exception handling ensures that the software can manage unexpected events without crashing. This includes catching exceptions where they are expected and providing meaningful error messages or recovery mechanisms. For example:

```
try:
    result = calculate_difference(minuend, subtrahend)
except ZeroDivisionError as e:
    print(f'Error: {e}')
```

Integrating these best practices into everyday programming routines not only improves the immediate quality of the codebase but also sets a strong foundation for future development and collaboration. Such meticulous attention to detail in coding practices ultimately contributes to software that is robust, scalable, and easier to maintain over time.

Chapter 6

Software Testing and Quality Assurance

Software testing and quality assurance are crucial for ensuring that software systems meet specified requirements and perform reliably. This chapter discusses various types of testing, including unit, integration, system, and acceptance testing, as well as testing techniques like black-box and white-box testing. It covers test planning and management, automated testing, performance testing, security testing, and usability testing. The chapter also explores debugging techniques, quality assurance standards, metrics, and tools used to achieve high-quality software, while highlighting best practices in software testing.

6.1 Introduction to Software Testing and Quality Assurance

Software testing and quality assurance (QA) play a fundamental role in the software development lifecycle. These practices ensure that software products meet the specified requirements and perform reliably in real-world conditions. Testing evaluates the functionality of the software, while quality assurance encompasses all the systematic activities implemented to ensure that the quality requirements for a product are fulfilled.

The primary objective of software testing is to identify defects and ensure that the resultant software is free from critical issues before it reaches the end-users. It is a structured process that involves executing a program or application with the intent of finding software bugs or errors. Software testing can be seen as a preventive measure (preventing defects) and a corrective measure (correcting software bugs).

Quality assurance, on the other hand, is a broader discipline that ensures the processes used in software development lead to quality products. QA focuses not only on the finished product but also on improving and optimizing the processes used during development to prevent defects in the initial stages.

Core Components of Software Testing:

- **Test Planning:** Test planning defines the strategy and approach to be adopted for testing a project. It involves specifying objectives, identifying resources and scheduling test activities.
- **Test Design and Development:** This component involves creating detailed test cases and procedures. Test designers specify inputs, expected results, and test conditions for each test case.
- **Test Execution:** In this phase, actual testing is performed based on the prepared test cases. Testers execute the software, record the outcomes, and compare the actual results with the expected ones.
- **Defect Reporting and Tracking:** Defects and issues identified during testing are documented and reported. Defect tracking tools help manage the lifecycle of each defect, from discovery to resolution.
- **Test Closure:** Test closure activities include summarizing and evaluating the overall test effort. Key activities include test completion reporting, lessons learned, and archiving test artifacts for future reference.

Quality Assurance Activities:

- **Quality Audits:** Periodic reviews of the project's processes and procedures to ensure compliance with defined standards.
- **Process Improvement:** Continuous monitoring and enhancement of the software development process to improve quality and efficiency.

- **Training and Workshops:** Regular training and capability-building activities for the development and testing teams.
- **Reviews and Inspections:** Peer reviews of work products such as requirement documents, design documents, and code to identify defects in the early stages.

Key Principles of Software Testing:

- **Testing shows presence of defects:** Testing can show that defects are present, but cannot prove that the software is defect-free.
- **Exhaustive testing is impossible:** It is not feasible to test all possible combinations of data inputs, conditions, and scenarios.
- **Early testing:** Testing activities should start as early as possible in the software development lifecycle to detect defects as soon as they occur.
- **Defect clustering:** A small number of modules usually contain most of the defects detected.
- **Pesticide paradox:** Repeating the same test cases will not find new defects. Test cases should be regularly reviewed and revised.
- **Testing is context-dependent:** Different software applications require different types of testing approaches, techniques, and strategies.
- **Absence-of-errors fallacy:** Even if no defects are found, it does not guarantee that the software meets the user needs and requirements.

Types of Software Testing:

Software testing is broadly classified into two categories: static testing and dynamic testing.

Static Testing:

- Static testing involves inspecting and reviewing the software's static aspects, such as code, requirement documents, and design documents. It can be done manually or through automated tools.

- Techniques include code reviews, walkthroughs, and inspections.

Dynamic Testing:

- Dynamic testing involves executing the software with a given set of test cases. It can be classified into various levels: unit testing, integration testing, system testing, and acceptance testing.
- Functional and non-functional testing are subsets where functional testing focuses on the business requirements and specifications, and non-functional testing addresses aspects like performance, usability, and reliability.

Significance of Test Automation:

Test automation supports repeated execution of tests to verify software functionalities and regression testing. Automating tests increases accuracy and saves time, primarily when the same tests need to be executed multiple times during development cycles. Automated test scripts mimic user interactions and validate responses from user interfaces or APIs.

Example of a basic test automation script in Python using the unittest framework:

```
import unittest

def add(a, b):
    return a + b

class TestMathOperations(unittest.TestCase):
    def test_add(self):
        self.assertEqual(add(1, 2), 3)

if __name__ == '__main__':
    unittest.main()
```

Executing the above script would yield:

```
.
----------------------------------------------------------------------
Ran 1 test in 0.001s

OK
```

Software Quality Assurance Standards:

- **ISO/IEC 9126:** International standard for software product quality, providing a framework for evaluating software quality in terms of six characteristics – functionality, reliability, usability, efficiency, maintainability, and portability.

- **CMMI (Capability Maturity Model Integration):** Framework for process improvement that provides organizations with essential elements for effectively managing processes.
- **IEEE Standards:** The Institute of Electrical and Electronics Engineers (IEEE) provides various standards related to software testing and quality assurance, such as IEEE 829 for test documentation and IEEE 1028 for software reviews and audits.

By understanding and implementing these core principles and activities, teams can ensure that their software products not only meet functional requirements but also achieve high standards of quality and reliability throughout the software's lifecycle.

6.2 Types of Testing: Unit, Integration, System, and Acceptance

Software testing is a multifaceted discipline, encapsulating various levels that progressively validate the constructed software system. Each testing level, from unit to acceptance testing, serves a specific purpose in the software development lifecycle (SDLC) and is essential for ensuring the software's quality, functionality, and performance.

Unit testing is typically the first level of testing and is carried out by developers. This type of testing focuses on individual components or units of the software, which are the smallest testable parts. A unit can be a function, method, procedure, module, or object. The goal of unit testing is to validate that each unit performs as expected in isolation. By identifying defects early, unit testing can significantly reduce the cost and effort required to fix issues in later stages.

Most unit tests are automated and implemented using unit testing frameworks such as JUnit for Java, NUnit for .NET, or pytest for Python. These frameworks facilitate the creation, execution, and reporting of tests. A typical unit test is written to cover specific scenarios, including both typical and edge cases. Consider the following example of a unit test in Python using the pytest framework:

```
import pytest
from my_module import add

def test_add():
    assert add(1, 2) == 3
    assert add(-1, 1) == 0
```

```
assert add(0, 0) == 0
assert add(-1, -1) == -2
```

Integration testing follows unit testing and aims to identify issues that arise when combining individual units. During integration testing, interactions between integrated units are tested to ensure they work together as intended. This type of testing can be performed using various strategies, such as big-bang, top-down, bottom-up, and sandwich testing approaches.

In the big-bang approach, all or most of the units are combined at once and tested together, which can make it difficult to pinpoint the source of a defect. Top-down integration testing begins with the top-level modules and progressively integrates submodules, facilitating early verification of high-level logic. Bottom-up integration testing, conversely, starts with the lower-level modules and ascends. The sandwich approach combines both top-down and bottom-up strategies to leverage the advantages of both.

An example of an integration test in a Java environment might look like this:

```
import org.junit.jupiter.api.Test;
import static org.junit.jupiter.api.Assertions.assertEquals;

public class CalculatorServiceIntegrationTest {

    @Test
    public void testAdditionOperation() {
        CalculatorService calculatorService = new CalculatorService(new
                AdditionService());
        int result = calculatorService.performOperation(5, 3);
        assertEquals(8, result);
    }
}
```

System testing is the next phase and is a comprehensive evaluation of the complete system. System tests are performed in an environment that closely mimics the production environment to assess the software's compliance with specified requirements. These tests cover end-to-end scenarios, checking that the system as a whole meets the functional and non-functional specifications. This includes user interactions, system interactions, interfaces, hardware/software configuration, and performance.

A system test might involve testing multiple integrated applications or services in real-world conditions. For instance, system testing for an e-commerce application might include verifying the entire purchase process, from adding items to the cart, through payment, to the generation of order confirmations and notifications.

```
[Test Case ID: ST-01]
Test Scenario: Purchase Process Verification
Pre-conditions: User is logged in
Steps:
1. Add item to cart
2. Proceed to checkout
3. Enter payment details
4. Confirm order
Expected Result:
Order is processed successfully, order confirmation is displayed, and confirmation email is received.
```

Acceptance testing is the final level of testing and is conducted to determine whether the system meets the acceptance criteria. This type of testing is usually performed by the end-users or clients and consists of user acceptance testing (UAT) and business acceptance testing (BAT). The primary objective is to validate that the software meets the business requirements and is ready for deployment.

Acceptance tests are not only concerned with functionality but also with usability, performance, and compliance with business processes. These tests are often derived from user stories or use cases, ensuring that each feature and functionality aligns with user expectations. User acceptance testing may involve real-world scenarios and can be facilitated by test scripts that mimic typical user actions.

Here is an example of an acceptance test for a login feature:

```
[Test Case ID: AT-01]
Test Scenario: User Login Verification
Pre-conditions:
User account exists and is active

Steps:
1. Navigate to the login page
2. Enter valid username
3. Enter valid password
4. Click the 'Login' button

Expected Result:
User is successfully logged in and redirected to the homepage.
```

Through unit, integration, system, and acceptance testing, software systems undergo rigorous validation at multiple levels, ensuring comprehensive coverage and alignment with requirements. Each level addresses different aspects of the software, from individual components to complete system functionality and user satisfaction, thus contributing to the overall quality and reliability of the software.

6.3 Testing Techniques: Black Box vs. White Box

Software testing techniques are categorized into two primary approaches: black-box testing and white-box testing. These techniques differ significantly in their methodology, focus, and level of detail. Understanding both approaches is essential for a comprehensive testing strategy.

Black-box testing, also referred to as functional testing, examines the external behavior of the software. The tester is unaware of the internal workings or structure of the code. Instead, tests are designed based on the requirements and specifications of the software. This approach is akin to testing a system from the user's perspective, ensuring that the software performs as expected. Key techniques under black-box testing include equivalence partitioning, boundary value analysis, decision table testing, and state transition testing.

Equivalence Partitioning involves dividing the input data into different partitions where all members of a partition are expected to be treated similarly by the software. This reduces the number of test cases to a manageable level while ensuring adequate coverage.

```
# Python Example of Equivalence Partitioning
def classify_number(num):
    if num < 0:
        return "negative"
    elif num == 0:
        return "zero"
    else:
        return "positive"

# Test Cases
print(classify_number(-1)) # Expected: negative
print(classify_number(0)) # Expected: zero
print(classify_number(1)) # Expected: positive
```

Boundary Value Analysis is an enhancement of equivalence partitioning. It involves testing at the edges of these partitions, which often reveal errors in boundary conditions.

```
# Test Cases for Boundary Value Analysis
print(classify_number(-1)) # Expected: negative (boundary value)
print(classify_number(0)) # Expected: zero (boundary value)
print(classify_number(1)) # Expected: positive (boundary value)
```

Decision Table Testing provides a structured way of testing combinations of inputs and states. It is useful where different combinations of inputs result in different outcomes.

Input A	Input B	Output
0	0	0
0	1	1
1	0	1
1	1	2

Table 6.1: Decision Table Example

State Transition Testing is used when the system can be in multiple states, and transitions between these states are governed by the input conditions. The tests ensure that the system responds correctly when transitioning from one state to another.

```
State Transition Diagram:

State1 --(Input A)--> State2
State2 --(Input B)--> State3
State3 --(Input C)--> State1

Tests:
1. State1 -> Input A -> State2
2. State2 -> Input B -> State3
3. State3 -> Input C -> State1
```

White-box testing, in contrast, is also known as structural or glass-box testing. This technique requires knowledge of the internal structure of the code. Tests are based on coverage of code statements, branches, paths, and conditions. The goal is to ensure that the internal operations are performed correctly and according to specification. Key methods in white-box testing include statement coverage, branch coverage, path coverage, and condition coverage.

Statement Coverage aims to ensure that every line of code is executed at least once. This method can help identify statements that are never reached in normal execution.

```
# Pseudocode for Statement Coverage
if condition:
    execute_statement_1
execute_statement_2

# Test Case
condition = True # Ensures both statements are executed
```

Branch Coverage ensures that every possible branch (e.g., both the 'if' and 'else' parts of a conditional) is executed.

```
# Pseudocode for Branch Coverage
if condition:
```

```
    branch_a
else:
    branch_b

# Test Cases
condition = True # Test branch_a
condition = False # Test branch_b
```

Path Coverage goes further by testing all possible paths through the control flow of the program. This is more thorough but can also be impractical for complex programs due to the combinatorial explosion of paths.

```
# Pseudocode for Path Coverage
if condition1:
    path1
else:
    path2

if condition2:
    path3
else:
    path4

# Test Cases
# 1. condition1 = True, condition2 = True -> Covers path1 -> path3
# 2. condition1 = True, condition2 = False -> Covers path1 -> path4
# 3. condition1 = False, condition2 = True -> Covers path2 -> path3
# 4. condition1 = False, condition2 = False-> Covers path2 -> path4
```

Condition Coverage checks that every Boolean sub-expression evaluated in the program has been tested for both true and false values.

```
# Pseudocode for Condition Coverage
if (condition1 && condition2):
    execute_action

# Test Cases
condition1 = True, condition2 = True # Both conditions true
condition1 = False, condition2 = True # Condition1 false, condition2 true
condition1 = True, condition2 = False # Condition1 true, condition2 false
condition1 = False, condition2 = False # Both conditions false
```

Combining black-box and white-box techniques allows for a robust testing strategy. Black-box testing ensures that the software fulfills the specified requirements without any bias towards the internal code structure, while white-box testing guarantees thorough verification of the code itself. By integrating both approaches, testers can achieve higher levels of software quality and reliability.

6.4 Test Planning and Management

Test planning and management are essential components in the software testing lifecycle, providing a structured approach for organizing, executing, and monitoring testing activities. A well-developed test plan outlines the strategy, scope, resources, and schedule of testing activities, ensuring objectives are met and risks are managed effectively.

Test planning starts with defining the scope and objectives of testing. The scope delineates what features and functionalities of the software will be tested. It involves understanding the requirements and specifications of the software product. Objectives address the criteria for success, such as validating all functional requirements, ensuring performance benchmarks, or achieving compliance with security standards.

A crucial element to consider is the test strategy that will guide the testing efforts. This includes the choice of techniques—such as manual or automated testing, exploratory or scripted testing—and the level of testing, like unit, integration, system, or acceptance testing. The strategy should align with the software development lifecycle model employed, be it Agile, Waterfall, or any hybrid model.

The resource allocation begins with identifying the skill set required for the testing team, including domain expertise, technical skills, and familiarity with specific testing tools. Resource planning also involves allocating the necessary infrastructure, such as test environments and hardware configurations. In distributed development scenarios, coordination mechanisms must be established to synchronize testing activities across different locations.

Creating a detailed test schedule is another pivotal aspect of test planning. The schedule should outline timelines for each phase of testing, from initiation through execution to closure activities. Critical milestones, checkpoints, and deliverables for each phase must be clearly defined. The schedule should incorporate contingency plans to address potential delays or unexpected challenges.

Risk management is integral to test planning. Identifying, assessing, and mitigating risks associated with testing activities helps in anticipating problems before they occur. Potential risks might include schedule slippage, resource availability, or technical challenges. Each identified risk should have a mitigation plan detailing the actions to be undertaken if the risk materializes.

```
import unittest
```

```
class TestArithmeticOperations(unittest.TestCase):
    def test_addition(self):
        self.assertEqual((1 + 2), 3)

    def test_multiplication(self):
        self.assertEqual((2 * 2), 4)

if __name__ == '__main__':
    unittest.main()
```

The above code illustrates a basic structure for defining test cases using Python's unittest framework. It exemplifies how test cases for addition and multiplication operations are structured. Diversifying the test cases to cover boundary conditions and erroneous inputs elevates the robustness of testing.

Test management extends the focus to enforcing the test plan, tracking the progress of testing activities, and ensuring quality control. Test management tools assist in managing test cases, recording and tracking defects, and generating testing metrics. These tools provide dashboards and reports that offer visibility into the test process, facilitating informed decision-making.

Test case design and execution are key tasks within test management. Test cases must be designed to comprehensively cover required functionalities and diverse scenarios, from typical to edge cases. Executing these test cases systematically ensures thorough evaluation of the software's capabilities.

Issues found during testing are logged as defects in a tracking system. Each defect should be documented with sufficient detail to facilitate reproduction and debugging. Attributes like severity, priority, status, and responsibilities are assigned to each defect to prioritize and manage their resolution effectively.

Test Report Summary	**Total Test Cases**	**Passed**	**Failed**
Test Report Summary:	100	85	10
Blocked:	5		

The example above shows a summarized test report generated after executing test cases. This report provides insight into the overall status of testing activities, highlighting the number of test cases that passed, failed, or were blocked. Effective test reporting helps in assessing the quality of the software product and identifying areas needing attention.

Regression testing is another critical aspect managed during test cycles. Whenever new functionalities are introduced or existing functionalities are modified, regression tests ensure that these changes have not adversely impacted previously working features. Automated regression testing is often employed to efficiently revalidate the software after each change.

Communication within the testing team and with other stakeholders is fundamental to test management. Regular meetings, status updates, and reviews facilitate collaboration and synchronization among team members. Clear communication of progress, issues, and risks ensures alignment and supports proactive problem resolution.

A successful test planning and management process culminates in well-executed testing phases, resulting in a software product that meets quality standards and satisfies user requirements.

6.5 Automated Testing

Automated testing represents an integral component of modern software development practices, aiming to enhance the efficiency, consistency, and repeatability of the testing process. Automated tests are scripts or programs designed to execute predefined test cases without human intervention. These scripts can be run frequently and systematically to ensure that the software behaves as expected under various conditions.

The primary motivation behind automated testing is the reduction of manual effort and the mitigation of human error, which are often significant factors in complex software systems. Automated tests are particularly beneficial for regression testing, where previously tested functionality is re-evaluated to ensure that new changes have not introduced any defects.

```
import unittest

class TestMathOperations(unittest.TestCase):
    def test_addition(self):
        self.assertEqual(add(2, 3), 5)

    def test_subtraction(self):
        self.assertEqual(subtract(5, 2), 3)

if __name__ == '__main__':
    unittest.main()
```

In the example above, 'unittest' is a standard library in Python used for writing and running tests. The 'TestMathOperations' class includes methods to test the addition and subtraction operations. Each method uses the 'assertEqual' function to validate the output. When executed, the test suite provides immediate feedback on the correctness of the code.

```
..
----------------------------------------------------------------------
Ran 2 tests in 0.000s

OK
```

Automated testing can be categorized into several types, each serving a distinct purpose within the development lifecycle:

- **Unit Testing:** Tests individual components or functions in isolation. It aims to verify that each piece of code performs as intended.
- **Integration Testing:** Examines the interaction between integrated units/modules to ensure their combined behavior is correct.
- **System Testing:** Evaluates the complete and integrated software system to ensure compliance with the specified requirements.
- **Acceptance Testing:** Confirms that the software meets the business requirements and is ready for deployment.

Each type of testing can benefit from automation to varying degrees. Unit testing is particularly amenable to automation due to its focus on small, discrete segments of code. However, integration and system testing can also be automated, provided that dependencies and external interfaces are appropriately managed.

Advantages of Automated Testing:

- **Speed:** Automated tests execute significantly faster than manual tests, allowing for rapid feedback and quicker iterations.
- **Reusability:** Test scripts can be reused across different versions and iterations of the software.
- **Consistency:** Automated tests provide consistent results, eliminating variability caused by human factors.
- **Coverage:** Extensive test coverage can be achieved by running a large number of tests, which might be impractical manually.

Challenges in Automated Testing:

- **Initial Setup Cost:** The initial effort and cost of creating automated tests can be high, requiring upfront investment.
- **Maintenance:** Automated tests require ongoing maintenance to remain effective, especially as the software evolves.
- **Test Flakiness:** Automated tests can sometimes yield unreliable results due to varying factors such as timing issues or environment inconsistencies.

To address these challenges, the use of robust frameworks and best practices is essential. Tools such as Selenium for web applications, JUnit for Java applications, and pytest for Python applications have become industry standards, promoting consistency and reliability in automated testing processes.

```
import org.junit.Test;
import static org.junit.Assert.assertEquals;

public class MathOperationTest {
    @Test
    public void testAddition() {
        assertEquals(5, MathOperation.add(2, 3));
    }

    @Test
    public void testSubtraction() {
        assertEquals(3, MathOperation.subtract(5, 2));
    }
}
```

```
..
Time: 0.004

OK (2 tests)
```

Incorporating automated testing into the Continuous Integration (CI) and Continuous Deployment (CD) pipelines further enhances the software development workflow. CI systems automatically run tests whenever code changes are committed, ensuring that integration occurs in small, manageable steps and that defects are caught early. CD systems can use the results of automated tests to decide whether to deploy the tested software to production environments, thus streamlining the release process and reducing the likelihood of defects reaching end-users.

Automation in testing does not eliminate the need for manual testing but complements it by handling repetitive and regression tests. This allows human testers to focus on exploratory testing, usability testing, and other areas where human intuition and creativity are invaluable.

The growing complexity of software and the increasing pace of development cycles make automated testing an essential practice for any software engineering team aiming for robust, high-quality software.

6.6 Performance Testing and Load Testing

Performance testing and load testing are integral aspects of software testing that focus on assessing the system's behavior under specific conditions. Performance testing aims to determine how a system performs in terms of responsiveness and stability under a particular workload. Meanwhile, load testing examines the system's capability to handle a predetermined load of concurrent users or transactions.

Performance testing encompasses several sub-disciplines, such as load testing, stress testing, endurance testing, and spike testing. These disciplines help in identifying performance bottlenecks and ensuring that the system can meet the required performance standards.

Key Objectives of Performance Testing:

- Assessing the system's response time, throughput, and utilization under varying conditions.
- Identifying performance bottlenecks in the system.
- Ensuring the system meets the specified performance criteria.
- Validating the scalability of the system.
- Ensuring the system's stability under peak loads.

Load Testing: Load testing specifically evaluates a system's performance by subjecting it to a given load of simultaneous users or requests. The primary objective is to determine whether the system can sustain the operational load without compromising performance. This involves simulating multiple users accessing the system simultaneously to uncover any performance issues.

Example Load Testing Procedure: 1. **Define Test Goals:** Establish what aspects of the system need testing, such as response time and maximum load. 2. **Create Test Scenarios:** Develop scenarios that represent realistic usage patterns. 3. **Set Up Test Environment:** Ensure that the testing environment mirrors the production environment. 4. **Implement Test Cases:** Use test scripts or tools to simulate user activities. 5. **Execute Tests:** Run the tests and monitor the system's performance. 6. **Analyze Results:** Evaluate the data collected to identify performance characteristics and bottlenecks.

```
from locust import HttpUser, task, between

class WebsiteUser(HttpUser):
    wait_time = between(1, 5)

    @task
    def index_page(self):
        self.client.get("/")

    @task
    def about_page(self):
        self.client.get("/about")
```

In the above example, Locust, a Python-based load testing tool, is used to simulate user behavior on a website. The index_page and about_page tasks simulate requests to the website's homepage and about page, respectively.

Stress Testing: Stress testing scrutinizes the system's behavior under extreme load conditions, beyond its specified operational capacity. The objective is to identify the breaking point at which the system fails to manage the load gracefully. This type of testing helps uncover vulnerabilities and ensure robustness.

Endurance Testing: Endurance testing, also known as soak testing, examines the system's performance over an extended period under a sustained load. The goal is to detect issues such as memory leaks, resource exhaustion, and other problems that may arise from prolonged operation.

Spike Testing: Spike testing focuses on the system's ability to handle sudden, sharp increases in load. This test type is crucial for understanding how the system deals with unexpected bursts of traffic or user activities.

Metrics in Performance and Load Testing:

- **Response Time:** The time taken by the system to respond to a user request.

- **Throughput:** The number of transactions processed by the system within a given time frame.

- **Peak Load:** The maximum number of users or transactions the system can handle.
- **Error Rate:** The rate at which errors occur under specific conditions.
- **Resource Utilization:** The extent to which system resources such as CPU, memory, and network are utilized during the test.

Understanding and analyzing these metrics is vital for identifying performance issues and optimizing the system's efficiency. Tools commonly used for performance and load testing include JMeter, LoadRunner, and Gatling.

Example Output of a Load Testing Report:

```
Load Test Report:
Test Duration: 60 minutes
Total Requests: 100,000
Response Time (Average): 200 ms
Response Time (95th percentile): 450 ms
Throughput: 1,666 requests/minute
Error Rate: 0.5%
CPU Utilization: 75%
Memory Utilization: 60%
```

The above output provides a snapshot of the system's performance under load, including key metrics such as response time, throughput, error rate, and resource utilization.

Performance testing and load testing are crucial for ensuring that systems can withstand real-world usage and maintain performance standards. Properly conducted performance testing identifies potential issues before deployment, ensuring a robust, reliable, and scalable software product.

6.7 Security Testing

Security testing is critical in ensuring that a software application remains protected from vulnerabilities, unauthorized access, and various forms of exploitation. The primary objective of security testing is to identify potential weaknesses in the system and to ensure that the mechanisms safeguarding data and resources are both effective and uncompromised.

To achieve comprehensive security, the testing process encompasses several key aspects: vulnerability assessment, penetration testing, security scanning, risk assessment, and ethical hacking. Each activity focuses on distinct aspects of security and collectively contributes to the robustness of the system.

Vulnerability Assessment involves systematically reviewing the software to identify known vulnerabilities. Tools such as Nessus and OpenVAS are employed to conduct automated scans against databases of known vulnerabilities.

```
$ openvas-start
$ openvas-scan --target=192.168.1.1 --report-format=html > vulnerability_report.html
```

The report generated from such scans highlights critical, high, medium, and low severity vulnerabilities, guiding developers on prioritizing remediation efforts.

Penetration Testing, or pen testing, simulates real-world attacks to identify potential exploitations. Conducted by ethical hackers, pen testing involves a series of steps: reconnaissance, scanning, exploitation, post-exploitation, and reporting. Tools like Metasploit and Burp Suite facilitate this multi-step approach.

```
$ msfconsole
msf5 > use exploit/windows/smb/ms17_010_eternalblue
msf5 exploit(windows/smb/ms17_010_eternalblue) > set RHOSTS 192.168.1.1
msf5 exploit(windows/smb/ms17_010_eternalblue) > exploit
```

Ethical hackers also carry out **Security Scanning**, which involves automated and manual techniques to detect system vulnerabilities. The objective is to uncover foundational weaknesses that could lead to security breaches. Security scanning covers both network security and application security.

Risk Assessment quantitatively or qualitatively evaluates the potential risks identified in the software. This practice involves identifying critical assets, potential threats, and the impact of vulnerabilities. Tools such as CRAMM and RiskWatch facilitate thorough risk assessments, helping stakeholders prioritize risk mitigation strategies.

Risk Impact	Action Required
High	Requires immediate action
Medium	Requires planned remediation
Low	Can be monitored and addressed in the future

Table 6.2: Summary of Risk Impact

Ethical Hacking from within an organization aims to emulate potential insider threats. By doing so, it assesses the effectiveness of internal controls and policies. Tools like Wireshark and Nmap are commonly used in this context.

Security testing also extends to **Code Review**, which involves scrutinizing the source code for vulnerabilities, such as buffer overflows, SQL injection, and cross-site scripting (XSS). Static analysis tools like SonarQube and Fortify SSC automate this process.

```
$ sonar-scanner \
  -Dsonar.projectKey=my_project \
  -Dsonar.sources=. \
  -Dsonar.host.url=http://localhost:9000 \
  -Dsonar.login=the_login_token
```

Results from static code analysis highlight potential security flaws at the code level, allowing developers to address these issues before they manifest into real vulnerabilities.

Dynamic analysis, which is another facet of security testing, examines the application's behavior during execution. Tools like OWASP ZAP (Zed Attack Proxy) can dynamically analyze web applications to find vulnerabilities such as XSS, CSRF (Cross-Site Request Forgery), and insecure deserialization.

```
$ zap-cli quick-scan http://example.com
$ zap-cli report -o zap_report.html -f html
```

Results from dynamic analysis complement static code analysis by highlighting runtime issues.

Additionally, **Fuzz Testing** or fuzzing, is used to identify security issues by inputting massive amounts of random data, or fuzz, to the application. Tools like AFL (American Fuzzy Lop) and Peach Fuzzer are widely used for this purpose.

```
$ afl-fuzz -i input_dir -o output_dir -- ./target_binary
```

Fuzzing can uncover vulnerabilities that occur at the boundaries of input specifications, identifying bugs related to memory corruption, crashes, and assertion failures.

Finally, **Security Compliance Testing** ensures that the software meets regulatory and industry standards such as GDPR, HIPAA, and PCI-DSS. Compliance testing is conducted by evaluating both documentation and the operational aspects to verify adherence.

The integration of these techniques forms a comprehensive security testing strategy, focusing on identifying, analyzing, and mitigating vulnerabilities across the software development lifecycle. This thorough approach safeguards against potential breaches, ensuring that the software meets both functional and security requirements.

6.8 Usability Testing

Usability testing is fundamental in ensuring that software products are not only functional but also user-friendly. This form of testing evaluates the software by observing real users as they interact with it, aiming to uncover usability issues that might not be evident through other forms of testing.

The primary goals of usability testing are to identify areas where users struggle to accomplish desired tasks, understand user satisfaction, and ensure that the software meets user needs and expectations. Unlike functional testing, which focuses on whether the software works correctly, usability testing emphasizes the user experience.

Usability testing typically follows a structured process:

- **Define Objectives**: Clearly delineate what aspects of usability are to be tested, such as ease of use, efficiency, and user satisfaction.
- **Select Participants**: Choose a representative sample of users, typically reflecting the diversity of the target audience of the software.
- **Design Tasks**: Develop specific tasks that users will perform during the test, ensuring they are representative of real-world usage scenarios.
- **Conduct Tests**: Facilitators observe and record users as they perform the tasks, noting any difficulties or confusion encountered.
- **Analyze Data**: Compile and interpret the observations and feedback to identify usability issues.
- **Report Findings**: Summarize the results and provide recommendations for improving the user experience.

- **Iterate**: Make necessary design changes based on the findings and conduct additional rounds of testing as needed.

1. Define Objectives

Defining clear objectives is the first step in usability testing. Objectives should focus on specific aspects of the user experience, such as the intuitiveness of the interface, the learning curve for new users, navigational efficiency, and overall satisfaction. For example, an objective might be to determine whether users can complete a set of tasks without assistance or significant delay.

2. Select Participants

The selection of test participants is crucial to the validity of usability testing. Participants should represent the end-users of the software, including demographic diversity (age, gender, experience level) to capture a broad spectrum of user interactions. Generally, a smaller group of participants, typically between 5 to 10 individuals, can reveal most usability problems due to the nature of qualitative research.

3. Design Tasks

Tasks should be designed to simulate real-world scenarios that users will likely encounter while using the software. These tasks should have clear goals but leave room for users to navigate the system freely. Examples of tasks include logging into the system, searching for a specific document, or completing a transaction. The complexity of tasks should reflect typical usage patterns to reveal authentic user challenges.

4. Conduct Tests

During the test sessions, facilitators guide users through tasks and observe their behavior. It's essential to create a comfortable environment where users feel free to express their thoughts and difficulties. Facilitators should avoid offering help or guidance during tasks to ensure that users' interactions with the software are genuine. Recording the sessions, either through screen recording or note-taking, can provide valuable data for subsequent analysis.

User: "I'm trying to find the settings option, but I can't see it."
Facilitator: (Notes the difficulty without intervening)
User: "Oh, here it is, found it under the profile menu."

5. Analyze Data

Analyzing the collected data involves identifying patterns and recurring issues faced by users. Common problems such as difficulty in navigation, unclear instructions, or misplaced functionalities become apparent.

Quantitative data, such as time taken to complete tasks or error rates, can also be helpful.

```
Observation: 4 out of 5 users struggled to locate the settings menu.
Time Analysis: Average time to find the settings menu was 2 minutes.
```

6. Report Findings

The findings from usability testing are compiled into a report that details the identified issues, their potential impact on user experience, and suggestions for improvements. The report should be clear and actionable, prioritizing issues based on their severity and the frequency with which they were encountered.

```
Issue 1: Difficulty in locating the settings menu.
Recommendation: Relocate settings menu to the main navigation bar.
```

7. Iterate

Usability testing is an iterative process. Once changes are made based on the findings, subsequent rounds of testing are necessary to ensure the implemented solutions effectively address the issues and do not introduce new problems. This cycle continues until the software provides an optimal user experience.

Integrating usability testing into the development process can significantly enhance the quality of the software. By systematically identifying and addressing usability issues, developers can create software that is not only functional but also delivers a satisfying and efficient user experience. Through careful planning, execution, and iteration, usability testing ensures that the final product aligns with user expectations and requirements.

6.9 Debugging and Problem-Solving Techniques

Debugging is an integral part of the software development lifecycle, involving the identification, analysis, and removal of errors or issues in code. Effective debugging ensures that software functions as intended, ultimately improving the reliability and quality of the product. This process requires a methodical approach and a deep understanding of the codebase, as well as the specific problem at hand.

First, we define debugging as the meticulous process of pinpointing the specific location and nature of defects within a software system and applying corrective measures to resolve those defects. Debugging is often interleaved with testing activities; while testing aims to identify the presence of defects, debugging is concerned with locating and fixing them.

The debugging process typically involves the following stages:

- **Reproduce the Issue:** The first step in debugging is to reproduce the issue reliably. This entails understanding the context in which the problem occurs and executing the same sequence of operations to observe the defect. Access to detailed error reports, logs, and a consistent test environment enhances the reproducibility of issues.

- **Diagnose and Narrow Down to the Error Source:** Once the issue has been reproduced, the next step is to diagnose the underlying cause. This involves systematically ruling out potential causes and isolating the defect. Techniques such as divide-and-conquer, where the problem area is progressively reduced, are commonly employed at this stage.

- **Apply Fixes:** After localizing the defect, the appropriate corrective measures must be applied to fix the issue. This may involve code corrections, adjustments to configurations, or changes in data. The fix should address the root cause of the problem without introducing new issues.

- **Verify the Fix:** Verification involves confirming that the applied fix resolves the identified issue without negatively impacting other system functionalities. Regression testing is crucial at this stage to ensure that new defects have not been introduced.

- **Document the Solution:** Proper documentation of the issue, its root cause, the applied fix, and any associated test cases is essential for future reference and to aid other developers who may encounter similar issues.

Several debugging techniques and tools can be leveraged to streamline this process:

Print Statements: One of the simplest and most common techniques involves inserting print statements in the code to display variable values or execution flow at different points. This method, although rudimentary, provides immediate visibility into the software's behavior.

```
def calculate_sum(a, b):
    print(f"Calculating sum of {a} and {b}")
    result = a + b
    print(f"Result: {result}")
    return result
```

Logging: Logging is a more sophisticated approach where log messages are automatically recorded during program execution, often at different levels (e.g., DEBUG, INFO, WARN, ERROR). Logging frameworks like Log4j (for Java) or the logging module in Python can be configured to provide detailed and context-specific information.

```
import logging
logging.basicConfig(level=logging.DEBUG)
logger = logging.getLogger(__name__)

def calculate_sum(a, b):
    logger.debug(f"Calculating sum of {a} and {b}")
    result = a + b
    logger.debug(f"Result: {result}")
    return result
```

Interactive Debugging: Interactive debugging involves using debuggers, which allow developers to pause execution, inspect variables, and step through code line-by-line. Tools such as gdb (for C/C++), pdb (for Python), and integrated debuggers in IDEs like Visual Studio and Eclipse offer powerful capabilities to facilitate this process.

A simple debugging session using pdb in Python might look like this:

```
import pdb

def calculate_sum(a, b):
    pdb.set_trace() # Pause execution and start the debugger
    result = a + b
    return result

calculate_sum(3, 5)
```

Upon execution, the debugger will pause at the specified trace point, allowing the developer to inspect the program state and step through the subsequent lines of code.

Automated Tools: Several automated tools are designed to assist in debugging by identifying common issues such as memory leaks, race conditions, or code violations. Tools like Valgrind (for memory debugging in C/C++), FindBugs (for static analysis in Java), and Pylint (for static analysis in Python) can highlight potential problems even before runtime.

Profiling: Profiling tools provide insights into the program's performance characteristics, helping to identify bottlenecks and performance-related issues. Profilers like gprof (for C/C++), cProfile (for Python), and JProfiler (for Java) offer detailed reports on function call frequency, execution time, and resource utilization.

```
import cProfile

def calculate_sum(a, b):
    result = a + b
    return result

cProfile.run('calculate_sum(3, 5)')
```

ncalls	tottime	percall	cumtime	percall	filename:lineno(function)
1	0.000	0.000	0.000	0.000	<ipython-input-26-9f40f5a0b6c4>:1(calculate_sum)
1	0.000	0.000	0.000	0.000	<string>:1(<module>)
1	0.000	0.000	0.000	0.000	built-in method builtins.exec
1	0.000	0.000	0.000	0.000	built-in method builtins.print

Table 6.3: Profiling Results for calculate_sum Function

Understanding and utilizing these techniques efficiently can significantly reduce the time and effort involved in debugging complex software. Moreover, problem-solving skills are crucial to systematically approach issues, explore alternative hypotheses, and synthesize solutions. When confronted with a challenging bug or problem, employing a combination of the mentioned techniques often yields the best results. The aim is to develop a robust understanding of the codebase and foster an environment conducive to effective problem resolution.

6.10 Quality Assurance Standards and Metrics

Quality assurance (QA) encompasses the systematic processes implemented to determine the quality of software products and ensure that they meet predefined criteria. Various standards and metrics provide guidance and benchmarks for achieving and measuring this quality. This section discusses the most widely recognized QA standards, elaborates on key metrics used for evaluating software quality, and explains their practical applications in the software development lifecycle.

Quality assurance standards set forth the protocols and guidelines that organizations follow to ensure the quality of their software products. Adhering to these standards helps in maintaining consistency, reliability, and efficiency across software projects. Some of the prominent standards include ISO/IEC 25010, ISO/IEC 12207, and Capability Maturity Model Integration (CMMI).

ISO/IEC 25010, known as the Systems and Software Quality Requirements and Evaluation model, provides a comprehensive framework for assessing software quality. It delineates eight quality characteristics: functional suitability, performance efficiency, compatibility, usability, reliability, security, maintainability, and portability. Each characteristic is further subdivided into sub-characteristics, providing a detailed structure for evaluation.

ISO/IEC 12207 establishes a framework for software lifecycle processes. It aims to be the standard framework defining all tasks required for developing and maintaining software. This standard covers the entire software lifecycle from conception through retirement, emphasizing the importance of process definition and control.

CMMI, on the other hand, is a process level improvement training and appraisal program. Administered by the CMMI Institute, it offers a set of best practices that focus on process improvement. CMMI's staged representation is divided into maturity levels, guiding organizations through an evolutionary improvement path from ad hoc processes to disciplined, mature processes.

Metrics play a crucial role in quality assurance by providing quantitative data to assess various aspects of software quality. Commonly used metrics include defect density, code coverage, mean time to failure (MTTF), and cyclomatic complexity.

- Defect density is the number of confirmed defects detected in a software module or system divided by the size of the software entity, often measured in lines of code (LOC) or function points. This metric helps in evaluating the quality of code and can highlight areas that require more rigorous testing.

```
def calculate_defect_density(defects, lines_of_code):
    return defects / lines_of_code

# Example usage
defects_found = 25
total_loc = 10000
density = calculate_defect_density(defects_found, total_loc)
print(f"Defect Density: {density} defects per LOC")
```

```
Defect Density: 0.0025 defects per LOC
```

- Code coverage is a measure indicating the extent to which the source code of a program is tested. It is typically expressed as a percentage. Higher code coverage suggests more comprehensive testing, though it does not guarantee the absence of defects.

```
def calculate_code_coverage(tested_cases, total_cases):
    return (tested_cases / total_cases) * 100

# Example usage
tested = 150
total = 200
coverage = calculate_code_coverage(tested, total)
print(f"Code Coverage: {coverage}%")
```

```
Code Coverage: 75.0%
```

- MTTF is the average time elapsed between the inherent failures of a system during operation. It is a reliability metric used to predict the performance and lifespan of a product.
- Cyclomatic complexity measures the complexity of a program by quantifying the number of linearly independent paths through the program's source code. High cyclomatic complexity may indicate complex, hard-to-maintain code.

Evaluating these metrics at various stages of development can provide insights into areas where improvements are needed, guiding the team toward more robust and reliable software solutions.

Understanding and implementing QA standards and metrics is fundamental for achieving high software quality. These tools and frameworks provide the structure needed to manage and measure the development process, and their consistent application helps ensure that software products meet the required standards of excellence. This approach not only builds confidence in the product but also enhances customer satisfaction and trust.

6.11 Tools for Software Testing and Quality Assurance

Tools for Software Testing and Quality Assurance (QA) play a pivotal role in ensuring that software systems meet the desired quality standards and perform reliably. These tools aid in various facets of the testing lifecycle, ranging from test management to automated test execution, performance monitoring, security assessment, and usability evaluation. This section explores some of the most widely used tools in the industry, providing an overview of their functionalities and applications.

Test Management Tools

Test management tools are critical for organizing, planning, and managing test cases, test execution, and reporting. They allow teams to track the progress of testing activities and ensure comprehensive coverage of requirements.

- **JIRA with Zephyr**: JIRA, when integrated with Zephyr, provides an extensive platform for test management. Users can create, view, edit, clone, and archive test cases, manage test cycles, and generate detailed reports. The integration of both tools offers seamless issue tracking and test management within a single interface.

```
# Sample JIRA Command for Creating a Test Issue
curl -D- -u username:password -X POST \
--data '{"fields": {"project": {"key": "PROJ"},"summary": "TEST Summary","
    description": "Creating a Test Issue","issuetype": {"name": "Test"}}}' \
-H "Content-Type: application/json" \
https://your-domain.atlassian.net/rest/api/2/issue/
```

- **TestRail**: TestRail is a web-based test case management tool that enables structured organization and management of test cases. It supports integration with issue tracking tools like JIRA and Bugzilla, allowing for efficient defect tracking and reporting.
- **HP ALM (Application Lifecycle Management)**: HP ALM provides comprehensive tools for test planning, test execution, and defect management. It supports the entire application lifecycle, making it suitable for large-scale enterprise applications.

Automated Testing Tools

Automated testing tools facilitate the execution of pre-scripted tests on the application under test. These tools are essential for regression testing, continuous integration, and continuous deployment pipelines.

- **Selenium**: Selenium is an open-source tool suite for automating web browsers. It offers multiple components, including Selenium WebDriver for executing scripts across different browsers and Selenium Grid for parallel test execution.

```
// Sample Selenium WebDriver Code in Java
import org.openqa.selenium.WebDriver;
import org.openqa.selenium.WebElement;
import org.openqa.selenium.chrome.ChromeDriver;

public class SeleniumExample {
    public static void main(String[] args) {
        System.setProperty("webdriver.chrome.driver", "path/to/chromedriver");
        WebDriver driver = new ChromeDriver();
        driver.get("http://www.example.com");

        WebElement element = driver.findElement(By.name("q"));
        element.sendKeys("Software Testing");
        element.submit();

        driver.quit();
    }
}
```

- **JUnit**: JUnit is a widely-used testing framework for Java applications. It enables the creation and execution of repeatable automated tests, making it integral to Test-Driven Development (TDD).

```
// Sample JUnit Test Case in Java
import org.junit.Test;
import static org.junit.Assert.assertEquals;

public class ExampleTest {
    @Test
    public void testAddition() {
        int result = 1 + 1;
        assertEquals(2, result);
    }
}
```

- **QTP/UFT (Unified Functional Testing)**: QTP/UFT by Micro Focus is a commercial tool designed for functional and regression testing. It supports a wide range of applications and technologies, enabling automated testing across various platforms.

Performance Testing Tools

Performance testing tools measure and evaluate the responsiveness, stability, and scalability of an application under load. These tools simulate multiple users to test the system's behavior under different conditions.

- **Apache JMeter**: JMeter is an open-source performance testing tool designed to load test functional behavior and measure performance. It can simulate a heavy load on servers, networks, or other objects to test their strength and analyze overall performance under different load types.

```
# Sample JMeter Command to Run a Test Plan
jmeter -n -t testplan.jmx -l test_results.jtl
```

- **LoadRunner**: LoadRunner by Micro Focus is a widely-used performance testing tool that predicts system behavior and performance. It supports a wide range of protocols and offers precise performance monitoring and analysis.
- **Gatling**: Gatling is an open-source load and performance testing tool for web applications. It provides detailed metrics and interactive reports to help identify performance bottlenecks efficiently.

Security Testing Tools

Security testing tools are designed to identify vulnerabilities, security flaws, and potential threats in software applications. These tools ensure that the application complies with security standards.

- **OWASP ZAP (Zed Attack Proxy)**: OWASP ZAP is an open-source penetration testing tool for finding vulnerabilities in web applications. It is highly configurable and supports both automated and manual testing.
- **Burp Suite**: Burp Suite is a comprehensive platform for web application security testing. It includes tools for performing automated scans, manual testing, and vulnerability assessments.

```
# Sample Python Code to Interact with Burp Suite API
import requests

url = "http://localhost:8080/burp/scan"
headers = {'Content-Type': 'application/json'}
payload = {'url': 'http://example.com'}
response = requests.post(url, json=payload, headers=headers)

print(response.json())
```

- **Nessus**: Nessus is a vulnerability scanner designed to automate the process of finding security flaws. It performs comprehensive assessments against a variety of threats and vulnerabilities.

Usability Testing Tools

Usability testing tools focus on evaluating how user-friendly and intuitive an application is. These tools help identify usability issues that could affect the end-user experience.

- **Optimal Workshop**: Optimal Workshop provides a suite of tools to conduct usability studies, including tree testing, card sorting, and first-click testing. These tools help improve the information architecture of a website or application.
- **UserTesting**: UserTesting is a platform for conducting remote usability testing. It provides insights into user behavior by recording real user interactions with the application and capturing their verbal feedback.
- **Lookback**: Lookback is a versatile usability testing tool that supports both moderated and unmoderated sessions. It offers real-time collaboration, session recording, and detailed analytics to understand user interactions better.

Each of these tools contributes significantly to various aspects of software testing and QA. Integrating the appropriate tools into the testing process helps ensure comprehensive test coverage, enhances testing efficiency, and ultimately leads to the delivery of high-quality software products.

6.12 Best Practices in Software Testing

Adhering to best practices in software testing is imperative to ensure the development of robust, reliable, and high-quality software systems. Implementing these practices not only helps in early detection and rectification of defects but also contributes to the efficiency and effectiveness of the testing process as a whole.

- **Early Integration of Testing Activities:** Engaging in testing activities from the early stages of the software development lifecycle can yield significant benefits. This approach, known as shift-left testing, advocates for the identification and resolution of defects during the requirements and design phases. This can be achieved through techniques such as static code analysis, peer reviews, and early prototyping. Detecting issues early helps in reducing the cost and effort required to fix them in later stages.
- **Comprehensive Test Planning:** A detailed test plan is the cornerstone of successful testing efforts. The plan should encompass clear objectives, the scope of testing, resource allocation,

schedule, deliverables, and risk management strategies. Additionally, it should outline the criteria for entry and exit, ensuring that all preconditions are met before testing begins, and all postconditions are verified before concluding the testing phase.

- **Test Automation:** Automation is a vital component in modern software testing practices. Automated tests improve the testing process by providing fast, consistent, and repeatable test execution. They are particularly effective for regression testing, where repeated testing of unchanged parts of the application is necessary. Automated testing tools like Selenium, JUnit, and TestNG can be integrated into the continuous integration (CI) pipeline to automate the execution of test suites.

```
import static org.junit.jupiter.api.Assertions.assertEquals;
import org.junit.jupiter.api.Test;

public class ExampleTest {
    @Test
    void testAddition() {
        int sum = Calculator.add(2, 3);
        assertEquals(5, sum, "2 + 3 should equal 5");
    }
}
```

- **Adequate Test Coverage:** Test coverage refers to the measure of the extent to which the source code is tested. Tools such as JaCoCo, Cobertura, and Clover can be used to determine the code coverage. It is essential to strive for high coverage, including condition coverage, decision coverage, and path coverage, ensuring that critical paths are tested and potential defects are identified.

- **Usage of Appropriate Testing Environments:** It is critical to conduct testing in environments that closely resemble the production environment. This practice ensures that tests produce realistic results and that the software behaves as expected under production-like conditions. Testing environments should be provisioned with the necessary hardware, software, datasets, and network configurations.

- **Robust Test Data Management:** Effective test data management involves the creation, maintenance, and usage of test data that authentically represent real-world scenarios. Test data should be anonymized to uphold data privacy and regulatory compliances. Establishing a strategy for test data management, including data generation, masking, and conditioning, aids in conducting meaningful tests.

- **Continuous Testing:** Continuous testing is a paradigm that integrates testing activities within the continuous integration/continuous deployment (CI/CD) pipeline. It ensures frequent validation of the software at every stage of its lifecycle. CI tools like Jenkins, GitLab CI, and Travis CI support continuous testing by automating test execution upon every code commit.

```
pipeline {
    agent any
    stages {
        stage('Build') {
            steps {
                sh 'mvn clean package'
            }
        }
        stage('Test') {
            steps {
                sh 'mvn test'
            }
        }
    }
    post {
        always {
            junit 'target/surefire-reports/*.xml'
        }
    }
}
```

- **Detailed Documentation:** Thorough documentation of test plans, test cases, test scripts, and test results is crucial for maintaining the transparency and repeatability of the testing process. Documents should be maintained in a centralized, version-controlled repository to ensure that they are accessible and up-to-date. Tools like TestRail, Zephyr, and qTest facilitate comprehensive test management and documentation.

- **Defining Clear Testing Metrics:** Testing metrics offer quantifiable measures to assess the efficacy and efficiency of the testing process. Key metrics include defect density, test case execution rate, test coverage percentage, mean time to detect (MTTD), and mean time to repair (MTTR). Regular monitoring of these metrics provides insights into the testing process and helps identify areas for improvement.

- **Adopting a Risk-Based Testing Approach:** Risk-based testing prioritizes test efforts based on the risk of failure and the impact of defects. By focusing on high-risk areas, testers can efficiently allocate resources and time, ensuring that the most critical aspects of the software are thoroughly tested. Risk assessment should consider factors such as defect history, complexity, and criticality of software components.

Employing these best practices in software testing fosters the development of high-quality software systems, minimizes risks, and enhances the overall effectiveness of the testing process. This approach ensures that the software meets its specified requirements and performs reliably in real-world conditions, ultimately leading to greater user satisfaction and reduced maintenance costs.

Chapter 7

Software Maintenance and Evolution

Software maintenance and evolution address the ongoing process of updating and improving software after its initial deployment. This chapter examines the different types of maintenance, including corrective, adaptive, perfective, and preventive, and outlines the maintenance process. It discusses the challenges associated with legacy systems, the impact of software changes, and the importance of reverse engineering and refactoring. The chapter also explores configuration management, metrics for measuring maintenance effectiveness, and tools and techniques to facilitate maintenance, along with real-world case studies.

7.1 Introduction to Software Maintenance and Evolution

Software maintenance and evolution represent critical phases in the lifecycle of any software system. Once software is operational, it is neither static nor complete. Continuous changes are typically necessary to correct faults, improve performance, adapt to a changing environment, or refine features based on user feedback and evolving requirements. These ongoing modifications ensure that the software remains reliable, functional, and relevant.

Maintenance is broadly categorized into four types: corrective, adaptive, perfective, and preventive. Each type addresses different aspects of the evolving software.

- **Corrective Maintenance** focuses on fixing defects found in the software post-deployment. It includes resolution of bugs that were not discovered during the initial testing phase. An example of corrective maintenance would be releasing a patch to resolve a security vulnerability that was exposed after the software's release. Consider the following code snippet used to fix a buffer overflow issue:

```
void secureFunction(char *input) {
    char buffer[25];
    strncpy(buffer, input, sizeof(buffer) - 1);
    buffer[sizeof(buffer) - 1] = '\0';
}
```

This code replaces a potentially unsafe strcpy call with strncpy, mitigating the risk of buffer overflow by ensuring the input size is controlled.

- **Adaptive Maintenance** involves making modifications to the software to ensure its compatibility with changing environments. This includes changes in the operating system, hardware, or any other peripheral software dependencies. For example, adapting software to a new version of an operating system might involve changes in API calls and handling new system features.

- **Perfective Maintenance** aims at enhancing the software by improving or adding new features without changing the existing functionality. This type of maintenance is driven by user feedback and changing requirements that necessitate additional capabilities or performance improvements in the software. For example, a software product might undergo perfective maintenance to enhance the user interface based on user feedback.

- **Preventive Maintenance** focuses on future fault prevention. It involves modifications to improve the maintainability and reliability of the software, making it more adaptable to future changes. This may entail code optimization, refactoring, and updating documentation. Consider the following refactoring example where code is restructured to enhance readability and maintainability:

```
# Original code
def calculate(input):
    result = 0
    for i in range(len(input)):
        if input[i] % 2 == 0:
            result += (input[i] ** 2)
        else:
            result -= (input[i] ** 2)
    return result

# Refactored code
def calculate(input):
    def compute_term(value):
        return value ** 2 if value % 2 == 0 else -value ** 2

    return sum(compute_term(num) for num in input)
```

In the refactored code, the computational logic is encapsulated in a separate function, making it more readable and easier to manage.

The scale and complexity of software systems today necessitate significant effort in software maintenance. Software is expected to operate efficiently over extended periods with minimal downtime, emphasizing the need for ongoing evolution. The maintenance process is not just about fixing errors but managing the entire lifecycle of system enhancements and environment adaptations.

- **Software Evolution** entails the incremental development and improvement of software over time. As user requirements and technologies evolve, the software must adapt. Factors influencing software evolution include changing business goals, technological advancements, and legislative changes. The evolution process involves not just adding features but also improving and optimizing existing functionalities based on usage patterns and performance metrics.

The processes and principles governing software maintenance and evolution underscore the importance of a structured approach to manage and execute necessary changes effectively. Key challenges in this domain include managing complexity, ensuring backward compatibility, minimizing downtime, and maintaining documentation. Each maintenance activity must be thoroughly tested and documented to avoid introducing new faults into the system.

- **Tools and Techniques** for software maintenance are essential in managing these activities efficiently. Version control systems, automated testing frameworks, and continuous integration tools play pivotal roles in facilitating seamless maintenance processes. Metrics and measurements are crucial for assessing the effectiveness and impact of maintenance activities, ensuring that continuous improvements lead to actual enhancements in performance and reliability.

Understanding software maintenance and evolution's intricacies can lead to better-managed projects, more reliable software systems, and ultimately, more satisfied users. This introduction lays the foundation for further exploration of the specific types of maintenance, methodologies, and tools that support these critical activities, which will be examined in subsequent sections.

7.2 Types of Software Maintenance: Corrective, Adaptive, Perfective, and Preventive

Software maintenance encompasses a broad range of activities, each targeting specific objectives to ensure the software system remains functional, efficient, and relevant over time. Maintenance activities can be categorized into four primary types: corrective, adaptive, perfective, and preventive. These types address distinct aspects of software upkeep and improvement.

Corrective Maintenance focuses on rectifying faults in software after they are detected. Faults can manifest as errors, bugs, or defects impacting the software's functionality or performance. Corrective maintenance is critical for restoring the software to its intended operational state and includes debugging and fixing issues in the code.

```
public class Calculator {
    public int add(int a, int b) {
        return a - b; // Bug: should be a + b
    }
}

// Corrected code
public class Calculator {
    public int add(int a, int b) {
        return a + b; // Fixed: corrected the operator
    }
}
```

The above example demonstrates a simple case where a bug in the addition operation is corrected by modifying the incorrect operator. Such fixes are essential to ensure accurate outputs and maintain confidence in the software's reliability.

Adaptive Maintenance involves modifying the software to accommodate changes in the external environment or operational settings. This type of maintenance ensures that the software can function correctly in new or altered hardware, operating systems, regulatory requirements, or market conditions.

```
# Original code using an outdated library version
import old_library

def process_data(data):
    result = old_library.process(data)
    return result

# Updated code using the new version of the library
import new_library

def process_data(data):
    result = new_library.process(data)
    return result
```

In this instance, adaptive maintenance adapts the software to use a new version of a library, ensuring compatibility and leveraging new features or improvements in the library.

Perfective Maintenance aims at enhancing the software to improve performance, maintainability, or other attributes without altering its primary functionality. This type of maintenance responds to user requests for additional features, optimizes code, and refactors design for efficiency.

```
function calculateSum(arr) {
    let sum = 0;
    for(let i = 0; i < arr.length; i++) {
        sum += arr[i];
    }
    return sum;
}

// Improved function using reduce for better performance and readability
function calculateSum(arr) {
    return arr.reduce((acc, current) => acc + current, 0);
}
```

By refactoring the code to use the reduce method, the function becomes more concise, potentially improving performance and readability, which are key goals of perfective maintenance.

Preventive Maintenance involves pro-actively identifying and addressing potential issues before they manifest as faults. It aims at improving software reliability and performance by regular updates, code reviews, and refactoring, thus preventing future issues.

```
@Deprecated
public void oldMethod() {
    // deprecated method implementation
}

public void newMethod() {
    // updated method implementation
}

public class Service {
    public void performAction() {
        oldMethod(); // Risky: using deprecated method
    }
}

// Updated code
public class Service {
    public void performAction() {
        newMethod(); // Safe: using updated method
    }
}
```

The code snippet showcases the replacement of a deprecated method with its modern counterpart to prevent potential issues arising from deprecated API usage, a key aspect of preventive maintenance.

Each type of maintenance plays an integral role in the software lifecycle, ensuring the software remains robust, adaptable, and aligned with evolving user needs and technological advancements. Through these maintenance activities, the long-term value and effectiveness of software systems are preserved and enhanced.

7.3 The Maintenance Process

The software maintenance process is an intricate and ongoing sequence of activities that ensure the software remains functional, reliable, and relevant to users' evolving needs. This process encompasses a variety of tasks from the identification and analysis of necessary changes to the implementation and documentation of these changes. A well-defined maintenance process is crucial for minimizing disruption, ensuring continuous improvement, and maintaining the overall integrity of the software system.

1. Identification of Maintenance Requirements:

The initial phase of the maintenance process involves identifying the requirements for maintenance. Changes may be driven by user feedback, bug reports, performance monitoring, or changes in the operational environment. The identification process can be facilitated through:

- **User Reports:** Users often provide valuable feedback regarding bugs, inefficiencies, or missing features.
- **Automated Monitoring Tools:** Tools that monitor software performance and usage statistics can provide insights into areas requiring maintenance.
- **Change Requests:** Formal request mechanisms within the organization allow stakeholders to request specific changes or enhancements.

2. Classification of Maintenance Requests:

Once the maintenance requirements are identified, they need to be classified into categories such as corrective, adaptive, perfective, or preventive maintenance. Proper classification helps in prioritizing the tasks and assigning the appropriate resources. For instance, corrective maintenance tasks that address critical bugs may take precedence over perfective tasks that aim at refining software features.

3. Impact Analysis:

Impact analysis determines the potential consequences of making the proposed changes. This step evaluates how the changes will affect existing functionalities, performance, and system dependencies. Impact analysis ensures risks are identified and managed prior to implementing changes. Key activities in this phase include:

- **Traceability Analysis:** Assessing relationships and dependencies between software components to understand the scope of change.
- **Risk Assessment:** Identifying and evaluating potential risks associated with changes, including technical, operational, and business impacts.
- **Cost-Benefit Analysis:** Comparing the costs of making changes against the expected benefits to justify the maintenance effort.

4. Planning:

Post impact analysis, a detailed plan is devised outlining the steps required to implement the changes. This includes resource allocation, scheduling, and defining success criteria. The planning phase also incorporates strategies for minimizing disruption during the maintenance activities. Considerations include:

- **Resource Management:** Assigning the right personnel with the necessary skills and expertise to perform maintenance tasks.
- **Scheduling:** Developing a timeline that accommodates the urgency of changes and minimizes operational downtime.
- **Backup and Recovery Plans:** Ensuring there are strategies for data backup and recovery to prevent data loss in case of failure.

5. Implementation:

The actual modifications to the software are carried out during the implementation phase. This involves coding, testing, and validating the changes. Key aspects of this phase include:

- **Coding:** Adhering to coding standards and best practices to ensure high-quality code.
- **Testing:** Extensive testing, including unit tests, integration tests, and regression tests, to verify that the changes work as intended without introducing new issues.
- **Code Review:** Peer reviews to ensure code quality and adherence to design specifications.

6. Validation and Verification:

Upon completing the implementation, the software undergoes validation and verification to ensure all requirements are met, and the changes are properly integrated. This phase may include:

- **Verification:** Confirming the modified software correctly implements specified requirements.
- **Validation:** Ensuring the software fulfills its intended purpose in the actual operational context.
- **User Acceptance Testing (UAT):** Engaging end-users to test the new changes and provide feedback to ensure the software meets their expectations.

7. Documentation:

Adequate documentation is essential for future maintenance and user support. Documentation should include:

- **Change Logs:** Detailed records of all changes made, including the rationale, implementation details, and any associated issues.
- **User Manuals:** Updated manuals reflecting the new features or changes to guide users.
- **Maintenance Reports:** Comprehensive reports that capture the maintenance activities, tools used, and outcomes.

8. Deployment:

After thorough testing and documentation, the changes are deployed to the production environment. Deployment must be managed carefully to avoid disruptions. This phase involves:

- **Release Management:** Coordinating the deployment process across different teams and stakeholders.
- **Version Control:** Maintaining control over different software versions to facilitate rollback if needed.
- **Monitoring:** Continuously monitoring the software post-deployment to ensure it is operating correctly and to detect any unforeseen issues.

9. Post-Deployment Review:

A review is conducted after deployment to assess the success of the maintenance activities. It includes evaluating whether objectives were met, reviewing user feedback, and identifying lessons learned for future maintenance efforts. Components of this review are:

- **Performance Evaluation:** Analyzing the performance of the software to ensure it meets predefined standards.
- **User Feedback:** Collecting feedback from users to understand their experience with the new changes.
- **Lessons Learned:** Documenting insights and lessons learned to improve future maintenance processes.

By adhering to a structured maintenance process, software engineering teams can effectively manage and implement changes, ensuring that the software remains robust, efficient, and capable of meeting evolving demands. This systematic approach is critical to maintaining the longevity and success of software systems in a constantly changing technological landscape.

7.4 Legacy Systems and Their Challenges

Legacy systems refer to outdated computer systems, software, or applications that are still in use, despite the availability of newer, more efficient alternatives. These systems often form the backbone of critical operations within an organization and have typically been in operation for many years. While they are crucial to business continuity, they pose numerous challenges that can complicate maintenance and evolution.

One primary challenge is the **technical debt** associated with legacy systems. Technical debt refers to the implied cost of future rework caused by choosing an easy solution now instead of using a better approach that would take longer. Legacy systems often have accumulated significant technical debt due to outdated technologies, poor documentation, and obsolete practices. This debt makes the systems brittle and challenging to modify, as changes are more likely to introduce new defects or failures.

Furthermore, **software architecture** in legacy systems may no longer align with current best practices or business requirements. The original design decisions made during development may not support modern functionality or integration with new systems. For instance, a legacy system may rely on monolithic architecture, where all functionalities are tightly coupled, making it hard to isolate and update specific components. In contrast, modern software design favors microservices architecture, where functionalities are loosely coupled and can be independently updated.

Another critical issue is the **software dependencies** inherent in legacy systems. These systems often depend on outdated libraries, frameworks, or third-party tools that are no longer supported. These dependencies can introduce security vulnerabilities and may not be compatible with new hardware or operating systems. Consequently, maintaining legacy systems involves considerable effort in identifying and managing these dependencies.

Documentation (or the lack thereof) is another significant challenge. Legacy systems are frequently poorly documented, with the original development team long gone, taking with them valuable knowledge about the system's inner workings. The absence of comprehensive and accurate documentation makes it arduous for current maintenance teams to understand the system fully, leading to delays and errors in implementing changes.

The **skill set** required to maintain legacy systems is often scarce. Many legacy systems are written in outdated programming languages, such as COBOL, FORTRAN, or older versions of Java, which are no longer widely taught or used. As experienced developers retire or leave the organization, finding skilled personnel to maintain and enhance these systems becomes increasingly difficult. This shortage can lead to higher labor costs and increased risk of errors and inefficiencies.

From a **business perspective**, legacy systems can impede agility and innovation. These systems may not support modern business practices or integration with new technologies, such as cloud-based services, mobile applications, or advanced data analytics. This limitation can prevent organizations from responding quickly to market changes or adopting innovative solutions that could provide competitive advantages. Additionally, the costs associated with maintaining and operating legacy systems, including hardware, software licenses, and personnel, can be significantly higher than those for modern systems.

Migration of legacy systems to more modern platforms or architectures is a common solution but presents its own set of challenges. The **migration process** is complex and risky, as it often involves redeveloping or reengineering large portions of the system while ensuring that critical business operations are not disrupted. This process requires careful planning, significant financial investment, and meticulous execution.

```
# Example of a script for migrating a database from an old system
import pyodbc

# Create a connection to the old database
old_db_conn = pyodbc.connect('DRIVER={SQL Server};'
                              'SERVER=old_server;'
                              'DATABASE=old_db;'
                              'UID=user;'
                              'PWD=password')

# Create a connection to the new database
new_db_conn = pyodbc.connect('DRIVER={SQL Server};'
                              'SERVER=new_server;'
                              'DATABASE=new_db;'
                              'UID=user;'
                              'PWD=password')
```

```
# Function to transfer data from old database to new database
def migrate_table(table_name):
    old_cursor = old_db_conn.cursor()
    new_cursor = new_db_conn.cursor()

    # Fetch data from the old table
    old_cursor.execute(f'SELECT * FROM {table_name}')
    rows = old_cursor.fetchall()

    # Insert data into the new table
    for row in rows:
        new_cursor.execute(f'INSERT INTO {table_name} VALUES (?, ?, ?, ?)', row)

    new_db_conn.commit()

# Example of migrating a specific table
migrate_table('example_table')

# Close connections
old_db_conn.close()
new_db_conn.close()
```

The output of the migration process can be monitored to ensure data integrity and completeness.

```
Migration started...
Transferring data from example_table
100 records transferred...
200 records transferred...
...
Migration completed successfully.
```

Security concerns are paramount with legacy systems. They are often built with outdated security paradigms and may not be capable of defending against modern cyber threats. This vulnerability is exacerbated by the fact that legacy systems rarely receive updates or patches, leaving known security holes unaddressed. Organizations must implement compensatory controls, such as network segmentation, firewalls, and intrusion detection systems, to mitigate these risks.

While legacy systems remain essential for many organizations, they present a multifaceted array of challenges. Addressing these issues requires a comprehensive strategy that includes careful management of technical debt, updating or replacing obsolete components, improving documentation, and ensuring that skilled personnel are available. Additionally, organizations must consider the potential benefits and risks associated with system migration, adopt robust security measures, and continuously evaluate the alignment of legacy systems with business objectives.

7.5 Impact of Software Changes

Software changes are an inevitable part of the software life cycle. These changes can stem from various sources, including new user requirements, bug fixes, performance enhancements, and adaptation to new hardware or software environments. Each change, regardless of its origin, can have a profound impact on the software system and its environment.

Software changes can be classified based on their impact into categories such as structural changes, behavioral changes, and performance changes. Structural changes affect the architecture of the software, including changes in data models, code structure, and module interactions. Behavioral changes alter the functional behavior of the system, such as changes in algorithms or user interface modifications. Performance changes relate to non-functional aspects such as speed, resource consumption, and scalability.

One of the primary impacts of software changes is on the system's reliability. Introducing a change can inadvertently introduce new bugs or expose latent defects that were previously undetected. Testing is crucial to mitigate this risk. Regression testing, in particular, is essential as it ensures that existing functionality remains unaffected by the new changes. Automated regression test suites are invaluable in this context as they allow for rapid and thorough testing.

Another significant impact is on the software's maintainability. Changes that are poorly designed or implemented can increase the complexity of the codebase, making future maintenance more difficult and error-prone. This impact is often measured using maintainability metrics such as cyclomatic complexity, coupling, and cohesion. High cyclomatic complexity can indicate complicated and hard-to-test code, while high coupling between modules can suggest that changes in one module will likely affect others. Conversely, high cohesion within modules is desirable as it indicates that the module's elements functionally belong together.

Maintainability issues are closely related to technical debt, which refers to the long-term costs incurred by taking shortcuts during software development. Quick fixes and patches that are implemented to address immediate problems but ignore best practices can accumulate into significant technical debt over time. Managing technical debt is crucial to ensure that software remains flexible and maintainable in the long term.

The impact on performance is another critical consideration. Changes aimed at improving performance can sometimes lead to trade-offs that affect other aspects of the system. For example, optimizing an algorithm for speed might increase memory usage, or vice versa. Profiling tools and performance benchmarks are essential to quantify such changes and their impact accurately. These tools can help identify performance bottlenecks and verify that performance improvements are realized without unintended side effects.

Software changes also impact documentation and user training. Any change in the software requires corresponding updates to user manuals, help files, and training materials. Failure to update these resources can lead to confusion and reduce the software's overall usability. Automated documentation tools and user feedback mechanisms can facilitate this process by ensuring that documentation is kept current.

In distributed systems and multi-tier architectures, the impact of changes can be more complex due to dependencies between various components and services. Service-oriented architectures (SOAs) and microservices, for example, involve numerous loosely coupled services that communicate over a network. A change in one service can affect other services that depend on it, making comprehensive integration testing and robust versioning strategies essential. Containerization technologies such as Docker and orchestration tools like Kubernetes can help manage these complexities by isolating changes within containers and orchestrating the deployment process.

Configuration management plays a vital role in managing the impact of software changes. By maintaining a well-documented and controlled configuration management system, teams can track changes, roll back to previous versions if needed, and ensure consistency across different environments. Version control systems (VCS) such as Git provide powerful features for branching, merging, and tracking change history, making it easier to manage multiple versions of the software concurrently.

Security is another domain where the impact of software changes is critical. Any change, especially those involving sensitive data or critical system functions, must be scrutinized for potential security vulnerabilities. Code reviews, static analysis tools, and security testing are essential practices to identify and mitigate security risks associated with changes.

Lastly, the impact of software changes is not limited to the technical aspects but also extends to the people and processes involved. Effective communication and collaboration within the development team and with stakeholders are vital in ensuring that changes are properly understood, implemented, and integrated. Agile methodologies, with their emphasis on iterative development and continuous feedback, can help in managing the impact of changes by fostering a culture of adaptability and continuous improvement.

```
# Original Function
def calculate_area(radius):
    return 3.14 * radius * radius

# Modified Function
def calculate_area(radius):
    pi = 3.141592653589793
    return pi * radius * radius
```

```
Before Change:
- Less accurate area calculation.

After Change:
- More accurate area calculation.
- Potentially impacted performance due to increased precision.
```

Understanding the multifaceted impact of software changes is crucial for effective software maintenance and evolution. By considering the various dimensions of change impact, including reliability, maintainability, performance, documentation, security, and collaboration, software engineers can better manage changes and ensure the long-term success of the software system.

7.6 Reverse Engineering and Refactoring

Reverse engineering and refactoring are critical activities in the software maintenance and evolution lifecycle. These practices are employed to enhance the understandability, quality, and performance of existing software without altering its externally observable behavior. They help maintainers in comprehending complex systems, identifying areas for improvement, and implementing changes effectively.

Reverse engineering involves analyzing a system to identify its components and their interrelationships, creating representations of the system at a higher level of abstraction. This process is essential for understanding legacy systems, especially when documentation is inadequate or missing. By contrast, refactoring focuses on improving the internal structure of the software. It involves restructuring the existing codebase to optimize performance, readability, and maintainability while preserving its functionality.

Reverse Engineering

Reverse engineering can be broken down into several sub-activities:

- **Extraction of Unified Models**: Creating abstract models that describe the overall design and behavior of the software system. This includes data flow diagrams, control flow graphs, and entity-relationship diagrams.
- **Program Slicing**: Dividing the program into parts based on specific criteria to isolate areas of interest. Program slicing helps in understanding specific functionalities and dependencies in the code.
- **Code Analysis**: Performing static and dynamic analysis to gather information about the code structure, data dependencies, and runtime behavior.

The following illustrates a basic example in C to demonstrate program slicing:

```c
#include <stdio.h>

int multiply(int a, int b) {
    return a * b;
}

int main() {
    int x = 5;
    int y = 10;
    int result = multiply(x, y);
    printf("Result: %d", result);
    return 0;
}
```

In this example, a slice with respect to the variable result would include the main function, excluding any unrelated code.

Program slicing helps reverse engineers focus on specific aspects of the program, improving their ability to understand and modify complex systems.

Refactoring

Refactoring encompasses a variety of techniques aimed at improving code without changing its external behavior. Common refactoring techniques include:

- **Code Smell Identification and Removal**: Identifying bad code practices, known as code smells, and rectifying them. Examples include long methods, large classes, and duplicated code.
- **Renaming Method and Variables**: Renaming methods and variables to make their purpose clearer. Clear naming conventions enhance code readability and maintainability.
- **Extract Method**: Creating new methods from sections of code to simplify complex methods and promote code reuse.

Consider a Java method that calculates the sum and average of an array of integers:

```
public class Statistics {
    public void calculate(int[] numbers) {
        int sum = 0;
        double average = 0;
        for(int number: numbers) {
            sum += number;
        }
        if(numbers.length > 0) {
            average = sum / numbers.length;
        }
        System.out.println("Sum: " + sum);
        System.out.println("Average: " + average);
    }
}
```

Refactoring by extracting methods for sum and average calculations, the code becomes more modular and easier to maintain:

```
public class Statistics {
    public void calculate(int[] numbers) {
        int sum = sum(numbers);
        double average = average(numbers, sum);
        System.out.println("Sum: " + sum);
        System.out.println("Average: " + average);
    }

    private int sum(int[] numbers) {
        int sum = 0;
        for(int number: numbers) {
            sum += number;
        }
        return sum;
    }

    private double average(int[] numbers, int sum) {
        if(numbers.length > 0) {
            return sum / (double) numbers.length;
        }
        return 0;
    }
}
```

Effective refactoring demands a thorough understanding of the existing code. Automated refactoring tools integrated into modern IDEs (Integrated Development Environments) assist developers in performing these changes safely by ensuring that all affected parts of the codebase are updated accordingly.

When applied together, reverse engineering and refactoring bolster the maintainability of legacy systems, making it feasible to evolve software in response to new requirements or technologies. Proper documentation and adoption of best practices during these processes cater to smoother transitions and long-term effectiveness in software maintenance and evolution.

7.7 Configuration Management in Maintenance

Configuration management (CM) is a critical aspect of software maintenance that ensures the integrity and traceability of software configurations throughout the lifecycle of a product. CM involves systematically handling changes to the software, maintaining consistency, and verifying that the system performs as intended. It is a discipline that supports the systematic control of changes to software products, allowing for the accurate reconstruction of every software version produced.

Key elements of configuration management include configuration identification, configuration control, configuration status accounting, and configuration audits.

- **Configuration Identification** involves defining and documenting the configuration items (CIs) within a system and their interrelationships. This process includes labeling and identifying the versions of software documents, hardware, and software components. Configuration items can range from entire systems to individual files and serve as the baseline for configuration control and audits.

- **Configuration Control** ensures that changes to a system are introduced in a controlled and coordinated manner. This involves the recording, assessment, approval, and implementation of changes. The process typically uses a Change Control Board (CCB) to oversee and authorize modifications, ensuring that changes do not negatively affect system integrity or performance. The change control process can be exemplified using the following steps:

```
# Current version of a function
def calculate_area(radius):
    return 3.14 * radius ** 2

# Updated version to improve precision
def calculate_area(radius):
    pi = 3.141592653589793
    return pi * radius ** 2
```

In this example, the change from a fixed value of π to a more precise value is tracked through the CM system, ensuring transparency and auditability.

- **Configuration Status Accounting** involves recording and reporting all necessary information about the configuration items and their changes. This provides visibility into what versions of software or hardware components are in use, what changes have been made, and the current status of configuration items. Configuration status accounting can involve generating detailed reports, such as build status reports or change request status updates, which are crucial for maintaining an accurate historical record.
- **Configuration Audits** are performed to ensure that the configuration items match their documented descriptions and satisfy the specified requirements. Audits help to verify that the CM process is being followed correctly and that all changes are properly implemented and recorded. This includes both functional audits, which confirm the proper implementation of configuration functions, and physical audits, which ensure the physical existence and correct version of the configuration items.

A practical tool for supporting configuration management is the use of version control systems such as Git. These systems manage the evolution of software artifacts and ensure that every change is documented and reversible. Through branching and merging, Git allows multiple developers to work concurrently on the same project without interfering with each other's work. An example of using Git for configuration management is shown below:

```
# Cloning a repository
git clone https://github.com/user/repo.git
```

```
# Creating a new branch for a feature
git checkout -b new-feature

# Adding changes to the staging area
git add modified_file.py

# Committing the changes
git commit -m "Enhanced area calculation precision"

# Merging the branch back into the main branch
git checkout main
git merge new-feature

# Pushing changes to the remote repository
git push origin main
```

Proper CM practices are particularly vital in environments where multiple versions of a software product must be maintained simultaneously. They ensure that patches and updates can be accurately applied to the correct versions without introducing new errors or inconsistencies.

Effective configuration management requires a combination of proper tools, processes, and discipline by the development and maintenance teams. By carefully managing configurations, teams can increase stability, consistency, and accountability within a project, ultimately leading to higher quality software products.

7.8 Metrics and Measurement in Software Maintenance

Accurate metrics and measurement are indispensable for effective software maintenance. They provide quantifiable data, enabling assessment of maintenance activities and guiding decision-making processes. The primary objectives of these metrics are to monitor and improve software quality, productivity, and the predictability of maintenance efforts.

A wide range of metrics exists, each shedding light on different aspects of software maintenance. The following detailed explanations will cover various categories of maintenance metrics, including product metrics, process metrics, and project metrics.

Product Metrics: Product metrics measure characteristics of the software product itself, such as size, complexity, and quality. These metrics provide insight into the structural attributes of the software, aiding in identifying potential problem areas.

- **Size Metrics:** Size metrics typically measure the physical size of the software codebase. Common size metrics include Lines of Code (LOC), Function Points (FP), and Code Churn.

```
# Example Python function to count the number of lines in a file.
def count_lines(filename):
    with open(filename, 'r') as file:
        return len(file.readlines())

print(count_lines('example.py')) # Outputs the number of lines in 'example.py'
```

```
# Output
52 # Indicates that the file contains 52 lines of code
```

- **Complexity Metrics:** Complexity metrics provide a measure of the intricateness of the code, which can affect maintainability. Cyclomatic Complexity, Halstead Metrics, and McCabe's Complexity are widely used.

```
# Example Python function to calculate Cyclomatic Complexity
import networkx as nx

def cyclomatic_complexity(graph):
    edges = graph.number_of_edges()
    nodes = graph.number_of_nodes()
    return edges - nodes + 2

# Create a directed graph representation of code
graph = nx.DiGraph()
graph.add_edges_from([(1,2), (1,3), (2,4), (3,4)])

print(cyclomatic_complexity(graph)) # Outputs the Cyclomatic Complexity
```

```
# Output
2 # Cyclomatic Complexity of the code represented by the graph
```

- **Quality Metrics:** Quality metrics measure the actual performance against desired qualities like reliability and maintainability. Defect Density and Mean Time to Repair (MTTR) are examples.

Process Metrics: Process metrics focus on the efficiency of the maintenance process itself, providing insights into resource utilization and workflows.

- **Effort Metrics:** These metrics measure the amount of time and resources dedicated to various maintenance tasks. Examples include effort hours, team size, and resource allocation.
- **Defect Metrics:** Tracking the number and severity of defects found during maintenance activities. Metrics such as Defect Removal Efficiency (DRE) and Defect Density during phases of maintenance are valuable.

- **Change Request Metrics:** This includes the number of change requests received, their nature (corrective, adaptive, etc.), and the time taken to address them. Change request age and backlog size are also important metrics.

Project Metrics: Project metrics encompass broader measures that assess aspects of the entire maintenance project, including cost, schedule, and overall return on investment.

- **Cost Metrics:** These metrics measure the financial resources required for maintenance activities. Examples include total maintenance cost, cost per function point, and cost overrun.

- **Schedule Metrics:** These metrics monitor the adherence to maintenance schedules. Examples are time to market for new releases, schedule variance, and the duration of maintenance loops.

- **Productivity Metrics:** This includes metrics like the number of function points delivered per person-month, code churn per iteration, and maintenance productivity index.

```
# Formula for Maintenance Productivity Index (MPI)
MPI = Size of the Improved Software / Effort Spent

# Example calculation
Size_of_the_Improved_Software = 1000 # Function Points
Effort_Spent = 50 # Person-Months

MPI = Size_of_the_Improved_Software / Effort_Spent
print(MPI) # Outputs Maintenance Productivity Index
```

Accurate measurement requires the proper collection and analysis of data associated with each metric. Tools and techniques such as version control systems, issue tracking systems, and analytical software play a pivotal role in gathering and interpreting these metrics. By deploying these metrics thoughtfully, software engineering teams can enhance their understanding of maintenance activities and drive improvements in both the software product and the maintenance process.

7.9 Tools and Techniques for Software Maintenance

Software maintenance is a critical phase in the software development lifecycle that ensures the software continues to operate efficiently and meets user requirements. The tools and techniques employed in this phase are essential for effective management, modification, and improvement of the software. This section delves into several of these tools and techniques, providing insights into their functionalities and applications.

Version Control Systems

Version control systems (VCS) are vital in software maintenance, facilitating the management of changes to source code over time. They enable multiple developers to collaborate on a project without conflicts. Popular VCS tools include Git, Subversion, and Mercurial.

```
# Cloning a repository
git clone https://github.com/user/repo.git

# Checking the status of the working directory
git status

# Adding changes to the staging area
git add .

# Committing changes
git commit -m "Commit message"

# Pushing changes to the remote repository
git push origin main
```

The execution of these commands ensures that changes are tracked accurately, providing a comprehensive history that is crucial for maintenance.

Integrated Development Environments (IDEs)

Integrated Development Environments (IDEs) are sophisticated tools that offer comprehensive facilities to software developers for software development and maintenance. IDEs like Eclipse, IntelliJ IDEA, and Visual Studio provide features such as code editing, debugging, and project management in an integrated manner. These features significantly improve productivity and code quality during the maintenance phase.

Refactoring Tools

Refactoring tools are used to improve the internal structure of the software without altering its external behavior. These tools help in maintaining and improving code readability, reducing complexity, and enhancing performance. Common refactoring tools include the built-in features of IDEs, as well as standalone tools like JRefactory and Refactoring Browser.

```
// Before Refactoring
public void process_data() {
    for (int i = 0; i < data.size(); i++) {
        if (data.get(i) % 2 == 0) {
            System.out.println("Even number: " + data.get(i));
        }
    }
}

// After Refactoring
public void process_data() {
    data.stream()
        .filter(number -> number % 2 == 0)
        .forEach(System.out::println);
}
```

The refactored code demonstrates improved readability and reduced complexity.

Static Analysis Tools

Static analysis tools examine source code for potential errors and ensure code quality without executing the program. Tools like SonarQube, FindBugs, and Checkstyle are employed extensively for identifying coding errors, potential vulnerabilities, and adherence to coding standards.

Automated Testing Tools

Automated testing tools are indispensable for ensuring that changes introduced during maintenance do not break existing functionality. These tools facilitate the execution of test cases without human intervention. Popular automated testing tools include JUnit, Selenium, and TestNG.

```
import org.junit.Test;
import static org.junit.Assert.assertEquals;

public class CalculatorTest {
    @Test
    public void testAdd() {
        Calculator calc = new Calculator();
        assertEquals(5, calc.add(2, 3));
    }

    @Test
    public void testSubtract() {
        Calculator calc = new Calculator();
        assertEquals(1, calc.subtract(5, 4));
    }
```

```
}
```

Executing these test cases ensures the robustness of the software by verifying that the recent changes have not negatively impacted its functionality.

Dependency Management Tools

Managing software dependencies correctly is crucial to ensure smooth operation. Dependency management tools automate the process of downloading, updating, and resolving project dependencies. Tools such as Maven, Gradle, and npm (Node Package Manager) are widely used in the industry.

```
<dependency>
    <groupId>org.springframework</groupId>
    <artifactId>spring-core</artifactId>
    <version>5.2.6.RELEASE</version>
</dependency>
```

These tools streamline the incorporation and maintenance of dependencies in a project, ensuring compatibility and reducing conflicts.

Continuous Integration/Continuous Deployment (CI/CD) Tools

CI/CD tools facilitate the automatic build, test, and deployment of code changes, leading to more frequent and reliable software releases. Jenkins, Travis CI, and CircleCI are popular CI/CD tools.

```
language: java
jdk:
  - openjdk11
before_script:
  - ./gradlew clean
script:
  - ./gradlew build
```

Utilizing CI/CD tools ensures that code changes are continuously integrated and deployed, reducing the chances of integration issues and expediting the delivery process.

These tools and techniques form the backbone of a robust software maintenance process, ensuring that software systems remain functional, efficient, and adaptable to changing requirements. By adopting these tools, developers can address the various challenges associated with software maintenance effectively.

7.10 Case Studies in Software Maintenance

Case studies offer critical insights into the real-world applications of software maintenance principles and methodologies. Through detailed examination of specific instances, we can better understand the challenges, strategies, and outcomes associated with maintaining and evolving software systems. This section delves into various case studies that highlight the complexities of software maintenance and the approaches employed to tackle them effectively.

Case Study 1: Migrating a Legacy Banking System to a Modern Architecture

A leading financial institution faced significant issues with its legacy banking system, which was built on an outdated mainframe architecture. The system suffered from performance bottlenecks, high maintenance costs, and difficulties in implementing regulatory changes. A comprehensive strategy was employed to migrate the system to a modern, scalable architecture.

The migration process began with an in-depth analysis of the existing system, involving reverse engineering techniques to understand the system's functionality and data flow. The following steps were executed:

- **Assessment and Planning:** Detailed assessment of business requirements and legacy system capabilities. Planning involved stakeholder consultations, risk assessments, and the creation of a migration roadmap.
- **System Decomposition:** Breakdown of the monolithic system into manageable components to facilitate understanding and re-engineering.
- **Data Migration:** Development of scripts and tools to safely transfer data from the legacy databases to modern relational databases, ensuring data integrity and consistency.
- **Incremental Migration:** Adoption of an incremental approach, migrating and validating one module at a time to minimize disruption and allow for continuous feedback and adjustments.
- **Refactoring and Optimization:** Extensive code refactoring and optimization to leverage modern programming paradigms and improve performance.

The final system demonstrated improved performance, reduced maintenance costs, and enhanced compliance with regulatory standards.

Case Study 2: Implementing Preventive Maintenance in an E-commerce Platform

An e-commerce company aimed to reduce system downtime and enhance user experience by implementing preventive maintenance measures. The company's platform, which handled millions of transactions daily, faced sporadic outages and performance degradation impacting user satisfaction.

Preventive maintenance was implemented as follows:

- **Regular System Audits:** Automated scripts were developed to conduct regular system audits, identifying potential vulnerabilities and performance bottlenecks.
- **Proactive Monitoring:** Deployment of advanced monitoring tools to track system metrics in real time, such as CPU usage, memory consumption, and transaction response times.
- **Scheduled Maintenance Windows:** Establishment of scheduled maintenance windows to perform updates, patch deployments, and infrastructure improvements without impacting peak usage times.
- **Incident Response Planning:** Development of comprehensive incident response plans to swiftly address any issues detected during preventive checks.
- **User Feedback Integration:** Collection and analysis of user feedback to identify and address recurrent issues proactively.

These measures resulted in a significant reduction in system downtime, improved system stability, and higher user satisfaction scores.

Case Study 3: Adaptive Maintenance in a Healthcare Management System

A healthcare provider needed to adapt its management system to comply with new healthcare regulations and integrate with external medical databases and equipment. The system was critical for patient record management, scheduling, and billing processes.

Adaptive maintenance included:

- **Interface Development:** Creation of new interfaces and APIs to enable seamless integration with external databases and equipment, ensuring the secure exchange of patient information.
- **Regulatory Compliance Updates:** Modification of the software to meet the latest regulatory requirements, including the implementation of enhanced security and privacy features.
- **User Training and Support:** Provision of extensive user training sessions and support to facilitate the transition to the updated system.
- **Testing and Validation:** Rigorous testing and validation phases to ensure the system met all functional and non-functional requirements, reducing the risk of post-deployment issues.

The adaptive maintenance efforts enabled the healthcare provider to offer improved services, maintain compliance with regulations, and better integrate with modern medical technologies.

Case Study 4: Corrective Maintenance in an Educational Management System

An educational institution used an outdated management system experiencing frequent bugs and system crashes, jeopardizing the administration of educational programs and student management. Corrective maintenance was necessary to restore the system to optimum functionality.

The corrective maintenance process involved:

- **Bug Tracking and Triage:** Employing a bug tracking system to log, prioritize, and manage reported issues based on their severity and impact on operations.
- **Root Cause Analysis:** Conducting root cause analyses for critical issues to identify underlying problems and prevent recurrence.
- **Patch Deployment:** Developing and deploying patches to resolve identified bugs, with thorough testing in a staging environment before production rollout.
- **User Communication:** Maintaining clear communication channels with users to inform them of ongoing maintenance activities and any temporary disruptions.

These corrective measures resulted in a more stable and reliable system, enhancing the overall efficiency of the institution's administrative processes.

Case Study 5: Perfective Maintenance in a Customer Relationship Management (CRM) System

A mid-sized enterprise sought to enhance its CRM system to improve user productivity and customer satisfaction. The perfective maintenance efforts were geared towards adding new features and optimizing existing functionalities based on user feedback.

The perfective maintenance activities included:

- **Feature Enhancement:** Adding new features such as advanced analytics, automated customer follow-up, and enhanced reporting capabilities based on user needs.
- **Code Optimization:** Refactoring and optimizing the existing codebase to improve performance and reduce technical debt.
- **Usability Improvements:** Redesigning the user interface for better usability and accessibility, incorporating modern design principles.
- **Feedback Loops:** Establishing feedback loops with end users to gather continuous input and ensure that new features met their needs.

The CRM system updates led to higher user adoption rates, improved customer satisfaction, and greater employee productivity.

Chapter 8

Project Management in Software Engineering

Project management in software engineering involves planning, organizing, and controlling resources to achieve specific software project goals. This chapter covers the project life cycle and its phases, including project planning, scheduling, resource management, and risk management. It discusses cost management and budgeting, quality management, and effective communication within project teams. The chapter also introduces Agile project management, various tools and techniques used in project management, and provides case studies to illustrate successful software project management practices.

8.1 Introduction to Project Management in Software Engineering

Project management in software engineering encompasses a structured approach towards planning, organizing, and controlling resources to realize specific objectives. It melds both the art and science of managing software projects, ensuring that goals are achieved within the constraints of time, budget, and quality. Project management ensures that projects are aligned with business objectives and delivered efficiently. This section elucidates the core principles and frameworks that underlie project management in the context of software engineering.

At the heart of project management lies the project life cycle, a series of phases that a project undergoes from initiation to closure. Understanding this life cycle is crucial for effectively managing a software project. The project life cycle traditionally comprises the following stages:

- **Initiation** This phase involves defining the project at a high-level, identifying the project's objectives, scope, purpose, and deliverables. Key activities include feasibility analysis, gathering initial requirements, and securing initial stakeholders' agreement and funding.
- **Planning** Once a project is initiated, detailed planning ensues. This phase involves defining a roadmap for achieving the project objectives. It includes creating detailed project plans, schedules, cost estimates, resource allocation, risk management plans, and communication plans. Tools like Gantt charts, PERT charts, and Work Breakdown Structures (WBS) are often employed.
- **Execution** During execution, resources are coordinated, and activities are conducted according to the project plan. This phase requires robust team management, communication, and monitoring to ensure adherence to timelines and budgets. Deliverables are developed and verified, meeting the predefined quality standards.
- **Monitoring and Controlling** Running concurrently with execution, this phase involves tracking, reviewing, and regulating project performance. Key Performance Indicators (KPIs) are monitored to ensure the project remains on track. Variances from the plan are identified, and corrective actions are implemented as required.
- **Closure** Upon project completion, closure entails finalizing all activities to formally close the project. This includes deliverable handover, documentation, resource release, and evaluating project success against its objectives. A project review or retrospective is often conducted to document lessons learned.

In the context of software engineering, project management requires a nuanced understanding of the software development process. Software projects are typically marked by rapid technology changes, evolving requirements, and significant uncertainties, necessitating adaptive and iterative approaches. Traditional methodologies, such as Waterfall, as well as Agile methodologies, such as Scrum and Kanban, are employed based on the project's nature and complexity.

A comprehensive project management strategy in software engineering involves multiple knowledge areas, each contributing to the project's overall success:

- **Scope Management** Controlling what is included and excluded from the project to ensure it meets its objectives.
- **Time Management** Ensuring timely completion through effective scheduling techniques like critical path method (CPM) and Gantt charts.
- **Cost Management** Planning, estimating, budgeting, and controlling costs to keep the project within the approved budget.
- **Quality Management** Ensuring the final product meets the desired quality standards, often using metrics like defect density and customer satisfaction.
- **Resource Management** Efficiently and effectively utilizing human, physical, and financial resources.
- **Risk Management** Identifying, analyzing, and responding to risks to minimize their impact on the project.
- **Communication Management** Facilitating optimal communication among stakeholders to ensure transparency and address issues promptly.
- **Procurement Management** Acquiring necessary services or products from external sources.
- **Stakeholder Management** Identifying and engaging with all individuals and organizations affected by the project to ensure their expectations are met.

Project management in software engineering also relies heavily on tools and techniques to enhance efficiency and effectiveness. Modern project management tools provide functionalities for task scheduling, resource management, risk assessment, and collaboration. Familiarity with industry-standard tools such as Microsoft Project, Jira, Trello, Asana, and others is indispensable for a project manager.

Risk management is particularly critical in the realm of software projects, given the high uncertainty and rapid technological evolution. Effective risk management strategies involve proactive identification of potential risks, thorough analysis, and devising mitigation plans. Quantitative risk analysis techniques such as Monte Carlo simulations and qualitative methods like SWOT analysis are frequently utilized.

Throughout history, many high-profile software projects have benefited from robust project management practices, illustrating their importance. The development of the Boeing 777's flight control software, managed by a meticulous project management regime, remains a landmark example of successful software project management.

Lastly, adaptive methodologies like Agile have gained prominence, offering iterative and incremental approaches to software development. Agile methodologies emphasize flexibility, continuous feedback, and collaboration, making them particularly suitable for complex and dynamic software projects.

```
# This script automates the creation of user stories and tasks in an Agile project
    management tool

import requests

def create_user_story(project_id, title, description):
    url = "https://api.projectmanagementtool.com/userStories"
    payload = {
        "project_id": project_id,
        "title": title,
        "description": description
    }
    headers = {
        "Authorization": "Bearer YOUR_API_TOKEN",
        "Content-Type": "application/json"
    }
    response = requests.post(url, json=payload, headers=headers)
    if response.status_code == 201:
        print("User story created successfully.")
    else:
        print("Failed to create user story.")
    return response.json()

def create_task(user_story_id, title, description):
    url = f"https://api.projectmanagementtool.com/userStories/{user_story_id}/tasks"

    payload = {
        "title": title,
        "description": description
    }
    headers = {
        "Authorization": "Bearer YOUR_API_TOKEN",
        "Content-Type": "application/json"
    }
    response = requests.post(url, json=payload, headers=headers)
    if response.status_code == 201:
        print("Task created successfully.")
```

```
    else:
        print("Failed to create task.")
    return response.json()

# Example usage
project_id = 1
user_story = create_user_story(project_id, "Implement Login", "User should be able
    to log in.")
create_task(user_story["id"], "Design Login UI", "Create wireframes for login screen.")
create_task(user_story["id"], "Develop Login Backend", "Implement authentication
    logic.")
```

Execution of this script results in the following output:

```
User story created successfully.
Task created successfully.
Task created successfully.
```

Understanding these concepts and applying them effectively elevates a software engineer's capability to contribute to and manage successful projects.

8.2 Project Life Cycle and Phases

The project life cycle is a systematic series of phases that all project efforts follow. This ensures effective project initiation, planning, execution, control, and closure. Each phase, acting as a framework, assists project managers in organizing tasks and resources to achieve project goals efficiently. This section elaborates on the typical phases encountered in most software engineering projects.

A standard project life cycle in software engineering consists of the following phases: **Initiation, Planning, Execution, Monitoring and Controlling**, and **Closure**.

Initiation Phase: This phase marks the beginning of the project and involves defining the project at a broad level. The primary focus is to identify the business need, problem, or opportunity. Here, stakeholders and the project manager will develop a project charter and a high-level project scope statement that identifies the project's objectives, constraints, assumptions, and deliverables. This phase may include feasibility studies, which assess the project's viability in terms of technology, cost, and market considerations.

The deliverables of the initiation phase typically include:

- Project Charter

- Initial Scope Statement
- Stakeholder Identification
- Feasibility Study
- Preliminary Project Plan

Planning Phase: Once the project receives the green light during initiation, it moves into the planning phase. This phase involves constructing the roadmap that will guide the team through the development and delivery of the software. Detailed plans are crafted to outline the project schedule, cost estimates, resource allocation, quality management, risk management, and communication management.

Key components and deliverables can include:

- Detailed Project Management Plan
- Work Breakdown Structure (WBS)
- Gantt Charts
- Resource Allocation Plan
- Detailed Budget/Cost Estimates
- Risk Management Plan
- Communication Plan
- Quality Management Plan

In this phase, substantial attention is also directed towards defining the project's scope in more detail, developing detailed technical requirements, and constructing initial system architecture plans.

Execution Phase: During the execution phase, the project plan is set into motion and the work required to complete the project is performed. As the project's longest phase, it involves the development of the actual deliverables. Teams execute their tasks, produce deliverables, and use many resources, including team members and budget allocations.

During this phase, project managers must ensure that tasks are completed within the defined scope, timeframe, and budget. Key activities include:

- Team Development and Management
- Executing Project Tasks as Defined in the Project Schedule
- Deliverable Production and Verification
- Quality Assurance Activities
- Status Reporting and Stakeholder Interaction
- Management of Stakeholder Expectations

Tools such as problem tracking systems, configuration management tools, and automated build systems are often employed to keep work on track. Additionally, effective change management processes ensure adaptive responses to any unforeseen changes required during execution.

Monitoring and Controlling Phase: This phase runs concurrently with the execution phase and focuses on measuring project performance to ensure that everything aligns with the project plan. The primary objective is to identify and rectify deviations from the plan at the earliest.

Essential activities in this phase include:

- Performance Reporting
- Risk Monitoring and Management
- Quality Control
- Scope Verification and Change Control
- Schedule and Budget Tracking

To facilitate these processes, project managers utilize various project management information systems (PMIS), dashboard interfaces, and performance metrics. By monitoring project activities continuously, project managers ensure adherence to scope, and take corrective actions when necessary.

Closure Phase: The closure phase marks the completion of the project. It includes handing over deliverables to the client, releasing project resources, and conducting post-project reviews to identify best practices and lessons learned.

Key activities and deliverables of the closure phase include:

- Final Project Documentation and Archiving
- Client Handover and Presentation
- Release of Project Resources
- Project Performance and Completion Reports
- Post-mortem Analysis and Lessons Learned

The post-project review is integral to enhancing future project outcomes by encapsulating both successful methodologies and failure points experienced during the project. It creates a repository of knowledge that fosters continual improvement across the organization.

Understanding and meticulously managing each phase of the project life cycle is essential to achieving successful outcomes in software engineering projects. Proper application of phase-based management allows for heightened precision in resource management, risk mitigation, and achievement of project goals.

8.3 Project Planning and Scheduling

Project planning and scheduling are critical activities in project management, where deliberate efforts are made to structure tasks, allocate resources efficiently, and achieve project goals within specified constraints. These activities involve defining the scope, devising work breakdown structures, scheduling tasks, and determining their dependencies. Effective planning and scheduling directly contribute to the successful delivery of a software project, ensuring its objectives are met on time and within budget.

Defining the Scope

The first step in project planning is defining the project scope, which establishes the boundaries and deliverables of the project. The scope includes detailed requirements, project goals, and constraints. Accurate scope definition prevents scope creep, where uncontrolled changes affect project progression.

Work Breakdown Structure (WBS)

A Work Breakdown Structure (WBS) is a hierarchical decomposition of the total scope of work to be carried out by the project team. It organizes and defines the work in manageable sections from the highest level down to the individual tasks:

- Project Goal
  - Milestone 1
    - Task 1.1.1
    - Task 1.1.2
  - Milestone 2
    - Task 1.2.1
    - Task 1.2.2

Creating a comprehensive WBS is essential to ensure all work elements necessary to complete the project are identified, and helps in tracking progress and managing resources effectively.

Gantt Charts

A Gantt chart is a vital tool for visualizing the project schedule. It represents tasks with bars plotted against time, illustrating task duration, start, and end dates, and dependencies:

```
ProjectSchedule <- data.frame(
  Task = c("Task 1", "Task 2", "Task 3"),
  Start = as.Date(c("2023-10-01", "2023-10-05", "2023-10-08")),
  End = as.Date(c("2023-10-10", "2023-10-15", "2023-10-20"))
)
gantt_chart(ProjectSchedule)
```

A Gantt chart allows project managers to monitor the progress of tasks, identify delays, and adjust schedules accordingly. Tools like Microsoft Project or online platforms like Asana support the creation and maintenance of Gantt charts.

Critical Path Method (CPM)

The Critical Path Method (CPM) is an algorithm for scheduling project tasks. It determines the longest sequence of activities in a project, known as the critical path, which dictates the shortest time possible to complete the project. Identifying the critical path is essential for understanding task dependencies and optimizing the project timeline:

```
Tasks <- data.frame(
  TaskID = c("A", "B", "C", "D"),
  Duration = c(4, 3, 2, 5),
  Dependencies = c(NA, "A", "A", "B")
)
critical_path(Tasks)
```

This method highlights critical and non-critical tasks, allowing for enhanced focus on activities that directly impact project finish dates.

PERT Analysis

Program Evaluation and Review Technique (PERT) is a statistical tool used to manage uncertain activities in a project. It involves three time estimates: optimistic, most likely, and pessimistic. By calculating the expected time for each task, PERT aids in developing a probabilistic project schedule:

```
Tasks <- data.frame(
  TaskID = c("A", "B", "C"),
  Optimistic = c(3, 2, 4),
  MostLikely = c(5, 3, 6),
  Pessimistic = c(7, 5, 8)
)
pert_analysis(Tasks)
```

PERT enhances the credibility of the project schedule by accounting for variability and providing a range of possible completion dates.

Resource Allocation and Leveling

Efficient resource allocation ensures that personnel, finances, and materials are used optimally throughout the project. Resource leveling is a technique to avoid overallocation by adjusting the start and finish dates based on resource constraints. Balancing resources prevents bottlenecks and ensures smooth project execution:

```
Resources <- data.frame(
  TaskID = c("A", "B", "C"),
  Resources = c("Team1", "Team2", "Team1")
)
resource_leveling(Resources)
```

Proper resource management helps in adhering to the project schedule and maintaining productivity.

Scheduling Tools and Techniques

Various tools and techniques are available for project scheduling, including manual scheduling, software tools like Microsoft Project, and cloud-based solutions such as Jira and Trello. These tools support the planning, tracking, and updating of project schedules:

```
# Scheduling using Microsoft Project
proj <- Project$new()
proj:add_task("Task 1", "2023-10-01", "2023-10-05")
proj:add_task("Task 2", "2023-10-06", "2023-10-10")
proj:add_task("Task 3", "2023-10-11", "2023-10-15")
proj$schedule()
```

These tools provide features like dependency management, critical path analysis, risk assessment, and collaborative capabilities.

Monitoring and Updating Schedules

Project schedules need regular monitoring to track progress and make adjustments. Variances from the planned schedule, such as delays or early completions, should be assessed. Schedule updating involves recalibrating the project timeline in response to these variances to keep the project on track:

```
Planned Start Date: 2023-10-01
Actual Start Date: 2023-10-02
Planned End Date: 2023-10-15
Actual End Date: 2023-10-20

Schedule Variance: -5 days
```

Effective monitoring ensures proactive management of scheduling risks and adherence to project timelines.

Project planning and scheduling are fundamental to the systematic progression of any software project, establishing a blueprint that guides teams through the execution phase and towards successful project completion.

8.4 Resource Management

Resource management in software engineering is a critical aspect of project management. It involves the efficient and effective deployment and allocation of an organization's resources when and where they are needed. These resources can include personnel, financial resources, technology, and physical resources. Effective resource management ensures that projects are completed on time, within budget, and with the required quality standards.

At the core of resource management are several principles and practices that aim to maximize resource efficiency. These include resource allocation, resource leveling, resource smoothing, and the management of multi-project environments. Each practice involves a detailed and thorough understanding of available resources, project requirements, and timelines.

Resource allocation is the process of distributing available resources to various tasks and activities within a project. Resource allocation aims to optimize the use of resources and avoid resource conflicts. A common method for resource allocation is the use of a resource breakdown structure (RBS), which depicts the hierarchy of resources and their allocation within a project. Consider the following example of a simple RBS:

- 1. Personnel
  - 1.1 Software Engineers
  - 1.2 Testers
  - 1.3 Project Managers
  - 1.4 UX/UI Designers
- 2. Technology
  - 2.1 Development Tools
  - 2.2 Testing Tools
  - 2.3 Deployment Infrastructure
- 3. Financial Resources
  - 3.1 Budget Allocation
  - 3.2 Contingency Funds

Resource allocation also involves utilizing tools that assist in managing and visualizing resource assignments. Gantt charts and resource histograms are particularly useful in visualizing resource allocation over time.

Resource leveling is a technique used to address resource conflicts by adjusting the start and finish dates of tasks based on resource constraints. Resource leveling seeks to balance resource demand with the available supply, preventing over-allocation. The goal is to ensure that resources are not over-extended, which could lead to burnout or project delays. However, this can sometimes result in extended project durations.

Resource smoothing is similar to resource leveling but differs in that the project end date must not be affected. With resource smoothing, the focus is on adjusting the work within specified date constraints, making sure that resource usage stays within defined limits. This technique is useful when maintaining the original project timeline is critical.

Efficient resource management also involves the management of multi-project environments. In many organizations, resources are shared across multiple projects. This necessitates the ability to prioritize projects, align resources with project priorities, and facilitate effective communication between project teams. The goal is to avoid resource bottlenecks and ensure that critical projects receive the necessary resources.

Project management software tools play a vital role in facilitating resource management. Tools like Microsoft Project, JIRA, and Trello offer functionalities to track resource availability, allocation, and utilization. For instance, consider the following task allocation for a software development project managed using a project management tool:

```
Task Allocation:
- Develop login module: Assigned to Alice (Software Engineer) [40 hours]
- Test payment gateway: Assigned to Bob (Tester) [20 hours]
- Design user interface: Assigned to Carol (UX/UI Designer) [30 hours]
```

Such tools also support the creation of resource calendars, which can display the availability of resources based on holidays, working hours, and other constraints. The project manager can thus ensure that resource allocation is both fair and effective.

To handle resource constraints, project managers may employ various strategies such as hiring temporary staff, outsourcing certain tasks, or adjusting project scopes. These strategies can provide the necessary flexibility to manage unforeseen changes in resource availability.

Risk management also intersects significantly with resource management. Identifying potential risks related to resource availability—such as the risk of key team members leaving the project or budget overruns—allows project managers to develop mitigation plans.

Advancements in technologies like Artificial Intelligence (AI) and Machine Learning (ML) are increasingly being leveraged to enhance resource management capabilities. For example, AI can be used to predict resource utilization patterns and suggest optimal resource allocation strategies.

Moreover, continuous improvement in resource management practices is key to long-term success. Collecting data on resource utilization and project outcomes provides valuable insights that can be used to refine and enhance planning processes. Establishing a culture of regular review and adaptation ensures that resource management remains aligned with organizational goals and evolving project needs.

Therefore, resource management is a multi-faceted discipline that requires a blend of strategic planning, tactical execution, and continuous improvement to ensure that resources are used effectively and projects are delivered successfully in software engineering.

8.5 Risk Management

Risk management is an essential component of project management in software engineering, focused on identifying, assessing, and mitigating risks that could adversely affect the project's outcomes. Understanding and effectively managing risks can significantly enhance the chances of project success. This section will cover the detailed processes involved in risk management, including risk identification, risk analysis, risk prioritization, risk response planning, and risk monitoring and control.

Risk management begins with **risk identification**, which involves recognizing potential risks that could affect the project. Various techniques can be employed for risk identification, including brainstorming sessions, expert interviews, and examination of risk checklists from past projects. Often, project managers will use tools such as SWOT (Strengths, Weaknesses, Opportunities, Threats) analysis or risk breakdown structures (RBS) to systematically identify risks.

- **Brainstorming:** Typically involves a facilitated group session where team members identify as many risks as possible without immediate judgment or discussion.
- **Expert Interviews:** Involve consulting with individuals who have significant experience and expertise in similar projects to elicit potential risks.
- **SWOT Analysis:** A strategic planning tool that helps in identifying the strengths, weaknesses, opportunities, and threats related to the project.
- **Risk Breakdown Structure (RBS):** A hierarchical decomposition of risks, similar to a Work Breakdown Structure (WBS), which helps categorize risks into various levels.

Once risks are identified, the next step is **risk analysis**, wherein each risk is assessed to understand its potential impact and likelihood of occurrence. There are two primary types of risk analysis: qualitative and quantitative.

Qualitative Risk Analysis involves prioritizing risks based on their impact and probability using a predefined rating system, often involving scales (e.g., low, medium, high). This can be represented visually using a risk matrix.

Probability/Impact	Low	Medium	High
High	Moderate*	High*	Extreme*
Medium	Low	Moderate*	High*
Low	Very Low	Low	Moderate

(*) Indicates high-priority risks that require attention.

Quantitative Risk Analysis involves numerically estimating the effects of identified risks on project objectives. This often requires more complex methods such as Monte Carlo simulations, sensitivity analysis, and decision tree analysis. For instance, Monte Carlo simulation uses probability distributions to model the uncertainty of risk events and their potential impact on project outcomes.

```
import numpy as np

# Define the simulation parameters
num_simulations = 10000
project_costs = []

# Run the simulations
for i in range(num_simulations):
    risk_event = np.random.choice(['event1', 'event2', 'event3'], p=[0.3, 0.5, 0.2])
    if risk_event == 'event1':
        project_costs.append(1000 + np.random.normal(0, 50))
    elif risk_event == 'event2':
        project_costs.append(2000 + np.random.normal(0, 75))
    else:
        project_costs.append(3000 + np.random.normal(0, 100))

# Output the results
cost_mean = np.mean(project_costs)
cost_std = np.std(project_costs)

print(f"Average Project Cost: ${cost_mean:.2f}")
print(f"Standard Deviation: ${cost_std:.2f}")
```

```
Average Project Cost: $1900.75
Standard Deviation: $825.47
```

Following risk analysis is **risk prioritization**, which involves ranking the identified risks based on their assessed impacts and probabilities. This ranking helps in focusing the project management efforts on the most significant risks. Risks that are ranked higher usually require more immediate and robust response strategies.

The next phase is **risk response planning**, where strategies are developed to mitigate identified risks. There are four major types of risk responses:

1. **Avoidance:** Changing the project plan to eliminate the risk or its impact.
2. **Mitigation:** Reducing the probability or impact of the risk through preventative actions.
3. **Transfer:** Shifting the impact of the risk to a third party, such as through insurance or outsourcing.
4. **Acceptance:** Acknowledging the risk and deciding to deal with it if it occurs, often because the cost of mitigation is higher than the expected impact.

Finally, **risk monitoring and control** is an ongoing process throughout the project life cycle. It involves tracking identified risks, monitoring residual risks, identifying new risks, and ensuring the execution of risk response plans. Project managers use tools such as risk registers and risk audits to effectively monitor and control risks.

Risk ID	Description	Probability	Impact	Response Strategy	Status
R1	Requirement changes	High	High	Mitigation	In progress
R2	Resource shortage	Medium	Medium	Transfer	Monitored
R3	Technology issues	Low	High	Acceptance	Monitored

Risk management is not a one-time activity but a continuous effort to ensure the project adapts to any uncertainties that arise. Proper risk management leads to proactive rather than reactive management, thereby enhancing the likelihood of project success.

8.6 Cost Management and Budgeting

Cost management and budgeting play a critical role in ensuring that a software project is completed within its financial constraints. Accurate cost management ensures resource availability, project feasibility, and stakeholder satisfaction. This section delves into fundamental concepts, methodologies, and tools essential for effective cost management and budgeting in software engineering projects.

Cost Estimation

Cost estimation is the process of predicting the costs associated with a software project. Accurate cost estimation involves considering all potential expenses, including development, testing, deployment, maintenance, and overhead costs such as personnel and infrastructure. There are several commonly used cost estimation techniques:

- **Expert Judgment**: Leveraging the experience and insights of experts who have handled similar projects. This method, while subjective, can yield valuable estimations when expert knowledge is robust.
- **Analogous Estimation**: Using historical data from similar projects to estimate costs. The accuracy of this method depends on the similarity between the current and previous projects.
- **Parametric Models**: Utilizing algorithms and statistical models to estimate project costs based on parameters like size, complexity, and team skills. One widely known parametric model is the Constructive Cost Model (COCOMO).
- **Bottom-Up Estimation**: Aggregating costs from detailed estimates of work packages or tasks. This method is more granular and can be more accurate but is also more time-consuming.

Cost Estimation Model Example: COCOMO

The COCOMO model predicts the effort and cost of a software project based on its size measured in thousands of delivered source instructions (KDSI). The basic COCOMO model is given by the formula:

$$E = a \times (KDSI)^b$$

Where:

- E is the effort in person-months.
- a and b are constants derived from historical project data and vary depending on the project type (organic, semi-detached, embedded).

Example:

For an organic project with $a = 2.4$ and $b = 1.05$:

```
KDSI = 100
E = 2.4 * (100 ^ 1.05) = 2.4 * 125.89 ~ 302.14 person-months
```

Budgeting

Budgeting involves the allocation of estimated costs to specific project activities. This ensures that necessary funds are available at the appropriate stages of the project. A comprehensive budget covers all types of costs:

- **Direct Costs**: Costs that can be directly attributed to project activities, such as developer salaries, tools, and software licenses.
- **Indirect Costs**: Costs that are not directly linked to a single project activity but are necessary for the project, like utility bills, administrative expenses, and rent.
- **Contingency Reserves**: Allocations for unforeseen costs or risks. Typically, a percentage of the total budget is reserved based on the project risk assessment.

Budget Allocation Example

Consider a software project with the following planned components:

- Development: USD 200,000
- Testing: USD 50,000
- Deployment: USD 30,000
- Maintenance: USD 20,000
- Contingency: 10% of total planned cost

The total budget will be calculated as:

```
Planned_Total = 200000 + 50000 + 30000 + 20000 = 300000
Contingency = 0.1 * Planned_Total = 0.1 * 300000 = 30000
Total_Budget = Planned_Total + Contingency = 300000 + 30000 = 330000
```

Cost Control

Cost control involves monitoring project expenses to ensure alignment with the budget. Techniques for effective cost control include:

- **Earned Value Management (EVM)**: A project performance measurement technique that integrates project scope, time, and cost data. Key metrics in EVM include:

  - **Planned Value (PV)**: The authorized budget assigned to scheduled work.
  - **Earned Value (EV)**: The value of work actually performed.
  - **Actual Cost (AC)**: The actual cost incurred for the work performed.

  The following formulas derive critical performance indices:

  - Cost Performance Index (CPI) = $\frac{EV}{AC}$
  - Schedule Performance Index (SPI) = $\frac{EV}{PV}$

- **Variance Analysis**: Identifying and analyzing variances between planned and actual performance to identify causes and take corrective actions.

Example of Earned Value Management (EVM)

Consider a software project with:

- PV = USD 100,000
- EV = USD 80,000
- AC = USD 90,000

The performance indices are calculated as:

$$CPI = EV \;/\; AC = 80000 \;/\; 90000 = 0.89$$
$$SPI = EV \;/\; PV = 80000 \;/\; 100000 = 0.8$$

CPI < 1 indicates cost overrun.
SPI < 1 indicates schedule delay.

Effective cost management and budgeting ensure that software projects are completed on time and within the allocated financial resources. Clear estimating, careful budgeting, and stringent cost control practices are imperative for project success.

8.7 Quality Management

Quality management in software engineering involves ensuring that a software product meets the specified requirements and satisfies customer expectations. This encompasses a wide array of activities aimed at preventing defects, evaluating process effectiveness, and improving overall product quality. Central components of quality management include quality assurance (QA), quality control (QC), and the implementation of various standards and best practices.

Quality Assurance (QA) refers to the systematic activities implemented within the quality system to provide confidence that the requirements for quality will be fulfilled. QA governs the whole development process, from specifications through design and implementation to documentation and release.

QA involves the use of a well-defined software development process, with the establishment of clear protocols and review processes at various stages of the software life cycle. This ensures that each phase of development adheres to predefined criteria, hence minimizing the risk of defects as the project progresses.

```
$ pylint my_module.py
************* Module my_module
my_module.py:1:0: C0114: Missing module docstring (missing-module-docstring)
my_module.py:1:0: C0103: Function name "myfunc" doesn't conform to snake_case
    naming style (invalid-name)
...
```

The tool used in the example above, *pylint*, is an example of a static code analysis tool that helps enforce coding standards and identify potential errors in Python code before execution, thus contributing to QA efforts.

Quality Control (QC) complements QA by focusing on the outputs. QC involves various activities designed to evaluate the final product. These evaluations ensure that the product complies with the requirements and standards defined during the QA process. QC typically includes techniques like testing, inspections, and code reviews.

```
import unittest

class TestMathFunctions(unittest.TestCase):
    def test_add(self):
        self.assertEqual(add(1, 2), 3)

if __name__ == '__main__':
    unittest.main()
```

```
$ python -m unittest test_module.py
.
----------------------------------------------------------------------
Ran 1 test in 0.000s

OK
```

In this example, *unittest* in Python is used to create unit tests. Running these tests regularly during development ensures that individual units of code function as expected, thus facilitating QC.

Software Testing constitutes a fundamental part of QC. Various testing methods are employed, depending on the context and requirements of the project, to ensure a comprehensive evaluation of the software product:

- **Unit Testing**: Involves testing individual components or functions of the software.
- **Integration Testing**: Focuses on testing the interactions between integrated units/modules.
- **System Testing**: Entails testing the complete, integrated system to evaluate compliance with specified requirements.
- **Acceptance Testing**: Conducted to determine if the system satisfies the business requirements and is ready for deployment.

Implementing Standards and Best Practices is crucial for maintaining high quality in software projects. Standards like ISO/IEC 9126, which defines software quality characteristics and related metrics, serve as benchmarks.

- **Functionality**: Refers to the software's ability to provide functions that meet stated and implied needs.
- **Reliability**: Measures the software's capability to maintain its performance under stated conditions for a specified period.
- **Usability**: Assesses how effectively and efficiently users can employ the software to achieve their goals.
- **Efficiency**: Pertains to the software's performance relative to the amount of resources used.
- **Maintainability**: Evaluates how straightforward it is to identify and fix defects in the software.
- **Portability**: Determines the effort required to transfer the software from one environment to another.

Continuous Improvement is fundamental in quality management. Adopting methodologies such as Total Quality Management (TQM) and Lean Six Sigma can enhance processes and reduce waste, leading to higher quality software products. These methodologies provide structured approaches to problem-solving and emphasize the importance of iterative process refinement based on feedback and metrics.

Quality management is integral throughout the software development life cycle to deliver a product that meets user expectations, adheres to standards, and functions reliably in its intended environment. Ensuring involvement of all stakeholders, from developers and testers to users, is vital for effective quality management.

8.8 Project Communication Management

Project Communication Management is a crucial part of project management in software engineering, ensuring that information is effectively and efficiently conveyed among project stakeholders. Communication is fundamental for coordinating efforts, keeping team members informed, fostering collaboration, and ensuring the project aligns with stakeholder expectations.

Communication management involves planning, executing, and monitoring communication strategies to ensure the timely and appropriate generation, collection, dissemination, storage, and ultimate disposition of project information. This section will delve into key aspects of project communication management: communication planning, information distribution, performance reporting, and stakeholder management.

Communication Planning is the initial step in project communication management. It involves identifying the information needs of project stakeholders and establishing the means of communication. A structured communication plan outlines the following:

- **Stakeholder Communication Requirements:** Determine the communication needs of all stakeholders, including the type of information required, the format, the level of detail, and the frequency of communication.
- **Information Form and Timing:** Define the format, content, and timing of information distribution, such as status reports, meeting agendas, and project updates.

- **Distribution Methods:** Specify the communication channels and methods, such as emails, meetings, newsletters, or project management software.
- **Responsibility Matrix:** Assign communication responsibilities to team members, ensuring clarity in who is responsible for preparing, delivering, and receiving information.
- **Feedback Mechanisms:** Establish mechanisms for stakeholders to provide feedback, ask questions, and express concerns.

Creating a comprehensive communication plan is pivotal for minimizing misunderstandings, ensuring consistency in information dissemination, and aligning stakeholders with project objectives.

Information Distribution pertains to the process of making necessary information available to project stakeholders in a timely manner. This involves both informal and formal communication, encompassing various formats such as written documents, verbal updates, and multimedia presentations. Effective information distribution ensures stakeholders have access to accurate and up-to-date information, enabling informed decision-making and fostering transparency. Key methods include:

- **Meetings:** Regularly scheduled meetings, such as status updates, team meetings, and stakeholder briefings, serve as platforms for discussing progress, addressing issues, and making collective decisions.
- **Status Reports:** Periodic reports documenting project health, progress, and outstanding issues. These reports may vary in detail and frequency, tailored to stakeholder needs.
- **Workshops and Training Sessions:** Organized events that provide stakeholders with detailed information, facilitate problem-solving, and enhance team skills.
- **Electronic Communication:** Emails, instant messaging, and collaboration tools (e.g., Slack, Microsoft Teams) that allow for rapid information exchange.

The choice of distribution method should align with stakeholder preferences and the nature of the information being communicated.

Performance Reporting involves the collection and dissemination of performance data to inform stakeholders of project status and progress. Key elements include:

- **Progress Reports:** Detailed reports tracking project milestones, completed tasks, and work in progress.
- **Variance Analysis:** Assessment of project performance by comparing planned progress against actual outcomes, identifying deviations, and taking corrective actions.
- **Trend Analysis:** Examination of project data over time to identify patterns, forecast potential issues, and guide decision-making.
- **Earned Value Management (EVM):** A method that integrates scope, schedule, and cost metrics to assess project performance and forecast future performance.

Effective performance reporting enables proactive management of the project, highlighting areas that require attention and facilitating continuous improvement.

Stakeholder Management is the process of managing project stakeholders' expectations and ensuring their continued engagement and satisfaction. It includes:

- **Identifying Stakeholders:** Through a stakeholder analysis, identify all individuals and organizations affected by the project and document their interests, influence, and expectations.
- **Stakeholder Engagement Plan:** Develop a plan to engage stakeholders through regular communication, updates, and involvement in decision-making processes.
- **Expectation Management:** Clearly communicate the project's goals, constraints, and progress to manage stakeholders' expectations realistically.
- **Conflict Resolution:** Implement strategies to address and resolve conflicts among stakeholders, ensuring alignment and cooperation.
- **Feedback Collection:** Continuously gather feedback from stakeholders to understand their concerns and incorporate their input into the project's planning and execution phases.

Effective stakeholder management ensures that stakeholders are informed, involved, and supportive, contributing to the project's overall success.

The following Python script, for example, could be used to automate the generation of project status reports by collecting data from various sources and compiling it into a PDF document for distribution:

```
import pandas as pd
from fpdf import FPDF

def generate_report(data_source):
    # Load data
    data = pd.read_csv(data_source)

    # Process data
    progress = data['Progress'].mean()
    issues = data[data['Status'] == 'Issue']

    # Create PDF
    pdf = FPDF()
    pdf.add_page()

    # Title
    pdf.set_font("Arial", size=12)
    pdf.cell(200, 10, txt="Project Status Report", ln=True, align='C')

    # Progress
    pdf.cell(200, 10, txt=f"Overall Progress: {progress:.2f}%", ln=True)

    # Issues
    pdf.cell(200, 10, txt="Issues:", ln=True)
    for index, issue in issues.iterrows():
        pdf.cell(200, 10, txt=f"- {issue['Description']}", ln=True)

    # Save PDF
    pdf.output("status_report.pdf")

generate_report("project_data.csv")
```

The output of this script would be a PDF document summarizing the current project status, which can then be distributed to stakeholders.

```
Project Status Report

Overall Progress: 75.30%
Issues:
- Incorrect data mapping in module X
- Delay in API integration
```

By implementing robust project communication management practices, project teams can ensure clarity, foster collaboration, and maintain alignment with stakeholders, ultimately contributing to the successful delivery of software projects.

8.9 Agile Project Management

Agile project management is an iterative and incremental approach to managing software development projects that emphasizes flexibility, collaboration, and customer feedback. Unlike traditional waterfall methodologies that follow a linear sequence of phases, Agile prioritizes the delivery of small, workable increments of the final product, allowing for frequent reassessment and adaptation of plans.

The primary values and principles of Agile are outlined in the **Agile Manifesto**:

- **Individuals and interactions** over processes and tools.
- **Working software** over comprehensive documentation.
- **Customer collaboration** over contract negotiation.
- **Responding to change** over following a plan.

Each of these values is supported by twelve principles, emphasizing aspects such as customer satisfaction, welcoming changes, frequent delivery of working software, daily cooperation between business and developers, motivated individuals, face-to-face conversation, working software as the principal measure of progress, sustainable development, technical excellence, simplicity, self-organizing teams, and regular reflections on how to become more effective.

Scrum, a popular Agile framework, consists of specific roles, artifacts, and ceremonies. The key roles in Scrum include the **Product Owner**, the **Scrum Master**, and the **Development Team**. Each role provides distinct responsibilities and contributions to the Agile process.

The Product Owner is responsible for defining and prioritizing the features of the product. They manage the **Product Backlog**, which is an ordered list of all necessary work to be completed. The Product Backlog is dynamic, constantly evolving based on feedback and changing requirements.

The Scrum Master acts as a facilitator, ensuring that the team adheres to Scrum practices. They help remove impediments and protect the team from external distractions. The Scrum Master also organizes the Scrum ceremonies and fosters an environment conducive to high performance.

The Development Team consists of professionals who work autonomously to develop the product increments. The team is cross-functional, possessing all the skills required to turn Product Backlog items into increments of value.

Scrum prescribes several ceremonies to ensure regular and structured communication:

- **Sprint Planning:** At the start of each sprint, the team collaborates with the Product Owner to select the highest-priority items from the Product Backlog and define the Sprint Goal. The team then plans how to accomplish this goal within the sprint.
- **Daily Stand-Up:** A short, time-boxed meeting (usually 15 minutes) held daily to synchronize team activities and address any impediments. Each team member answers three questions: What did I do yesterday? What will I do today? What impediments do I face?
- **Sprint Review:** At the end of the sprint, the team demonstrates the working product increment to stakeholders, gathers feedback, and discusses potential future enhancements.
- **Sprint Retrospective:** This reflective meeting allows the team to assess the sprint's performance, identify what went well, what didn't, and what can be improved in the next sprint.

Scrum also utilizes several artifacts to track and maintain transparency:

- **Product Backlog:** A prioritized list of all features, enhancements, bug fixes, and tasks needed to develop the product.
- **Sprint Backlog:** A subset of the Product Backlog, chosen during Sprint Planning, along with a plan for delivering the sprint increment.
- **Increment:** The sum of all completed Product Backlog items at the end of a sprint. Each increment must be a usable product, meeting the Definition of Done.

Kanban is another Agile methodology that focuses on visualizing work, limiting work in progress, and enhancing flow. The Kanban Board is an essential tool, displaying columns representing various stages of the workflow, such as "To Do," "In Progress," and "Done." Each task is represented by a card that moves through the columns as it progresses.

Key principles of Kanban include:

- **Visualize the workflow:** Make the work visible, including all steps from task creation to completion.
- **Limit work in progress (WIP):** Set limits on the number of tasks in each workflow stage to increase focus and reduce bottlenecks.
- **Manage flow:** Ensure smooth movement of tasks through the workflow, identifying and addressing any delays promptly.
- **Make process policies explicit:** Clearly define rules and guidelines for how work is performed.
- **Implement feedback loops:** Regularly review the process and performance, incorporating feedback for continuous improvement.
- **Improve collaboratively:** Use data-driven analysis and team collaboration to optimize processes systematically.

Some critical success factors for implementing Agile methodologies include:

- **Strong leadership support:** Effective Agile adoption requires commitment and support from leadership to provide the necessary resources and foster a culture of collaboration and continuous improvement.
- **Training and onboarding:** Teams need adequate training in Agile principles and practices to work efficiently and effectively.
- **Tools and infrastructure:** Employ tools that support Agile practices, such as Kanban boards, task management software, and collaboration platforms.
- **Cultural alignment:** Ensure that the organization's culture supports Agile values, such as openness, trust, and a focus on delivering value.
- **Iteration and feedback:** Regularly iterate on processes and incorporate feedback to enhance performance and address any issues or impediments.

The implementation of Agile methodologies can lead to shorter development cycles, better alignment with customer needs, improved product quality, and increased team morale. As software development environments continue to evolve, Agile project management endures as a vital and adaptive approach for managing complex and dynamic projects.

8.10 Tools and Techniques for Project Management

In the domain of software engineering, the efficacy of project management is often determined by the tools and techniques employed. These tools streamline operations, enhance communication, and provide robust frameworks for planning, execution, and monitoring of projects. This section delves into various classes of tools and techniques pivotal to project management, highlighting their functionalities and best use cases, ensuring the readers can apply these tools to their own projects effectively.

1. Project Management Software

Modern project management software offers comprehensive platforms for managing diverse aspects of projects. Tools such as **JIRA**, **Microsoft Project**, and **Trello** help in organizing tasks, tracking progress, and facilitating team collaboration. Below is an example of how tasks might be organized using **JIRA**:

```
# Create Task: Implement login module
# Description: Develop a secure login system with email authentication
# Assignee: John Doe
# Due Date: 2023-10-15

# Create Task: Develop user profile management
# Description: Build functionalities for updating user profiles with proper validations
# Assignee: Jane Smith
# Due Date: 2023-10-20
```

The output might look like this in JIRA's interface:

```
Task: Implement login module | Assignee: John Doe | Due Date: 2023-10-15
Task: Develop user profile management | Assignee: Jane Smith | Due Date: 2023-10-20
```

2. Gantt Charts and Network Diagrams

Gantt charts and network diagrams are essential for visualizing project schedules. While Gantt charts are used to represent the timeline of project tasks, network diagrams (or PERT charts) illustrate task dependencies and project flow. Here is a sample Gantt chart representation created using **Microsoft Project**:

Task Name	Start Date	End Date	Duration
Project Planning	2023-10-01	2023-10-05	5 days
Requirement Analysis	2023-10-06	2023-10-10	4 days
Design Phase	2023-10-11	2023-10-20	10 days
Development Phase	2023-10-21	2023-11-10	20 days
Testing Phase	2023-11-11	2023-11-20	9 days
Deployment	2023-11-21	2023-11-30	10 days

This chart aids in tracking the project's progress against predefined milestones.

3. Collaboration Tools

Effective communication within project teams is facilitated by collaboration tools like **Slack**, **Microsoft Teams**, and **Asana**. These platforms offer real-time messaging, video conferencing, and document sharing capabilities. For example, a Slack conversation discussing a project issue might look like this:

```
John Doe [10:00 AM]: The login module has a security vulnerability.
Need to apply additional encryption.
Jane Smith [10:05 AM]: I agree. Let's review the current implementation
and fix this by today.
Sarah Lee [10:10 AM]: I'll prepare a quick security review
document and share it in 30 minutes.
```

4. Version Control Systems

Version control systems like **Git**, **SVN**, and **Mercurial** are indispensable in managing source code versions and collaborative development. Using Git, for instance, developers can efficiently track changes, branch out for new features, and merge codebases:

```
# Clone a repository
git clone https://github.com/user/repo.git

# Create a new branch
git checkout -b new-feature

# Commit changes
git add .
git commit -m "Implemented login module with security enhancements"

# Push to the repository
git push origin new-feature
```

The repository would then reflect these changes, allowing other developers to sync their local copies.

5. Agile and Scrum Boards

Agile methodologies necessitate the use of Scrum boards to visualize and manage work items through sprints. **Kanban** boards in JIRA or Trello provide a real-time visual representation of the workflow, enabling teams to manage work-in-progress efficiently. An example of a Scrum board in Trello:

```
To Do               In Progress            Done
-----------------------------------------------------
[ ] Login Module    [ ] User Profile        [X] Database Setup
[ ] API Integration [ ] Frontend Design       [X] Deployment Scripts
```

6. Automated Testing and CI/CD Tools

Continuous integration and continuous deployment (CI/CD) tools like **Jenkins**, **CircleCI**, and **Travis CI** automate testing and deployment processes, ensuring code integrity and accelerating delivery pipelines. A Jenkins pipeline script might look like this:

```
pipeline {
    agent any
    stages {
        stage('Build') {
            steps {
                sh 'npm install'
            }
        }
        stage('Test') {
            steps {
                sh 'npm test'
            }
        }
        stage('Deploy') {
            steps {
                sh 'npm run deploy'
            }
        }
    }
}
```

The output of the Jenkins build process:

```
[Pipeline] Start of Pipeline
[Pipeline] npm install
[Pipeline] npm test
All tests passed!
[Pipeline] npm run deploy
Deployment successful!
[Pipeline] End of Pipeline
```

These examples illustrate the vast array of project management tools and techniques available to software engineers. Selecting and integrating the right tools can significantly enhance project outcomes, improve team collaboration, and ensure timely delivery of high-quality software.

8.11 Case Studies in Software Project Management

Case studies provide concrete examples of software project management in practice, elucidating the principles and techniques discussed in the preceding sections. By examining real-world scenarios, we can derive valuable insights into effective practices, common challenges, and innovative solutions in software project management.

Case Study 1: Development of a Mobile Banking Application

Project Overview:

A prominent financial institution undertook the development of a mobile banking application to enhance customer engagement and provide seamless banking services. The project aimed to create an intuitive, secure, and feature-rich application supporting various functionalities such as account management, funds transfer, bill payments, and customer support.

Project Planning and Scheduling:

The project was meticulously planned using the Waterfall model, focusing on clearly defined stages:

- Requirements Analysis
- Design
- Implementation
- Integration and Testing
- Deployment
- Maintenance

The Gantt chart below outlines the project's timeline, demonstrating the sequence and duration of each phase:

Resource Management:

A multidisciplinary team was assembled, comprising:

- Project Manager
- Lead Developer

Stage	Duration	Start - End
Requirements Analysis	4 weeks	Jan 1 - Jan 28
Design	6 weeks	Feb 1 - Mar 14
Implementation	10 weeks	Mar 15 - May 24
Integration and Testing	8 weeks	May 25 - Jul 19
Deployment	2 weeks	Jul 20 - Aug 2
Maintenance	Ongoing	After Deployment

Table 8.1: Project Timeline

- UI/UX Designer
- Quality Assurance Specialist
- Security Expert
- Database Administrator

Effective resource allocation ensured that each team member's skills were optimally utilized. Regular stand-up meetings facilitated clear communication and coordination.

Risk Management:

Several risks were identified and mitigated, including:

- Data Security: A security protocol was implemented, including encryption and multi-factor authentication.
- Project Delays: A buffer period was added to the timeline to accommodate unforeseen delays.
- Technical Challenges: Training sessions on new technologies were conducted for the development team.

Cost Management and Budgeting:

A detailed budget was prepared, considering:

- Personnel costs (salaries, benefits)
- Software and hardware expenses
- Licensing costs
- Contingency funds

Cost tracking tools were used to ensure adherence to the budget, and surplus funds were redirected to enhance application features.

Quality Management:

Quality was a critical focus, achieved through:

- Adherence to coding standards
- Rigorous testing (unit, integration, and user acceptance tests)
- Regular code reviews

Feedback loops were established with end-users to continually improve application quality and functionality.

Project Communication Management:

Effective communication was maintained through:

- Weekly progress meetings
- Detailed project reports
- Collaborative platforms (e.g., Slack, Jira)

The communication plan ensured transparency and allowed stakeholders to provide timely feedback.

Agile Project Management:

To adapt to changing requirements, Agile techniques were incorporated post-deployment for continuous improvement. Bi-weekly sprints and Scrum meetings facilitated iterative development and rapid response to user feedback.

Outcome:

The mobile banking application was successfully launched, receiving positive feedback for its user-friendly interface and robust security features. The project's success was attributed to comprehensive planning, effective resource management, proactive risk mitigation, meticulous cost management, and strong communication.

Case Study 2: E-commerce Platform Upgrade

Project Overview:

A leading e-commerce company embarked on upgrading its existing platform to enhance scalability, performance, and user experience.

The upgrade aimed to integrate cutting-edge technologies, improve site speed, and add new functionalities to support expanding business operations.

Project Planning and Scheduling:

The project followed an Agile methodology:

- Sprint Planning
- Backlog Refinement
- Sprint Execution
- Review and Retrospective

The project was divided into multiple sprints, each focusing on incremental improvements. The timeline was flexible to adapt to ongoing changes and refinements.

Resource Management:

The project team included:

- Scrum Master
- Product Owner
- Development Team (Front-end and Back-end Engineers)
- QA Team
- DevOps Engineer

Collaborative tools like Confluence and Jira facilitated effective resource coordination and task tracking.

Risk Management:

Key risks and their mitigation strategies were:

- Performance Degradation: Regular performance testing and monitoring tools were employed.
- User Data Integrity: A robust backup and data recovery plan was established.
- Feature Creep: A well-defined project scope and prioritization of backlog items helped manage expectations.

Cost Management and Budgeting:

The budget was dynamically managed to align with the Agile framework, allowing for flexible allocation as new requirements emerged. A continuous review of costs ensured financial control.

Quality Management:

Quality was ensured through:

- Automated testing frameworks
- Continuous Integration/Continuous Deployment (CI/CD) pipelines
- Peer code reviews

Project Communication Management:

Transparent communication was maintained using:

- Daily stand-ups
- Sprint reviews and demos
- Documentation and progress updates

Outcome:

The platform upgrade was completed on schedule, significantly improving site speed and user satisfaction. The adoption of Agile practices facilitated flexibility and responsiveness to user needs, contributing to the project's overall success.

These case studies underscore the significance of tailored project management strategies in achieving successful project outcomes in software engineering. Properly implemented, these strategies can mitigate risks, optimize resource use, manage costs efficiently, and ensure high-quality deliverables, all of which are crucial for the success of any software project.

Chapter 9

Software Engineering Tools and Environments

Software engineering tools and environments are essential for streamlining the software development process and enhancing productivity. This chapter explores various categories of tools, including integrated development environments (IDEs), version control systems, build and continuous integration tools, testing tools, and project management tools. It also discusses requirements management, design and modeling tools, configuration management, and collaboration and communication tools. The chapter emphasizes the importance of selecting the right tools for specific projects and examines future trends in software engineering tools.

9.1 Introduction to Software Engineering Tools and Environments

Software engineering tools and environments are fundamental to managing the complexity of modern software development. They facilitate tasks ranging from coding to project management, enabling developers to work more efficiently and collaboratively. This section provides an overview of the types and roles of these tools, emphasizing their importance in the software engineering lifecycle.

Software engineering tools can be broadly categorized based on their functionality within the software development process. These categories include:

- Integrated Development Environments (IDEs)
- Version Control Systems
- Build and Continuous Integration Tools
- Testing Tools
- Project Management Tools
- Requirements Management Tools
- Design and Modeling Tools
- Configuration Management Tools
- Collaboration and Communication Tools

Each category serves a distinct purpose, contributing to the overall productivity and quality of software developed.

Integrated Development Environments (IDEs) are essential for writing, testing, and debugging code. IDEs provide a comprehensive suite of tools in one application, including a source code editor, build automation tools, and a debugger. Popular examples include Eclipse, IntelliJ IDEA, and Visual Studio Code. By consolidating these functionalities, IDEs streamline the development process, reducing the need for context switching and thus increasing efficiency.

Version Control Systems (VCSs) are crucial for managing changes to source code over time. They enable multiple developers to work on a project simultaneously without overwriting each other's work. Git and Subversion are widely used VCSs. Version control is essential for maintaining a history of changes, enabling rollback to previous versions, and facilitating collaboration through branching and merging.

Build and Continuous Integration Tools automate the process of compiling source code into executable programs. These tools also integrate code changes from various developers, ensuring that the codebase remains consistent and functional. Examples include Jenkins, Travis CI, and CircleCI. Continuous integration tools help in identifying integration issues early, thus reducing the time and effort needed to resolve them.

Testing Tools are designed to validate the correctness, performance, and security of software. They include unit testing frameworks like JUnit, integration testing tools, and performance testing tools such as JMeter. Automated testing tools enable developers to run extensive test suites with minimal manual intervention, ensuring that code meets quality standards.

Project Management Tools assist in planning, tracking, and managing software projects. These tools, such as Jira and Trello, provide features for issue tracking, project planning, and team collaboration. Effective project management tools help in monitoring project progress, identifying bottlenecks, and ensuring that projects are completed on time and within budget.

Requirements Management Tools are used to capture, track, and manage software requirements throughout the development lifecycle. Tools like IBM DOORS and Jama Connect ensure that all stakeholders have a clear understanding of what the software is intended to achieve. Effective requirements management minimizes the risk of scope creep and ensures that the final product meets the user's needs.

Design and Modeling Tools enable the creation of architectural blueprints and system designs. Tools such as Rational Rose and Enterprise Architect allow for the modeling of software systems using standardized notations like UML. These tools provide a visual representation of the system, facilitating understanding and communication among stakeholders.

Configuration Management Tools help manage and control changes in software configuration items. Tools like Ansible, Puppet, and Chef automate configuration management tasks, ensuring that software environments are consistent and reproducible. This is particularly important for maintaining consistency across development, testing, and production environments.

Collaboration and Communication Tools enhance communication and collaboration among team members. Tools such as Slack, Microsoft Teams, and Confluence provide platforms for real-time communication, file sharing, and documentation. Effective collaboration tools are essential for maintaining coordination, especially in distributed or remote teams.

The selection and integration of these tools into a cohesive development environment are critical for maximizing the benefits they offer. A well-configured development environment not only enhances productivity but also improves the quality of the software product. As the field of software engineering evolves, new tools and technologies continue to emerge, offering enhanced capabilities and efficiencies.

Future sections will delve deeper into each category of tools, providing detailed insights and practical guidance on their usage. These tools collectively form the backbone of modern software engineering practices, enabling teams to meet the demands of increasingly complex and rapidly evolving software projects.

9.2 Integrated Development Environments (IDEs)

Integrated Development Environments (IDEs) play a crucial role in modern software development by providing comprehensive facilities to programmers for software production. An IDE typically consists of a source code editor, build automation tools, and a debugger. Many IDEs also offer intelligent code completion, version control integration, and various other functionalities that streamline the development workflow and enhance productivity. This section delves into the components, functionalities, and benefits of IDEs, alongside examining some popular IDEs used in the industry.

An IDE serves as an all-in-one tool where developers can write, compile, execute, and debug their code in a unified environment. Developers benefit from the integration of multiple tools and services, which allows for a cohesive and efficient development process. Key components of an IDE include:

- **Source Code Editor**: The editor forms the core of an IDE, providing capabilities for writing and editing code. Advanced features include syntax highlighting, code folding, and snippets. Syntax highlighting improves code readability by displaying text in different colors and fonts based on the category of terms.
- **Build Automation Tools**: These tools automate the process of compiling source code into executable applications. They manage complex build processes, including dependency management and incremental builds, improving efficiency and reducing human error.
- **Debugger**: A debugger helps identify and fix errors in the source

code by allowing developers to execute the code step-by-step, inspect variables, and evaluate expressions at runtime.

- **Intelligent Code Completion**: Also known as "autocomplete," this feature suggests possible code completions based on the current code context. It speeds up coding by reducing the amount of typing required and helps avoid syntax errors.
- **Version Control Integration**: IDEs support integration with version control systems such as Git and Subversion, enabling developers to commit, branch, and merge code directly within the environment.
- **Plugins and Extensions**: IDEs offer support for various plugins and extensions that add extra functionality, support multiple programming languages, and customize the development experience to specific project needs.

Key Functionalities

The functionalities of IDEs extend beyond the basic components described above. A non-exhaustive list includes:

- **Code Navigation**: Features such as "Go to Definition," "Find All References," and "Code Outline" enable developers to quickly navigate large codebases.
- **Refactoring Tools**: These tools assist in restructuring existing code without changing its external behavior. This might include renaming variables, extracting methods, and organizing imports.
- **Testing Framework Integration**: IDEs often incorporate testing frameworks for unit tests, integration tests, and other testing methodologies, providing a seamless testing and debugging experience.
- **Integrated Terminal**: A terminal emulator integrated into the IDE allows developers to access the command line and execute scripts and commands without leaving the development environment.
- **Profiling and Performance Analysis**: Tools to measure the performance of applications by analyzing memory usage, CPU utilization, and other metrics.

- **User Interface Builders (for GUI applications)**: Visual editors that help design graphical user interfaces, making it easier to build and modify the UI elements interactively.

Popular IDEs

Several IDEs are widely used in the industry, each with unique features suitable for different programming languages and development needs. Some of the most popular ones include:

- **Eclipse**: An open-source IDE primarily for Java development, Eclipse supports numerous other languages and platforms via plugins.
- **Visual Studio**: A robust IDE from Microsoft, well-suited for .NET development as well as languages like C++, Python, and TypeScript. It provides advanced debugging and profiling tools.
- **IntelliJ IDEA**: Known for its intelligent code completion and powerful refactoring tools, IntelliJ IDEA, by JetBrains, is popular for Java development and other JVM languages.
- **PyCharm**: Also from JetBrains, PyCharm is tailored for Python development and offers extensive support for web development with Django.
- **Xcode**: Apple's IDE for macOS and iOS development, supporting languages such as Swift and Objective-C. It includes a suite of tools for performance measurement and optimization.
- **NetBeans**: Another popular open-source IDE, NetBeans supports Java, PHP, C/C++, and HTML5 development.

Benefits of Using an IDE

Utilizing an IDE provides several benefits that can significantly improve software development efficiency and code quality:

- **Increased Productivity**: Integrated tools and automation features (e.g., compilation, testing, version control) reduce context switching and streamline the development workflow.
- **Error Reduction**: Syntax highlighting, intelligent code completion, and real-time error detection help catch and correct errors early in the development process.

- **Consistent Environment**: An IDE provides a consistent development environment across different projects and teams, simplifying setup and configuration.
- **Enhanced Collaboration**: Features like version control integration, shared templates, and project settings foster better collaboration among team members.
- **Learning and Improvement**: By providing tutorials, code examples, and documentation within the IDE, developers can learn new languages and frameworks more efficiently.

Code Example

To illustrate an example of code written in an IDE, consider the following Java program using IntelliJ IDEA:

```
// Simple Java program to display "Hello World"
public class HelloWorld {
    public static void main(String[] args) {
        System.out.println("Hello, World!");
    }
}
```

Output:
Hello, World!

IDE Configuration and Customization

Most modern IDEs offer extensive configuration options to tailor the development environment to the individual needs of developers. Customizable settings typically include:

- **Code Style**: Enforcing specific coding standards by configuring code formatting and style guidelines.
- **Keyboard Shortcuts**: Customizable key bindings improve productivity by offering quick access to frequently used commands.
- **Themes and Appearance**: Personalizing the IDE's UI with themes, fonts, and color schemes to reduce eye strain and enhance focus during long coding sessions.
- **Plugins and Extensions**: Adding or removing functionalities via a plugin marketplace to support additional languages, tools, and frameworks.
- **Build Configurations**: Defining multiple build and run configurations to manage different environments (e.g., development, testing, production).

An integrally important aspect of modern software engineering, IDEs consolidate development tasks within a single interface, significantly boosting efficiency, accuracy, and collaboration among developers. Understanding and harnessing the power of an IDE is fundamental for any software engineer aiming to improve their productivity and the quality of their codebase.

9.3 Version Control Systems

Version control systems (VCS) are software tools that help manage changes to source code over time. By tracking modifications, these systems provide a historical record of the project, which includes who made specific changes and allows developers to revert to previous versions when necessary. This section delves into the importance of version control, describes different types of VCS, provides usage examples, and highlights best practices in version control.

A VCS is crucial for both individual developers and teams. For individuals, it provides a robust mechanism to backup their work, experiment with new ideas without the risk of losing stable progress, and keep a log of their development activity. For teams, a VCS coordinates work, prevents conflicts when multiple people modify the same code, and tracks who made changes for accountability.

Centralized Version Control Systems (CVCS)

CVCS, such as Subversion (SVN) and Concurrent Versions System (CVS), use a central server to store all versions of a project. Developers commit their changes to this central repository and update their working copies:

```
# Committing changes to a central repository in SVN
svn commit -m "Description of the changes"
```

- Simplified management due to a single repository.
- Typically easier to set up and get started with for small teams.

- Single point of failure – if the central server goes down, no one can commit or update their work.
- Limited offline capabilities – operations like committing changes require access to the central server.

Distributed Version Control Systems (DVCS)

DVCS, such as Git and Mercurial, store the entire history of the project in each developer's local repository. This allows for greater flexibility and enhances performance. Key operations can be performed locally, and changes can be shared among repositories:

```
# Committing changes to a local repository in Git
git commit -m "Description of the changes"
```

```
# Pushing changes to a remote repository in Git
git push origin main
```

- Every copy of the project repository is a full backup.
- Users can commit, branch, and explore history offline.
- Better support for parallel development due to powerful branching and merging capabilities.

- Larger initial clone size as the entire history is fetched.
- Some learning curve due to more complex operations and flexible branching/merging.

Common Workflows in Version Control

Feature Branch Workflow: This workflow involves creating a new branch for each feature or bug fix. Changes are made in this branch and merged back into the main branch once they are complete. This allows for isolated development and easier collaboration:

```
# Creating a new feature branch in Git
git checkout -b feature-branch
```

```
# Merging the feature branch back to the main branch in Git
git checkout main
git merge feature-branch
```

Forking Workflow: Common in open source projects, this workflow involves developers forking a public repository, making changes in their fork, and then submitting pull requests to the original repository. Repository maintainers review the requests and merge them if they meet the project standards:

```
# Cloning a forked repository in Git
git clone https://github.com/username/repository.git
```

Gitflow Workflow: A well-defined branching strategy using different branches for feature development, releases, and hotfixes. This workflow defines a detailed process for code development and release management, involving branches like 'develop', 'release', and 'hotfix'.

```
# Creating a release branch in Gitflow
git checkout -b release-v1.0 develop
```

Best Practices for Version Control

- **Commit Often:** Frequent commits with descriptive messages make it easier to track changes and understand the project history.
- **Write Meaningful Commit Messages:** Each commit message should concisely describe what changes have been made and why.
- **Use Branches:** Leverage branches to work on features or bug fixes independently of the main codebase.
- **Merge Regularly:** Merging regularly helps avoid large conflicts and keeps the codebase coherent.
- **Review Code:** Use pull requests to review and discuss code changes before they are merged into the main branch.

```
$ git log --oneline
e5837d4 (HEAD -> main) Fix issue #42 by correcting file path
a7c9d12 Add unit test for user authentication
d2e43f5 Merge branch 'feature-branch'
```

In practice, version control systems are indispensable in modern software development. They enhance collaboration, maintain project history, and provide mechanisms to efficiently manage code changes. By adopting best practices, developers ensure smoother workflows and higher-quality code management.

9.4 Build and Continuous Integration Tools

Build and continuous integration (CI) tools are critical components in modern software development workflows. They facilitate the automation of repetitive tasks, ensure consistency across different environments, and contribute to maintaining the integrity of the codebase. This section will delve into the fundamental concepts of build automation and continuous integration, illustrate their significance, and provide detailed insights into some of the widely used tools in these domains.

Build automation involves the scripting of tasks related to software compiling, packaging, and testing. Automated builds aid developers by reducing manual interventions, minimizing errors, and speeding up the software release cycle. A typical build pipeline includes steps such as fetching dependencies, compiling source code, packaging binaries, running unit tests, and generating documentation.

One of the primary tools used for build automation is *Apache Maven*. Maven uses a pom.xml file to define project structure, dependencies, build logic, and plugins. Here's an example of a simple Maven pom.xml configuration:

```
<project xmlns="http://maven.apache.org/POM/4.0.0"
  xmlns:xsi="http://www.w3.org/2001/XMLSchema-instance"
  xsi:schemaLocation="http://maven.apache.org/POM/4.0.0
  http://maven.apache.org/maven-v4_0_0.xsd">
  <modelVersion>4.0.0</modelVersion>
  <groupId>com.example</groupId>
  <artifactId>my-app</artifactId>
  <packaging>jar</packaging>
  <version>1.0-SNAPSHOT</version>
  <name>My First Maven Project</name>
  <url>http://maven.apache.org</url>

  <dependencies>
    <dependency>
      <groupId>junit</groupId>
      <artifactId>junit</artifactId>
      <version>4.12</version>
      <scope>test</scope>
    </dependency>
  </dependencies>
</project>
```

Continuous integration refers to the practice of integrating code changes into a shared repository several times a day, each integration being verified by an automated build and automated tests. The primary goal is to detect integration issues early, reduce integration problems, and allow teams to develop cohesive software more rapidly.

Jenkins is a popular open-source automation server used in continuous integration. It supports various plugins to integrate with numerous other tools in the CI/CD pipeline. A straightforward Jenkins pipeline can be scripted using its Groovy-based domain-specific language (DSL). Here's an example of a Jenkins Pipeline script:

```
pipeline {
  agent any
```

```
    stages {
        stage('Build') {
            steps {
                echo 'Building...'
                sh 'mvn -B -DskipTests clean package'
            }
        }
        stage('Test') {
            steps {
                echo 'Testing...'
                sh 'mvn test'
            }
        }
        stage('Deploy') {
            steps {
                echo 'Deploying...'
            }
        }
    }
}
```

This script defines a pipeline with three stages: Build, Test, and Deploy. Each stage contains steps that execute shell commands or other predefined actions. Jenkins, along with its plugins, provides a robust platform to automate an entire software delivery process.

Another important aspect of CI is continuous delivery/deployment (CD), which automates the release of code changes. Continuous delivery ensures that code is always in a deployable state, while continuous deployment extends this by automatically deploying every change that passes the CI pipeline to production.

Travis CI is another widely-used CI/CD service that integrates seamlessly with GitHub. It uses a .travis.yml file to configure the CI/CD pipeline:

```
language: java
jdk:
  - openjdk11

script:
  - mvn clean install
  - mvn test
```

The .travis.yml file specifies that the project uses the Java programming language and OpenJDK 11. Under the script section, it defines the commands to clean, build, and test the project.

While the tools and configurations vary, the principles behind CI/CD remain consistent: automating the build, test, and deployment processes to ensure quality and reduce time-to-market. Integration of these tools can greatly enhance a team's efficiency and product reliability, crucial for competitive software redevelopment.

9.5 Testing Tools

Testing is a critical activity in the software development lifecycle that ensures the quality and reliability of the software product. Testing tools provide a structured approach to planning, executing, and assessing the results of tests. These tools facilitate various types of testing, including unit testing, integration testing, system testing, and acceptance testing.

One prominent category of testing tools is **Unit Testing Tools**. These tools are designed to test the smallest units of code, such as functions, methods, or classes, to ensure they work as expected. Frameworks like JUnit for Java and pytest for Python are widely used for unit testing. They provide mechanisms to define test cases, assert expected results, and report outcomes. An example of a unit test in Python using pytest is shown below:

```
# test_calculator.py
def test_add():
    from calculator import add
    assert add(1, 2) == 3

def test_subtract():
    from calculator import subtract
    assert subtract(2, 1) == 1
```

When executed, pytest generates a report indicating the pass or fail status of each test case. Example output:

```
=========================== test session starts ============================
collecting ... collected 2 items

test_calculator.py ..                                    [100%]

============================ 2 passed in 0.01s =============================
```

Integration Testing Tools extend testing to interaction between multiple units or components. They ensure that combined parts work together as intended. An example of an integration testing tool is Selenium, which is often used to automate web browser testing. Selenium allows developers to write scripts in various programming languages, such as Java, Python, and C#, to simulate user interactions with web applications. Below is an example of a simple Selenium test in Python:

```
from selenium import webdriver

def test_google_search():
    driver = webdriver.Chrome()
    driver.get("http://www.google.com")
    search_box = driver.find_element_by_name("q")
    search_box.send_keys("pytest")
    search_box.submit()
    assert "No results found." not in driver.page_source
```

```
driver.quit()
```

The test launches a Chrome browser, navigates to Google, performs a search, and asserts that no error message is displayed.

System Testing Tools focus on validating the behavior of the entire system against requirements. Tools like TestComplete and HP Quality Center provide comprehensive environments for automating and managing system tests. These tools often include features for test case management, test data generation, and detailed reporting.

Acceptance Testing Tools are used to determine whether a system meets the business requirements and is ready for deployment. Tools such as Cucumber facilitate behavior-driven development, allowing stakeholders to define requirements in plain language. These specifications are then automated into test scripts. An example of a Cucumber feature file is shown below:

```
Feature: Search functionality on the website

  Scenario: User searches for an item
    Given the user is on the homepage
    When the user enters "laptop" in the search bar
    And clicks the search button
    Then search results for "laptop" should be displayed
```

Alongside these specific types of testing tools, **Test Automation Tools** deserve mention. Automation reduces the human effort in repetitive testing tasks, increases the speed of test execution, and improves coverage. Tools like Jenkins, which serve as a continuous integration system, can be configured to trigger automated tests after each build. This integration ensures that any changes in the codebase are tested promptly. An example Jenkins pipeline script for running unit tests:

```
pipeline {
    agent any

    stages {
        stage('Build') {
            steps {
                echo 'Building...'
                // Compile code, etc.
            }
        }
        stage('Test') {
            steps {
                echo 'Testing...'
                sh 'pytest'
            }
        }
    }
```

```
    post {
        always {
            junit 'test-results/*.xml'
        }
    }
}
```

Apart from functional testing tools, non-functional testing tools such as **Performance Testing Tools** and **Security Testing Tools** play an essential role in ensuring the quality of software. Performance testing tools like Apache JMeter simulate various user loads to test the responsiveness, speed, and stability of systems. An example JMeter test plan might specify a number of users and a series of HTTP requests to simulate activities.

Security testing tools like OWASP ZAP help identify vulnerabilities in a web application by performing automated security scans.

Code Coverage Tools are another important category. Tools such as JaCoCo for Java and Coverage.py for Python measure the extent to which the source code is executed during testing. These tools highlight untested parts of the code, thereby guiding developers to write additional tests to improve coverage. An example of using Coverage.py:

```
$ coverage run -m pytest
$ coverage report -m
$ coverage html
```

This generates a report indicating the percentage of code executed and identifies untested lines. These reports can also be visualized in HTML format for easier analysis.

The use of testing tools is integral to a robust software engineering process, providing capabilities to ensure thorough validation of code, seamless integration of components, and compliance with requirements. Effective use of these tools ultimately leads to higher quality products and boosts overall development efficiency.

9.6 Project Management Tools

Project management tools provide a structured framework to plan, execute, and manage software development projects. These tools help coordinate tasks, track progress, manage resources, and ensure that project deliverables are completed on time and within budget. Modern project management tools offer a wide range of functionalities, from simple task management to complex resource allocation and performance tracking.

Task Management

At the core of any project management tool is task management. Task management involves the creation, assignment, and tracking of tasks that need to be completed to achieve project goals. Tasks can often be organized into hierarchies, allowing for the breakdown of large tasks into smaller, more manageable sub-tasks.

```
Task task1 = new Task("Design Database Schema");
Task subtask1 = new Task("Define Tables");
task1.addSubtask(subtask1);
```

Effective task management is crucial in maintaining clear workflows, ensuring that team members understand their responsibilities, and identifying bottlenecks early.

Gantt Charts and Timelines

Gantt charts provide a visual representation of the project timeline, displaying tasks along a linear time scale. They are useful for understanding the sequence of activities and their dependencies. This helps project managers and teams to identify the critical path, ensuring that tasks that directly affect the project's completion date are given priority.

Task	**Start Date**	**Duration**
Requirements	01/01/2023	10 days
Design	11/01/2023	15 days
Implementation	26/01/2023	30 days
Testing	25/02/2023	20 days

Table 9.1: Project Gantt Chart

Tools like Microsoft Project, Trello, and Asana offer built-in Gantt chart functionality.

Resource Management

Resource management involves the allocation and utilization of project resources, such as team members, hardware, software, and financial resources. Effective resource management ensures that resources are available when and where they are needed, and it helps to avoid over-allocation, which can lead to team burnout and project delays.

```
Resource dev1 = new Resource("Developer 1", ResourceType.HUMAN);
Resource dev2 = new Resource("Developer 2", ResourceType.HUMAN);
task1.assignResource(dev1);
```

```
task1.assignResource(dev2);
```

Time Tracking and Reporting

Time tracking capabilities allow teams to log the hours spent on various tasks. This data is valuable for project managers to monitor team performance, manage workloads, and ensure accurate billing for client projects. Reporting tools generate insights from this data, providing information on project progress, resource utilization, and potential risks.

```
Task: Design Database Schema
Time Spent: 45 hours
Developers: Developer 1 (25 hours), Developer 2 (20 hours)
```

Risk Management

Risk management tools help identify, assess, and mitigate risks that could impact the project. These tools support the creation of risk logs, risk assessment matrices, and the formulation of contingency plans. By systematically managing risks, projects can avoid or minimize unexpected issues that could derail progress.

Collaboration and Communication

Modern project management tools incorporate features for enhanced collaboration and communication, recognizing the importance of seamless interaction among team members. Features such as chat, discussion forums, document sharing, and integration with communication platforms like Slack and Microsoft Teams enable real-time collaboration.

```
Message teamMessage = new Message("Please review the latest design document.");
teamMessage.sendTo(teamMembers);
```

Agile and Scrum Support

Supporting Agile methodologies is common in contemporary project management tools. These tools typically offer boards (like Kanban boards), sprint planning, and backlog management features that align with Scrum practices. JIRA, for example, is widely used for managing Agile projects, providing facilities to track story points, sprints, and epics.

Examples of Project Management Tools

Some prominent project management tools include:

- **JIRA**: Offers robust support for Agile project management, including scrum and kanban boards.

- **Asana**: Provides a flexible platform for task, project, and workflow management with an intuitive user interface.
- **Microsoft Project**: Known for its powerful Gantt chart features and extensive project planning capabilities.
- **Trello**: Uses boards, lists, and cards to organize tasks in a visually compelling way, often employed for smaller projects.
- **Basecamp**: Emphasizes simplicity and team communication, offering tools for task management, document sharing, and scheduling.

Selecting the appropriate project management tool should consider factors such as team size, project complexity, preferred methodologies, and specific feature requirements. Integration with other tools and platforms is also a key consideration, ensuring a seamless workflow across different tools used in the software development lifecycle.

9.7 Requirements Management Tools

Requirements management is a crucial aspect of the software development lifecycle, aiming to ensure that the end product meets the needs and expectations of stakeholders. Requirements Management Tools (RMTs) facilitate this process by offering functionalities that centralize, organize, and trace requirements throughout the project.

Centralization of Requirements: RMTs provide a repository where all requirements can be stored centrally. This centralization ensures that all project members have access to the latest requirements and reduces the risk of inconsistencies. Centralized requirements management also allows for easier collaboration, as team members can work on the same set of requirements simultaneously.

Requirement Organization: Requirements can be categorized and organized in various ways within RMTs. Common methods of organization include:

- **Hierarchical Structuring:** Requirements are often structured hierarchically, enabling project managers to break down high-level requirements into more granular, actionable items.

- **Categorization by Type:** Requirements can be categorized by type, such as functional, non-functional, technical, and business requirements.
- **Prioritization:** Requirements can be prioritized based on their importance and impact on the project, which aids in resource allocation and planning.

Traceability and Impact Analysis: One significant feature of RMTs is the ability to trace requirements throughout the project lifecycle. Traceability features allow developers and project managers to:

- **Link Requirements to Design and Implementation:** Traceability links can connect requirements to design artifacts, code, test cases, and other project elements. This helps ensure that each requirement is accounted for in subsequent stages of the development process.
- **Perform Impact Analysis:** When a requirement changes, impact analysis features help assess the potential impact of the change on other requirements, design components, and tests. This assessment is crucial for managing change effectively and minimizing risks.

Version Control and History: Version control features in RMTs allow for tracking changes to requirements over time. Each change to a requirement is logged, along with the user who made the change and the reason for the change. This version history provides an audit trail that can be invaluable for understanding the evolution of requirements and for compliance purposes.

Collaboration and Communication: RMTs often include collaboration tools that enable team members to discuss requirements, provide feedback, and collaborate in real-time. Features such as:

- **Commenting and Annotations:** Team members can add comments and annotations to requirements, facilitating discussions and clarifications.
- **Notifications and Alerts:** Users can receive notifications and alerts when requirements are updated or when discussions take place, ensuring that everyone stays informed.

Requirement Validation: Validation features in RMTs help ensure that requirements are complete, unambiguous, and verifiable. Tools may include:

- **Checklists and Templates:** Predefined checklists and templates ensure that requirements adhere to standards and best practices.
- **Review Workflows:** Reviewing workflows enforce a systematic approach to requirement validation, involving stakeholders and domain experts in the review process.

Consider the example of an RMT in action using code snippets and their corresponding outputs. Below is a fictitious command script for setting up a new requirement in a simplified RMT interface:

```
# Command to add a new requirement
add_requirement --id REQ-001 --title "User Authentication" --type "Functional" --
    priority "High"

# Command to link requirement to design item
link_requirement --id REQ-001 --design-item "LoginModule"

# Command to add a comment to the requirement
add_comment --id REQ-001 --comment "Need to consider two-factor authentication"

# Command to perform impact analysis on requirement change
impact_analysis --requirement REQ-001
```

These commands result in the following entries in the requirement management tool:

Requirement ID	REQ-001
Title	User Authentication
Type	Functional
Priority	High
Linked Design Item	LoginModule
Comments	"Need to consider two-factor authentication"
Impact Analysis Result	Changes may affect: LoginModule, SecurityTests, UserDoc

Integration with Other Tools: Modern RMTs often integrate seamlessly with other software engineering tools. This integration allows for smoother workflows and enhanced traceability across different stages of the project. Common integrations include:

- **Integrated Development Environments (IDEs):** Automatically synchronize requirements with code documentation in IDEs.

- **Version Control Systems (VCS):** Link requirements to specific code commits and version histories.
- **Testing Tools:** Align requirements with test cases and test results.
- **Project Management Tools:** Connect requirements to project plans, timelines, and resource management.

By leveraging these tools and features, software development teams can maintain clear, organized, and traceable requirements, ultimately leading to higher quality software that meets stakeholder expectations.

9.8 Design and Modeling Tools

Design and modeling tools play a pivotal role in the software engineering lifecycle, specifically during the system design and architectural phases. These tools facilitate the visualization, specification, construction, and documentation of the artifacts required for the software development process. Utilizing design and modeling tools can significantly enhance the precision of the software design, reduce development time, and improve quality and maintainability. Central to these tools is their capability to handle complex modeling languages, such as the Unified Modeling Language (UML), which represents the backbone of many modern software design methodologies.

Unified Modeling Language (UML)

The Unified Modeling Language (UML) is a standardized general-purpose modeling language in the field of software engineering. UML provides a set of graphic notation techniques to create visual models of object-oriented software-intensive systems. UML encompasses a wide range of diagrams, each serving different purposes:

- *Class Diagrams*: Illustrate the static structure of a system by depicting classes, their attributes, operations, and relationships.
- *Use Case Diagrams*: Represent the functional requirements of a system by showcasing the interactions between users (or actors) and system components.
- *Sequence Diagrams*: Capture the sequence of messages exchanged between objects to fulfill a particular use case.

- *Activity Diagrams*: Model the dynamic aspects of the system by representing the workflow of activities and actions.
- *State Machine Diagrams*: Define state transitions of system components based on events.

The utility of UML in software design lies in its ability to create a unified representation of the system, enabling different stakeholders to communicate effectively and unambiguously.

Popular Design and Modeling Tools

Enterprise Architect (Sparx Systems)

Enterprise Architect is a comprehensive modeling tool designed primarily for UML-based design. It supports model-driven architecture (MDA), allowing developers to generate code directly from models. Its features include:

- *Rich Diagramming*: Supports all UML diagrams and provides additional diagram types such as BPMN, ArchiMate, and SysML.
- *Code Generation*: Enables forward and reverse engineering for various programming languages.
- *Team Collaboration*: Facilitates concurrent model editing and version control integration.

IBM Rational Rose

IBM Rational Rose is one of the legacy tools for visual modeling using UML. It integrates with IBM's broader Rational suite for lifecycle management. Key attributes include:

- *Visual Modeling*: Supports comprehensive UML modeling.
- *Round-Trip Engineering*: Facilitates synchronization between design models and code.
- *Integration*: Seamlessly integrates with other IBM Rational tools for requirements management and testing.

Visual Paradigm

Visual Paradigm excels in providing tools for both agile and traditional software development processes. Its key features include:

- *Diagram Types*: Includes support for UML, ERD, DFD, and BPMN diagrams.
- *Agile Tools*: Provides user story mapping, sprint planning, and Kanban board integration.
- *Plugins and Integrations*: Extensive integrations with IDEs, version control, and CI/CD tools.

Model-Driven Development (MDD)

Model-Driven Development (MDD) emphasizes the use of models as primary artifacts in the development process. The main goal is to increase the level of abstraction in programming, allowing developers to focus more on business logic than on technical implementation details. MDD tools typically support:

- *Model Transformation*: Convert high-level models into executable code or lower-level representations.
- *Code Generation*: Automatically generate source code from abstract models.
- *Validation and Verification*: Ensure models comply with specified standards and constraints.

MetaEdit+ (MetaCase)

MetaEdit+ is a domain-specific modeling environment that allows users to define their own modeling languages and constructs. This tool provides:

- *Customization*: Create custom notations and rules tailored to specific domains.
- *Multilevel Modeling*: Support for hierarchical and multi-perspective modeling.
- *Integration*: Works with various IDEs and version control systems for seamless workflow integration.

Evaluating and Selecting Design Tools

When selecting a design and modeling tool, several factors should be considered to ensure that the chosen tool aligns with project requirements and team workflows. These factors include:

- *Scalability and Performance*: Ability to handle complex models without significant performance degradation.
- *Usability*: Intuitive interface and ease of use for both novice and experienced users.
- *Collaboration Features*: Support for team collaboration, including version control and concurrent editing.
- *Integration*: Compatibility with other tools in the software development lifecycle, such as IDEs, requirements management, and CI/CD systems.
- *Cost*: Licensing fees and total cost of ownership, considering both initial and recurring expenses.

The cornerstone of effective software design lies in the strategic use of these modeling tools to create, verify, and communicate design aspects coherently across the development team. Leveraging the right design and modeling tools can yield significant improvements in the consistency, clarity, and maintainability of software systems, ultimately enhancing the overall quality and success of the project.

9.9 Configuration Management Tools

Configuration management tools are indispensable in the realm of software engineering for managing codebases, system settings, and environments across multiple stages of the software development lifecycle. These tools ensure that configurations are consistently maintained, facilitate the replication of environments, and help in tracking changes systematically.

Configuration management encompasses versioning, building, packaging, deploying, and monitoring configurations. Modern configuration management tools provide functionalities that automate these processes, minimize human errors, and improve efficiency.

Version Control in Configuration Management

Version control systems are a foundational aspect of configuration management. These systems not only manage source code but also handle environment configurations, scripts, and other project artifacts. By integrating configuration files into a version control system, development teams can track changes, audit history, and automatically apply updates across environments.

Popular version control systems used in configuration management include:

- **Git:** An open-source distributed version control system. Git's branching and merging capabilities allow teams to manage multiple configuration versions.
- **Subversion (SVN):** A centralized version control system that supports versioning of directories and configurations. Though less flexible than Git, it remains useful in managing configurations in environments where centralization is necessary.

Automation and Orchestration Tools

Configuration management tools intertwine with automation and orchestration tools to achieve Continuous Integration and Continuous Deployment (CI/CD). These tools reduce the burden of manual deployments and ensure consistent configuration across environments.

- **Ansible:** An agentless automation tool compatible with various IT environments. It uses simple YAML scripts called "playbooks" to manage configurations and deployments.
- **Chef:** Utilizes Ruby-based scripts termed "recipes" to automate configuration tasks. Chef's server-client model ensures configurations are consistently applied across nodes.
- **Puppet:** Employs a declarative language to define configurations. Puppet agents continuously enforce the desired state defined in configuration manifests.
- **Terraform:** Specializes in defining infrastructure as code. Terraform uses a declarative configuration language (HCL) to provision and manage resources across various cloud providers.

Infrastructure as Code (IaC)

Infrastructure as Code (IaC) is a practice where system configurations and environmental setups are written as code and stored in version control systems. This allows for reliable deployment and reproducibility.

Example: Provisioning a Server with Ansible

Below is an example of an Ansible playbook used to install and configure a web server.

```
---
- name: Configure web server
  hosts: webservers
  become: yes

  tasks:
  - name: Install Apache
    apt:
      name: apache2
      state: present

  - name: Start Apache service
    service:
      name: apache2
      state: started
      enabled: true
```

Execution of this playbook can be initiated using the following command:

```
ansible-playbook -i inventory webserver.yml
```

This command will install and start the Apache web server on all hosts listed in the 'inventory' file.

Monitoring and Compliance

Maintaining compliance with organizational policies and regulations mandates continuous monitoring of configurations. Configuration management tools offer auditing capabilities to track configuration changes and ensure compliance.

- **OTRS:** This tool helps in tracking changes, managing incidents, and ensuring compliance with ITIL (Information Technology Infrastructure Library) standards.
- **Nagios:** Extensively used for monitoring networks, systems, and configurations, Nagios provides alerts on configuration drifts.

Effective configuration management tools streamline the process of maintaining consistent configurations across development, testing, and production environments. They play a critical role in ensuring stable deployments and enabling rapid scaling of infrastructure. These tools collectively embody the principles of DevOps by fostering collaboration, automating repetitive tasks, and enhancing overall project delivery quality.

9.10 Collaboration and Communication Tools

Effective collaboration and communication are critical components of successful software engineering projects, particularly in distributed and agile environments. These tools facilitate teamwork, enhance productivity, and ensure that all team members are aligned with project goals and timelines.

Instant Messaging and Chat Platforms

Instant messaging (IM) and chat platforms provide real-time communication channels for teams. Popular tools such as Slack, Microsoft Teams, and Mattermost allow team members to send messages, share files, and engage in threaded conversations, which are vital for quick decision-making and problem resolution. Advanced features include integrations with other software engineering tools (e.g., version control systems, continuous integration servers), bots for automated tasks, and channels for focused discussions.

Video Conferencing Tools

Video conferencing tools enable face-to-face communication, which is essential for remote teams to maintain a sense of connection and collaboration. Tools such as Zoom, Google Meet, and Microsoft Teams offer high-definition video, screen sharing, and recording capabilities. These tools also provide scheduling features, integration with calendar applications, and options for virtual whiteboarding, enhancing their utility in collaborative environments.

Email Clients

Despite the rise of modern communication tools, email remains a cornerstone of professional communication. Email clients like Microsoft Outlook, Gmail, and Thunderbird offer robust features for managing communications. They support various protocols (POP3, IMAP, SMTP), and provide capabilities for filtering, labeling, and archiving messages. Integration with other collaboration tools, such as task management systems and calendaring, further augments their functionality in a software development context.

Project Management and Issue Tracking Tools

Project management and issue tracking tools are indispensable for handling tasks, bugs, and feature requests throughout the software development lifecycle. Tools such as JIRA, Asana, and Trello offer a range of features from simple to complex workflow management. These tools support agile methodologies, including Scrum and Kanban, by providing boards, sprints, backlog management, and burndown charts. Issue tracking functionality helps in documenting bugs, assigning them to developers, and tracking their resolution status.

```
# Example: Creating a Task in Jira Using Python API
import requests
import json

url = 'https://your-domain.atlassian.net/rest/api/3/issue'
headers = {
    'Accept': 'application/json',
    'Content-Type': 'application/json'
}
auth = ('email@example.com', 'API_TOKEN')

payload = json.dumps({
    "fields": {
        "project": {
            "key": "PROJ"
        },
        "summary": "This is a test task",
        "description": "Creating an issue from a script",
        "issuetype": {
            "name": "Task"
        }
    }
})

response = requests.post(url, headers=headers, auth=auth, data=payload)

print(response.json())
```

Version Control System Integrations

Version control systems such as Git and Subversion are not only for source code management but also provide collaboration features. Platforms like GitHub, GitLab, and Bitbucket offer issue tracking, merge requests (or pull requests) with code reviews, and continuous integration capabilities. Collaboration is further enhanced with features such as mention notifications, code discussion threads, and integration with chat tools.

Documentation Tools

Maintaining comprehensive documentation is crucial for long-term project success. Tools like Confluence, Notion, and SharePoint provide robust platforms for creating, managing, and sharing documents. Features include version histories, collaborative editing, templates, and integrations with other tools. Markdown support, LaTeX for formulas, and embedding media or interactive content enhance the versatility of these platforms.

```
# Example: Creating a Page in Confluence Using Python API
url = 'https://your-domain.atlassian.net/wiki/rest/api/content'
headers = {
    'Accept': 'application/json',
    'Content-Type': 'application/json'
}
auth = ('email@example.com', 'API_TOKEN')

payload = json.dumps({
    "type": "page",
    "title": "Sample Page",
    "space": {
        "key": "DOCS"
    },
    "body": {
        "storage": {
            "value": "<p>This is a sample page created via script.</p>",
            "representation": "storage"
        }
    }
})

response = requests.post(url, headers=headers, auth=auth, data=payload)
print(response.json())
```

Whiteboarding and Diagramming Tools

Visual collaboration using whiteboards and diagramming tools can significantly enhance the clarity of ideas and design processes. Online tools such as Miro, Lucidchart, and Microsoft Whiteboard allow team members to collaboratively draw diagrams, flowcharts, and sketches in real-time. These tools support embedding images, linking to other documents, exporting to various formats, and integrating with project management tools for seamless workflow.

Continuous Integration Communication

Continuous integration (CI) systems, like Jenkins, Travis CI, and CircleCI, often include communication hooks to notify teams about the status of builds and deployments. These notifications can be configured to send updates via email, chat channels, or dashboards, ensuring that team members are promptly informed of any issues that need attention.

Code Collaboration Tools

Tools such as Visual Studio Live Share and CodePen facilitate synchronous coding sessions among developers. These platforms enable real-time code editing, debugging, and sharing sessions, making pair programming and technical interviews more interactive and productive. Additional features include voice calls, session persistence, and integration with IDEs to streamline the development process.

Careful selection and integration of collaboration and communication tools are essential for maximizing team efficiency and ensuring successful project outcomes. Each tool's features and capabilities should align with the team's specific needs and workflows to enable seamless and effective collaboration.

9.11 Selecting the Right Tools for Your Project

Selecting the appropriate tools for a software development project is a critical decision that can influence the success of the project significantly. The choice of tools should be aligned with the project requirements, team skills, and the development process being adopted. This section delves into the major considerations for selecting software engineering tools, evaluating their advantages and limitations, and the strategies for effective tool integration.

Understanding Project Requirements

The initial step in selecting the right tools involves a thorough understanding of the project requirements. These requirements include the scope of the project, the expected functionality, performance constraints, and security needs. For instance, a project with strict security mandates might prioritize tools that offer robust encryption and compliance features.

Assessing Team Skills and Experiences

The selected tools should complement the skills and experiences of the development team. If the team has extensive experience with certain tools or programming languages, it could be beneficial to leverage that expertise to enhance productivity. However, this does not preclude the need for occasionally adopting new tools that may be better suited for specific tasks, provided adequate training is available.

Compatibility with Development Methodologies

The tools should be compatible with the chosen development methodology, whether it is Agile, Waterfall, DevOps, or any other approach. For example, Agile development benefits significantly from tools that support iterative development, continuous integration, and automated testing. Conversely, Waterfall projects may require more robust requirements management and design tools to handle the sequential phases of development.

Integration with Existing Systems

Consider whether the new tools will integrate seamlessly with existing systems and tools in use. This includes integration with version control systems, continuous integration pipelines, project management tools, and communication platforms. Incompatibilities can lead to workflow disruptions and inefficiencies.

Scalability and Performance

Evaluate whether the tools can scale as the project grows. Scalability encompasses the tool's ability to handle increased workload, additional team members, and larger codebases without a degradation in performance. For example, a version control system should efficiently manage repositories of various sizes and support concurrent operations by multiple users without conflict.

Cost and Licensing

Financial considerations play a crucial role in tool selection. Examine the cost implications of licensing, maintenance, and potential hidden expenses. Open-source tools can be a cost-effective alternative, but they may require additional resources for support and maintenance. Proprietary tools, while often more expensive, may come with professional support and more comprehensive documentation.

Usability and User Interface

The usability of the tool and its user interface design can significantly impact productivity. Tools with intuitive interfaces and proper documentation ensure that team members can effectively leverage their features without excessive learning curves.

Vendor Support and Community

Assess the level of vendor support and the activity of user communities around the tool. Tools with active communities provide a wealth of shared knowledge, plugins, and extensions that can enhance functionality and troubleshoot issues. Vendor support ensures that any critical issues can be addressed swiftly.

Security Features

Security is a paramount concern in software development. Ensure that the tools provide adequate security features, such as access control, encryption, and compliance with relevant standards. Consider tools that have undergone rigorous security testing and have a reputation for security resilience.

Evaluating Tool Effectiveness

Conducting an evaluation or trial period can provide practical insights into how well the tools meet project needs. Create a list of core functionalities and performance metrics to test during this period. Examples of such metrics include response time, ease of integration, user satisfaction, and how effectively the tool supports the intended workflow.

Feedback and Continuous Improvement

Gather feedback from all stakeholders including developers, testers, project managers, and other users of the tool. Use this feedback to refine tool usage strategies and make informed decisions about continuing, replacing, or complementing the tool with additional tools. Continuous improvement is vital in maintaining an effective toolkit that evolves with project needs.

Strategic Alignment

Align the selection of tools with the broader strategic goals of the organization. This includes considerations regarding long-term support, alignment with the company's technological direction, and the capacity for the tools to adapt to emerging trends and practices in the industry.

Selecting the right tools for a project involves a multifaceted evaluation process tailored to the specific needs and characteristics of the project. By meticulously considering all these factors, the team can enhance productivity, ensure workflow compatibility, and ultimately, drive the project to a successful completion.

9.12 Future Trends in Software Engineering Tools

Advancements in software engineering tools are shaping the future of software development, transforming processes, and enabling developers to deliver high-quality products more efficiently. As these tools evolve, several emerging trends are worth noting, including increased automation, integration of artificial intelligence and machine learning, enhanced collaboration features, and greater emphasis on security and privacy.

The automation of software engineering tasks continues to grow, reducing manual efforts and minimizing the risk of human error. Tools that automate code generation, testing, deployment, and maintenance allow developers to focus more on design and innovation. For instance, automated code review tools such as SonarQube perform static code analysis to identify potential issues early in the development lifecycle. Similarly, continuous integration and continuous deployment (CI/CD) pipelines automated using tools like Jenkins or GitHub Actions streamline the path from code commit to production deployment.

```
# Example of an automated CI/CD pipeline configuration using GitHub Actions
name: CI/CD Pipeline

on: [push]

jobs:
  build:
    runs-on: ubuntu-latest
    steps:
    - name: Checkout code
      uses: actions/checkout@v2
    - name: Set up Node.js
      uses: actions/setup-node@v2
      with:
        node-version: '14'
    - name: Install dependencies
      run: npm install
    - name: Run tests
      run: npm test
    - name: Build project
      run: npm run build
```

Artificial intelligence (AI) and machine learning (ML) are being increasingly integrated into software engineering tools to further improve productivity and code quality. AI-powered code completion tools like GitHub Copilot assist developers by suggesting contextually relevant code snippets, reducing the number of keystrokes required and accelerating the coding process. Additionally, AI-based testing tools such as Testim leverage machine learning to create, maintain, and execute tests more effectively, adapting to changes in the application with minimal human intervention.

```
# Example of AI-powered code suggestion with GitHub Copilot in Python
def add(a, b):
    """
    Add two numbers together.

    Parameters:
    a (int|float): The first number.
    b (int|float): The second number.

    Returns:
    int|float: The sum of the two numbers.
    """
    return a + b
```

The trend towards enhanced collaboration features in software engineering tools addresses the increasing need for remote and distributed development teams. Collaborative platforms such as Visual Studio Live Share enable real-time code-sharing and editing, allowing team members to navigate and edit codebases together, regardless of their physical locations. Tools like Slack and Microsoft Teams integrate with development environments to facilitate seamless communication and project management, keeping teams aligned and informed.

```
# Example of integration with Slack to notify team members of deployment status
curl -X POST -H 'Content-type: application/json' --data '{"text":"Deployment
    successful!"}' https://hooks.slack.com/services/your/webhook/url
```

Security and privacy have become paramount in the development of new tools, owing to the increasing frequency and sophistication of cyber-attacks. Modern software engineering tools emphasize secure coding practices and integrate security checks throughout the development lifecycle. DevSecOps, an extension of DevOps that includes security as a key component, embodies this trend. Tools like Snyk and OWASP ZAP facilitate the identification and remediation of vulnerabilities in code and dependencies early in the development process.

```
# Example of using Snyk CLI to test for vulnerabilities
snyk test
```

These trends reflect a move towards creating more intelligent, efficient, and secure software engineering environments. As tools continue to advance, they will undoubtedly bring further improvements, empowering developers to meet the ever-changing demands of the software industry.

Chapter 10

Current Trends and Future Directions in Software Engineering

Current trends and future directions in software engineering involve the adoption of cutting-edge practices and emerging technologies. This chapter covers developments such as Agile and DevOps, microservices architecture, cloud computing, and Software as a Service (SaaS). It also explores the integration of artificial intelligence and machine learning, blockchain technology, the Internet of Things (IoT), and advancements in cybersecurity. Additionally, the chapter discusses the implications of quantum computing and the future of software engineering research, highlighting the skills and education necessary to stay relevant in this evolving field.

10.1 Introduction to Current Trends in Software Engineering

The landscape of software engineering is inherently dynamic, characterized by the rapid evolution of practices, methodologies, and technologies. Keeping abreast of current trends is essential for practitioners, researchers, and organizations to remain competitive and innovative.

This section provides a detailed examination of the predominant trends shaping the contemporary field of software engineering, laying the foundation for more specific discussions in subsequent sections. We delve into the significance of Agile and DevOps practices, advancements in microservices and service-oriented architectures, the proliferation of cloud computing and Software as a Service (SaaS), and the integration of artificial intelligence and machine learning into software development processes.

Agile methodologies emphasize iterative development, collaboration, and flexibility, which directly contrast with traditional, linear development models such as the Waterfall model. Agile's significance lies in its ability to produce functional software increments within shorter timeframes, thereby enabling faster feedback cycles and more responsive adjustments to changing requirements. Core practices within Agile, including Scrum and Kanban, provide structured frameworks to enhance team productivity and project transparency.

To demonstrate an Agile practice in action, consider the following pseudocode representing a simplified sprint planning script using the Scrum methodology:

```
class Sprint:
    def __init__(self, sprint_id, sprint_goal, tasks):
        self.sprint_id = sprint_id
        self.sprint_goal = sprint_goal
        self.tasks = tasks

class Task:
    def __init__(self, task_id, description, assignee, status="To Do"):
        self.task_id = task_id
        self.description = description
        self.assignee = assignee
        self.status = status

def create_sprint(sprint_id, sprint_goal, task_list):
    sprint = Sprint(sprint_id, sprint_goal, task_list)
    return sprint

def add_task(sprint, task):
    sprint.tasks.append(task)

def update_task_status(task, new_status):
    task.status = new_status

# Example usage
task1 = Task(task_id=1, description="Implement feature X", assignee="Dev A")
task2 = Task(task_id=2, description="Fix bug Y", assignee="Dev B")
sprint = create_sprint(sprint_id=101, sprint_goal="Complete core functionalities",
        task_list=[task1, task2])

# Update task status
update_task_status(task1, "In Progress")
```

DevOps, a cultural and professional movement, integrates development and operations teams to enhance collaboration and productivity. By automating and monitoring every step of the software development lifecycle, from integration and testing to deployment and infrastructure management, DevOps aims to deliver high-quality software continuously and more reliably. The practice of Continuous Integration/Continuous Deployment (CI/CD) pipelines exemplifies DevOps principles, automating the build, test, and deployment phases to ensure rapid delivery and feedback.

Microservices architecture advocates for designing systems as a suite of independently deployable services, each with a distinct business functionality. This architectural style enhances scalability, fault isolation, and the ability to deploy changes incrementally. In contrast to monolithic architectures, microservices offer modularity and the flexibility to use different technologies within different services. The following diagram depicts a typical microservices architecture for an e-commerce application:

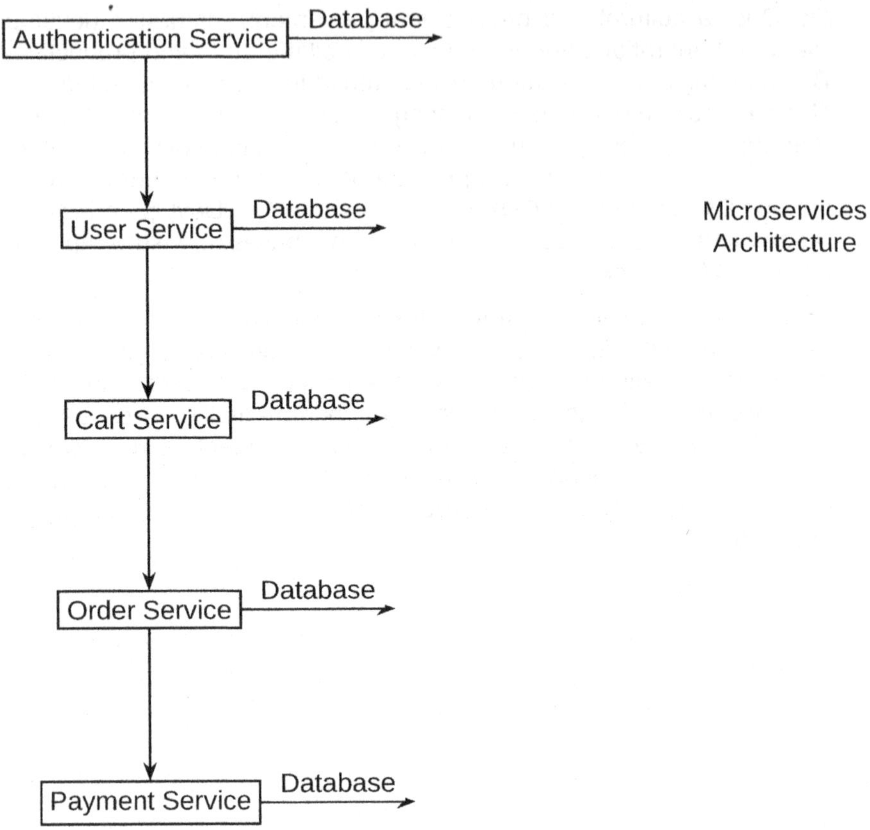

Cloud computing and SaaS have substantially transformed how software applications are developed, deployed, and consumed. Cloud computing offers scalable computing resources over the internet, allowing software systems to handle varying loads without direct investment in physical infrastructure. SaaS, a cloud-based service model, delivers software applications over the internet on a subscription basis. SaaS vendors manage the infrastructure, reducing the overhead for clients. Common examples of SaaS include office productivity suites, customer relationship management (CRM) systems, and collaborative tools.

Artificial Intelligence (AI) and Machine Learning (ML) are increasingly integrated into software engineering processes to enhance the automation and intelligence of systems. AI offers the capability to automate complex decision-making processes, while ML provides algorithms to learn from data and improve over time. Applications of AI/ML in software engineering include automated code generation, predictive analytics for bug detection, and natural language processing for user interface improvements.

```
from sklearn.datasets import load_iris
from sklearn.model_selection import train_test_split
from sklearn.ensemble import RandomForestClassifier
from sklearn.metrics import accuracy_score

# Load dataset
iris = load_iris()
X = iris.data
y = iris.target

# Split data into training and testing sets
X_train, X_test, y_train, y_test = train_test_split(X, y, test_size=0.3,
    random_state=42)

# Initialize and train the model
model = RandomForestClassifier(n_estimators=100)
model.fit(X_train, y_train)

# Make predictions
y_pred = model.predict(X_test)

# Evaluate accuracy
accuracy = accuracy_score(y_test, y_pred)
print("Accuracy: {:.2f}%".format(accuracy * 100))
```

Understanding these trends and their practical implications offers valuable insight for navigating the evolving landscape of software engineering efficiently. As each of these trends continues to develop, they collectively contribute to the ongoing transformation of the field, setting the stage for future innovations.

10.2 Agile and DevOps Practices

Agile and DevOps have revolutionized the way software development and operations teams collaborate and deliver software. Their fundamental principles focus on enhancing flexibility, improving communication, and accelerating software delivery cycles while maintaining high-quality standards.

Agile methodologies advocate for iterative development, where requirements and solutions evolve through the collaborative effort of cross-functional teams. The Agile Manifesto emphasizes individuals and interactions over processes and tools, working software over comprehensive documentation, customer collaboration over contract negotiation, and responding to change over following a plan. Key Agile frameworks include Scrum, Kanban, Extreme Programming (XP), and Lean Software Development.

Scrum is one of the most popular Agile frameworks. It structures work in cycles of up to a month, known as sprints, during which a predetermined set of features is developed. The main roles in Scrum include the Product Owner, Scrum Master, and the Development Team. The Product Owner is responsible for defining the features of the product and prioritizing them in the product backlog. The Scrum Master ensures that the Scrum framework is followed and that obstacles are removed to facilitate the team's progress. Development Teams are cross-functional, self-organizing units that collaboratively build the product. Essential Scrum ceremonies comprise Sprint Planning, Daily Stand-ups, Sprint Reviews, and Retrospectives.

Kanban, on the other hand, focuses on continuous delivery by limiting the work in progress and allowing teams to visualize their workflow on a Kanban board. Work items move through various stages such as 'To Do', 'In Progress', and 'Done'. It enables teams to optimize their flow of work, identify bottlenecks, and improve efficiency gradually.

Extreme Programming (XP) stresses technical excellence and suitable engineering practices like Test-Driven Development (TDD), Continuous Integration, Pair Programming, and frequent releases in short development cycles. Lean Software Development, derived from lean manufacturing principles, targets waste reduction, amplifies learning, and delivers as fast as possible with the least effort.

DevOps bridges the gap between development and operations, aiming for faster deployment, greater reliability, and higher-quality software. Key principles of DevOps include Continuous Integration (CI), Continuous Delivery (CD), automation, and infrastructure as code.

Continuous Integration (CI) involves automatically integrating code changes from multiple contributors frequently, at least once a day. This process triggers automated builds and tests, allowing teams to detect and address issues early. An example of setting up a CI pipeline using Jenkins, a popular CI/CD tool, is illustrated below:

```
pipeline {
   agent any
   stages {
       stage('Build') {
           steps {
               sh 'mvn clean install'
           }
       }
       stage('Test') {
           steps {
               sh 'mvn test'
```

```
            }
        }
        stage('Deploy') {
            steps {
                sh 'scp target/myapp.jar user@host:/deployments/'
            }
        }
    }
    post {
        success {
            echo 'Pipeline completed successfully!'
        }
        failure {
            mail to: 'team@example.com',
                 subject: 'Pipeline Failed',
                 body: 'Please check the logs.'
        }
    }
}
```

In the script above, the pipeline is defined as having build, test, and deploy stages. Each stage consists of steps that execute shell commands. The post block contains actions triggered by the success or failure of the pipeline.

Continuous Delivery (CD) extends CI by automating the release process, ensuring that software can be reliably released at any time. CD pipelines involve a series of steps, including build, test, and deploy to production-like environments, with frequent deployments and minimal manual intervention.

Automation in DevOps encompasses various activities such as environment provisioning, configuration management, deployment automation, and monitoring. Tools like Ansible, Chef, and Puppet facilitate the automation of repetitive and complex tasks, enabling rapid and consistent infrastructure management.

Infrastructure as Code (IaC) treats infrastructure configuration and provisioning similarly to software development. With IaC, infrastructure is defined through code, which is versioned, tested, and deployed. Terraform is a widely used IaC tool that allows for defining and provisioning data center infrastructure using a declarative configuration language. An example of a Terraform configuration file to set up an AWS EC2 instance is shown below:

```
provider "aws" {
    region = "us-west-2"
}

resource "aws_instance" "example" {
    ami = "ami-0c55b159cbfafe1f0"
    instance_type = "t2.micro"
```

```
  tags = {
    Name = "example-instance"
  }
}
```

This configuration specifies the AWS provider and defines an EC2 instance resource with a specific AMI and instance type. On applying this configuration, Terraform interacts with AWS APIs to provision the defined infrastructure.

Combining Agile methodologies with DevOps practices establishes a seamless and efficient development pipeline. Agile facilitates adaptive planning and iterative delivery, while DevOps enhances collaboration, continuous feedback, and automation across the software lifecycle. This integration leads to faster and more reliable software delivery, enabling organizations to respond swiftly to changing market demands.

To transition to Agile and DevOps effectively, organizations must embrace cultural change, adopt appropriate tools, and ensure continuous learning and improvement. Key success factors include management support, training teams in Agile and DevOps practices, and fostering a culture of collaboration and transparency.

10.3 Microservices and Service-Oriented Architectures

The evolution of software architecture has progressed significantly with the advent of microservices and service-oriented architectures (SOA). These paradigms offer solutions to many limitations found in traditional monolithic architectures, providing a structured approach that enhances scalability, flexibility, and maintainability of complex systems.

A traditional monolithic application is typically built as a single unified codebase. While this approach simplifies deployment, it often results in tightly coupled components, leading to several drawbacks such as difficulty in scaling parts of the application independently, increased risk of system-wide failures, and complex deployment processes. Microservices and SOA aim to address these issues by decomposing the application into smaller, loosely coupled services.

Microservices Architecture is an architectural style that structures an application as a collection of small, autonomous services modeled around a specific business domain. Each microservice is an independent entity that encapsulates a specific piece of functionality and interacts with other services through well-defined APIs, often using lightweight communication mechanisms such as HTTP/REST or messaging queues. The primary characteristics of microservices include:

- **Independent Deployment:** Each service can be deployed, updated, replaced, or scaled independently of other services.
- **Decentralized Data Management:** Every microservice manages its own database or data source, enabling more straightforward scaling and database schema changes.
- **Technology Heterogeneity:** Microservices allow different services to be built using various programming languages and technologies, ideally suited to the specific needs of each service.
- **Fault Isolation:** Failures in one service generally do not impact other services, increasing the overall system's resilience.

Consider the following simplified implementation of a microservice using Python's Flask framework:

```
from flask import Flask, jsonify

app = Flask(__name__)

@app.route('/health', methods=['GET'])
def health_check():
    return jsonify({'status': 'OK'}), 200

@app.route('/api/data', methods=['GET'])
def get_data():
    data = {
        'id': 1,
        'name': 'Sample Data'
    }
    return jsonify(data), 200

if __name__ == '__main__':
    app.run(host='0.0.0.0', port=5000)
```

Upon running the code above, the output when accessing the service might look like this:

```
$ curl http://localhost:5000/health
{"status": "OK"}

$ curl http://localhost:5000/api/data
{"id": 1, "name": "Sample Data"}
```

Service-Oriented Architecture (SOA) predates the microservices architecture and shares several principles yet differs in its approach and granularity. In SOA, the software design is based on discrete services that provide business capabilities and communicate over a network. Each service performs a specific function and is discoverable and invocable independently. Key principles of SOA include:

- **Loose Coupling:** Services maintain independence from one another, minimizing dependencies.
- **Service Contract:** Each service has a formal contract, which specifies the provided functionality and how it can be accessed.
- **Discoverability:** Services can be discovered and invoked using a directory service.
- **Reusability:** Services are designed to be reusable across different applications and contexts.

An example of an SOA implementation can be found in the use of SOAP (Simple Object Access Protocol) Web Services. The following code shows a basic SOAP service in Java:

```
import javax.jws.WebMethod;
import javax.jws.WebService;
import javax.jws.soap.SOAPBinding;
import javax.xml.ws.Endpoint;

@WebService
@SOAPBinding(style = SOAPBinding.Style.DOCUMENT, use = SOAPBinding.Use.
    LITERAL)
public class SimpleSOAPService {

    @WebMethod
    public String getStatus() {
        return "Service is running";
    }

    public static void main(String[] args) {
        Endpoint.publish("http://localhost:8080/soapservice", new SimpleSOAPService
            ());
    }
}
```

The response from invoking the service might look like this:

```
$ curl -X POST -H "Content-Type: text/xml" -d @request.xml http://localhost:8080/soapservice
<soap:Envelope xmlns:soap="http://schemas.xmlsoap.org/soap/envelope/">
  <soap:Body>
    <getStatusResponse>
      <return>Service is running</return>
    </getStatusResponse>
  </soap:Body>
</soap:Envelope>
```

The choice between microservices and SOA depends on various factors such as organizational structure, project requirements, and technological constraints. Microservices typically favor agile practices and continuous integration/deployment (CI/CD) pipelines, enabling rapid development and iterative updates. SOA, in contrast, is often used in environments where interoperability and standard protocols are paramount, particularly in large enterprises with existing infrastructure investments.

As software engineering continues to evolve, the adoption of microservices and SOA offers robust methodologies that align well with modern development practices.

10.4 Cloud Computing and Software as a Service (SaaS)

Cloud computing has revolutionized the landscape of software engineering, offering dynamic and scalable resources via the internet. Traditionally, organizations were constrained by the necessity to maintain physical infrastructure for computing resources. With cloud computing, resources such as servers, storage, databases, networking, software, and analytics are provided over the cloud, allowing businesses to innovate faster and leverage elastic scalability.

At its core, cloud computing can be broadly categorized into three primary service models: Infrastructure as a Service (IaaS), Platform as a Service (PaaS), and Software as a Service (SaaS).

IaaS provides virtualized computing resources over the internet. Users can provision processing power, storage, and networking capabilities on demand without worrying about physical hardware. PaaS offers a platform allowing developers to build, run, and manage applications without dealing with the infrastructure complexities associated with developing and deploying applications. SaaS delivers software applications over the internet, on a subscription basis, reducing the need for organizations to handle installation and maintenance of hardware and software.

Software as a Service (SaaS) is particularly transformative in how organizations deploy and use software solutions. SaaS applications are accessible via web browsers, eliminating the need for extensive setup and enabling users to access sophisticated functionalities with minimal technical expertise.

```
import requests

url = "https://api.example-saasyservice.com/v1/data"
headers = {
    "Authorization": "Bearer YOUR_ACCESS_TOKEN"
}

response = requests.get(url, headers=headers)

# Check response status
if response.status_code == 200:
    data = response.json()
    print("Data fetched successfully")
else:
    print(f"Failed to fetch data: {response.status_code}")
```

In the example above, a typical interaction with a SaaS API involves making HTTP requests using an access token for authentication. This highlights the simplicity of integrating SaaS solutions into existing systems.

SaaS offers several advantages:

- **Cost-Effectiveness**: SaaS reduces the financial burden related to purchasing, installing, and maintaining hardware and software. The subscription model often makes it easier for businesses to manage budgets.
- **Accessibility**: As SaaS applications are cloud-based, they can be accessed from anywhere with an internet connection, supporting the modern demand for remote work and mobility.
- **Scalability**: SaaS can easily scale to accommodate a growing number of users or increasing data volumes without significant changes to the software or hardware infrastructure.
- **Up-to-Date Software**: Providers manage software updates and patches, ensuring that the latest features and security enhancements are available to users without individual action required.

The underlying technologies that enable SaaS include virtualization, multi-tenancy, service-oriented architecture (SOA), and web APIs. Virtualization allows for efficient utilization of physical resources by creating virtual instances. Multi-tenancy ensures that a single software instance serves multiple customers with data isolation and security. SOA applies modularity principles, allowing reusable services to integrate seamlessly, while web APIs facilitate interoperability between different software systems.

The role of **microservices** within SaaS cannot be understated. Microservices decompose applications into smaller, independently deployable services, which communicate over well-defined APIs. Each microservice focuses on a specific business capability, enhancing agility and scalability. The following is an example architectural diagram of a SaaS application built using microservices:

```
+-----------+
| User Client |
+------+------+
|
v
+-----------+-----------+
| API Gateway/Router |
+-----------+-----------+
|
+-----------------------+-----------------------+
| | |
v v v
+-----------+ +-----------+ +-----------+
| AuthService | | DataService | | NotificationSvc|
+-----------+ +-----------+ +-----------+
```

In this architecture, the API Gateway serves as the entry point for all client requests, directing traffic to the appropriate microservice such as AuthService for authentication, DataService for handling data operations, and NotificationSvc for managing notifications.

Data security and privacy are critical considerations for SaaS providers. Compliance with regulations such as GDPR, HIPAA, and SOC 2 ensures that providers handle data responsibly. Encryption, both at rest and in transit, access controls, and regular security audits are necessary practices.

Cloud computing and SaaS continue to advance, driven by innovations like edge computing and AI integration. These will further reduce latency, improve performance, and bring intelligent functionalities closer to the data source. As the software engineering landscape evolves, the adoption and optimization of SaaS solutions remain pivotal.

10.5 Artificial Intelligence and Machine Learning in Software Engineering

Artificial intelligence (AI) and machine learning (ML) have emerged as significant components of contemporary software engineering practices. The infusion of AI and ML into software engineering introduces new dimensions in automation, predictive analysis, and efficient handling of complex data sets. This section delves into the mechanisms, applications, and up-to-date trends surrounding AI and ML within the context of software engineering.

AI refers to the simulation of human intelligence in machines that are programmed to think and learn. These capabilities include reasoning, problem-solving, and learning from experience. ML, a subset of AI, focuses on the development of algorithms that enable computers to learn from and make predictions based on data. The synergistic combination of AI and ML models facilitates enhanced decision-making processes and optimized solutions in software engineering projects.

In the software development lifecycle (SDLC), AI and ML augment various stages from requirements gathering to maintenance. During the requirements analysis phase, natural language processing (NLP) algorithms can be applied to parse and understand user requirements. NLP uses techniques from computational linguistics and machine learning to process and analyze large corpuses of natural language data. For instance, the extraction of requirements from unstructured data such as interview transcripts or user stories can be automated, thereby reducing the manual effort and ambiguity.

For illustration:

```
import spacy

# Load the large English NLP model
nlp = spacy.load("en_core_web_lg")

# Define the user requirements text
text = ("The system shall allow users to login using a username and password. "
        "The user profile should be easily editable with drag-and-drop features.")

# Process the text with the NLP model
doc = nlp(text)

# Extract entities and display them
for ent in doc.ents:
    print(ent.text, ent.label_)
```

The output of this code will be the critical entities recognized within the user requirements, which can then be used to inform the subsequent stages of development.

```
The system shall allow users to login using a username and password. (REQUIREMENT)
The user profile should be easily editable (FEATURE) with drag-and-drop features. (FUNCTIONALITY)
```

Moving on to the design and implementation stages, AI algorithms can assist in automatic code generation. By leveraging deep learning models, specifically neural networks trained on vast code repositories, developers can generate boilerplate code, spot potential bugs, and even suggest code improvements. Consider the utility of recurrent neural networks (RNNs) or transformer models like GPT-3 in code synthesis, assisting developers by predicting the subsequent lines of code based on learned patterns.

```
import openai

# OpenAI GPT-3 setup
openai.api_key = 'your-api-key-here'

# Define the code prompt
prompt = "def factorial(n):"

# Generate code completion
response = openai.Completion.create(
    engine="davinci-codex",
    prompt=prompt,
    max_tokens=50
)

# Print the generated code
print(response.choices[0].text.strip())
```

The probable output extends the function definition to include complete implementation details of the factorial function, enhancing development efficiency.

```
def factorial(n):
    if n == 0:
        return 1
    else:
        return n * factorial(n-1)
```

During the testing phase, AI methodologies such as reinforcement learning can optimize testing strategies. These intelligent systems identify the most susceptible portions of the code to errors, thereby prioritizing test cases to focus efforts where they are most needed. Predictive analytics models evaluate historical data from previous tests to anticipate potential faults and performance bottlenecks.

AI-driven code review tools facilitate static code analysis by identifying potential vulnerabilities and ensuring adherence to coding standards. Here is how a simple ML-based static analysis tool might operate:

```
from sklearn.feature_extraction.text import TfidfVectorizer
from sklearn.linear_model import LogisticRegression

# Sample code snippets - 'X' and their corresponding labels - 'y'
X = [
    "def add(a, b):\n\treturn a+b",
    "def add(a, b):\n\treturn a-b" # contains a logical flaw
]
y = [1, 0] # 1: correct, 0: flawed

# Transform the code snippets into a TF-IDF vector
vectorizer = TfidfVectorizer()
X_vectorized = vectorizer.fit_transform(X)

# Train a simple logistic regression model on the data
model = LogisticRegression()
model.fit(X_vectorized, y)

# Predicting new sample
new_code_snippet = ["def subtract(a, b):\n\treturn a-b"]
new_vector = vectorizer.transform(new_code_snippet)
prediction = model.predict(new_vector)

print("Prediction:", "Correct" if prediction[0] == 1 else "Flawed")
```

The aforementioned model, albeit simple, aims to classify code based on its logic. The integration of AI in code analysis enhances the ability to identify potential issues early in the software development process.

AI and ML also contribute significantly to software maintenance by enabling predictive maintenance. By analyzing system logs and usage patterns, AI models can predict when a component is likely to fail and recommend preemptive actions to avoid downtimes. Tools powered by ML for anomaly detection help in continuous monitoring of the software system's health.

From a broader perspective, AI and ML exemplify the transformation of software engineering workflows fostering more intelligent, adaptive, and efficient methodologies. The continuous evolution of these technologies promises further advancements, making them indispensable in the future landscape of software engineering.

10.6 Blockchain Technology

Blockchain technology has emerged as a revolutionary approach to data integrity and security. It operates on a decentralized network wherein information is authenticated and maintained by multiple nodes, ensuring transparency and immutability of records. The core principles of blockchain, such as cryptographic hashing, distributed consensus, and smart contracts, are instrumental in validating transactions and discouraging fraudulent activities.

A blockchain consists of a series of blocks that store transactional data. Each block contains a cryptographic hash of the previous block, a timestamp, and transaction data. This structure forms a chain, hence the term blockchain. The cryptographic hash function is pivotal as it converts data of arbitrary size to a fixed size, making it infeasible to regenerate the original data from the hash value. The hashing ensures that any alteration to the block data results in a different hash, immediately indicating tampering.

```
import hashlib

def hash_transaction(transaction):
    return hashlib.sha256(transaction.encode()).hexdigest()

# Example usage
transaction_data = "UserA sends 5 BTC to UserB"
hash_value = hash_transaction(transaction_data)
print("SHA-256 Hash:", hash_value)
```

```
SHA-256 Hash:
4f983d2b6eba5374c237a7f44c4dbd2a5d2d4e4f40268d5ecae44f08b0790d7a
```

The decentralized nature of blockchain is maintained through a consensus mechanism. Proof-of-Work (PoW) and Proof-of-Stake (PoS) are the two commonly used algorithms. PoW requires participants to solve a computationally intensive puzzle, thereby proving that they have invested significant resources in processing power. This approach, while secure, is energy-intensive. In contrast, PoS operates by selecting validators based on their stake in the network, determined by the number of tokens held. Validators are selected to forge new blocks, thus consuming less energy compared to PoW.

Proof-of-Work Algorithm Pseudocode:

```
while (block not valid)
{
    nonce++;
    hash = SHA-256(previous_block_hash + transactions + nonce);
}
add_block_to_chain(block);
```

The functionality of blockchain can be extended through smart contracts, which are self-executing contracts with the terms of the agreement directly written into code. These contracts automatically enforce and execute the conditions of an agreement when predetermined criteria are met, reducing the need for intermediaries and enhancing trust. Ethereum is one of the prominent platforms that facilitate smart contract deployment using its Solidity programming language.

```
pragma solidity ^0.5.0;

contract SimpleStorage {
    uint storedData;

    function set(uint x) public {
        storedData = x;
    }

    function get() public view returns (uint) {
        return storedData;
    }
}
```

Beyond financial transactions, blockchain technology has wide-ranging applications. In supply chain management, it ensures the traceability and transparency of goods from origin to delivery. In healthcare, it secures patient records and facilitates data sharing across institutions while preserving privacy. Moreover, blockchain is shaping digital identity management, providing individuals control over their credentials without the need for centralized authorities.

As blockchain technology continues to evolve, it is essential to address its challenges, including scalability, interoperability, and regulatory considerations. Scalability concerns relate to the ability of blockchain networks to handle a growing number of transactions per second. Interoperability denotes the capability of disparate blockchain networks to communicate and exchange data. Regulatory compliance involves creating frameworks that balance innovation with protection against misuse and fraud. Research and development in these areas are crucial for the continued advancement and adoption of blockchain technology in various sectors.

10.7 Internet of Things (IoT)

The Internet of Things (IoT) refers to the network of physical objects—devices, vehicles, buildings, and other entities—embedded with sensors, software, and connectivity capabilities that enable these objects to collect and exchange data. IoT significantly alters the landscape of software engineering by integrating the physical and virtual worlds, thereby creating unprecedented opportunities and challenges. This section will delve into core IoT concepts, architectural considerations, and specific technologies that are currently influencing IoT development and deployment.

IoT systems consist of three main components: devices (or things), communication networks, and cloud-based applications. These components interact to perform tasks and services. Devices include a wide variety of entities, from household appliances to industrial machines, equipped with sensors and actuators. These devices collect data about their environment and perform actions based on the information they receive.

Devices: IoT devices can range from simple sensors to complex systems. Each device typically includes:

- **Sensors:** Devices with sensors can monitor various physical parameters such as temperature, humidity, light intensity, motion, and more.
- **Actuators:** Devices with actuators can perform actions based on commands, such as turning on a light or adjusting a thermostat.
- **Microcontrollers or Microprocessors:** These manage the sensors and actuators, process data, and facilitate communication.

Communication Networks: Devices communicate with each other and with centralized systems via networks. This communication can occur through various protocols such as Wi-Fi, Bluetooth, Zigbee, and cellular networks. The choice of protocol depends on factors like range, power consumption, and data rate requirements.

Cloud-Based Applications: Centralized applications often run on cloud infrastructure, offering scalable storage, data processing, and analytical capabilities. These applications collect and analyze data from IoT devices, apply machine learning algorithms if required, and control the devices based on analytical insights.

IoT Architecture: IoT systems typically follow a layered architecture comprising the following layers:

- **Perception Layer:** This is the hardware layer incorporating sensors and actuators interfacing with the physical world.
- **Network Layer:** Facilitates connectivity and data transmission from devices to cloud services or local servers.
- **Middleware Layer:** Handles data processing and database management. It often includes edge computing capabilities to process data closer to the source.

- **Application Layer:** Represents IoT applications delivering various services, such as smart home control or industrial automation.

Security Considerations: Given the pervasive nature of IoT, security is paramount. Potential challenges include:

- **Device Vulnerabilities:** IoT devices often have limited computational resources, making implementation of stringent security measures difficult.
- **Data Privacy:** Ensuring that data collected by IoT devices is not misused or accessed without permission.
- **Network Security:** Protecting data as it travels over networks from devices to the cloud.

IoT Use Cases in Software Engineering:

- **Smart Homes:** Automation of household devices for enhanced convenience, security, and energy efficiency.
- **Industrial IoT (IIoT):** Boosting manufacturing and supply chain efficiencies through predictive maintenance, asset tracking, and process automation.
- **Healthcare IoT:** Mobile health applications for real-time monitoring of patient vitals and administration of treatments.
- **Smart Cities:** Urban planning and management through efficient transportation systems, waste management, and energy usage monitoring.

Programming and Development for IoT: Developing software for IoT involves several specialized tools and platforms. For example:

```
import Adafruit_DHT

# Define the sensor type and the GPIO pin it is connected to
sensor = Adafruit_DHT.DHT22
gpio_pin = 4

# Read the humidity and temperature data
humidity, temperature = Adafruit_DHT.read_retry(sensor, gpio_pin)

# Check if reading was successful
if humidity is not None and temperature is not None:
    print('Temp={0:0.1f}*C Humidity={1:0.1f}%'.format(temperature, humidity))
else:
    print('Failed to get reading from the sensor. Try again!')
```

In this example, Python is used to read data from a DHT22 sensor connected to a Raspberry Pi. The output might look like:

```
Temp=23.4*C  Humidity=45.0%
```

Future Directions: The fusion of IoT with other emerging technologies like artificial intelligence (AI), blockchain, and edge computing is broadening the horizon for innovation in software engineering. These integrations support enhanced data security, real-time processing, and automated decision-making capabilities.

Through continuous advancements in IoT, software engineering practices are evolving to include more robust, scalable, and secure solutions. Professionals in the field need to be proficient in both hardware and software aspects of IoT systems to fully harness its potential.

10.8 Cybersecurity Trends

The field of cybersecurity is rapidly evolving, driven by the increasing complexity and frequency of cyberattacks. This section elucidates the prevailing trends within cybersecurity, highlighting crucial practices and technologies essential for safeguarding modern software systems.

Zero Trust Architecture: A fundamental shift in cybersecurity, the Zero Trust model operates under the premise that threats could originate both outside and within an organization's network. Under Zero Trust principles, every access request is thoroughly authenticated, authorized, and validated before granting access to the requested resource. This approach significantly deviates from traditional perimeter-based security models by constantly validating users and devices, mitigating risks associated with internal threats and lateral movement of attackers. Key implementation aspects include micro-segmentation, least privilege access, and continuous monitoring.

Artificial Intelligence and Machine Learning Applications: Utilizing artificial intelligence (AI) and machine learning (ML) is becoming increasingly prevalent in cybersecurity strategies. AI and ML algorithms assist in identifying patterns and anomalies in large datasets, enabling early detection of potential threats. Techniques such as behavior analysis and anomaly detection are instrumental in recognizing deviations that could signify security breaches. Additionally, predictive analysis helps in foreseeing potential vulnerabilities and proactively fortifying defenses. Below is a sample Python code demonstrating anomaly detection using ML:

```
# Import necessary libraries
from sklearn.ensemble import IsolationForest

# Sample data (feature sets)
data = [[-1.1], [0.3], [0.5], [100]]

# Fit the model
clf = IsolationForest(contamination=0.1)
clf.fit(data)

# Predict anomalies
predictions = clf.predict(data)
print(predictions)
```

The output, which indicates normal and anomalous data points:

```
[ 1,  1,  1, -1]
```

Ransomware Defense: Ransomware attacks have surged, necessitating robust defensive measures. Ransomware employs malicious software to encrypt crucial data and demands a ransom for decryption keys. To combat ransomware, organizations are adopting comprehensive backup solutions, segmenting networks to reduce spread potential, and educating employees on identifying phishing attempts. Endpoint detection and response (EDR) systems, coupled with real-time intelligence sharing across sectors, enhance the ability to detect and mitigate ransomware threats swiftly.

Security Automation and Orchestration: Leveraging automation to bolster incident response and threat mitigation is gaining prominence. Security orchestration, automation, and response (SOAR) tools automate repetitive tasks, streamline workflows, and integrate various security technologies, allowing security teams to respond to incidents more efficiently. For instance, automating the collection and analysis of threat intelligence data can significantly reduce response times and minimize human error.

Cloud Security: As organizations migrate to cloud environments, securing cloud infrastructure and services is paramount. Cloud providers and customers share responsibility for security, where providers secure the infrastructure, and customers secure the data hosted on cloud services. Implementing robust identity and access management (IAM), encrypting data both in transit and at rest, and enforcing strong configuration management practices are critical to maintaining cloud security. Below is an example of creating an IAM policy using AWS CLI:

```
aws iam create-policy --policy-name MySecurityPolicy --policy-document file://
    security_policy.json
```

A sample policy document (security_policy.json):

```
{
    "Version": "2012-10-17",
    "Statement": {
        "Effect": "Allow",
        "Action": "s3:*",
        "Resource": "arn:aws:s3:::my-bucket/*"
    }
}
```

Privacy-Enhancing Technologies: In response to increasing regulatory requirements and consumer privacy concerns, privacy-enhancing technologies (PETs) are being integrated into cybersecurity strategies. Examples include homomorphic encryption, which allows computation on encrypted data without decryption, and differential privacy, which ensures that statistical analyses do not expose sensitive information about individuals within a dataset. Incorporating PETs into data processing workflows enhances compliance with regulations such as GDPR and CCPA.

Threat Intelligence Sharing: Fostering collaboration between organizations through threat intelligence sharing is vital for preempting cyber threats. Platforms facilitating the exchange of threat data (Indicators of Compromise, Tactics, Techniques, and Procedures) enable organizations to enhance their defensive postures based on collective knowledge. Standards such as STIX (Structured Threat Information Expression) and protocols like TAXII (Trusted Automated Exchange of Intelligence Information) underpin these collaborative efforts, promoting interoperability between security tools and stakeholders.

Quantum-Safe Cryptography: The advent of quantum computing poses significant challenges to current cryptographic methods. Quantum computers, with their potential to factorize large numbers efficiently, could undermine widely used encryption algorithms such as RSA and ECC. Research into quantum-safe cryptographic algorithms, including lattice-based, multivariate polynomial, and hash-based schemes, is essential to future-proofing cybersecurity infrastructure against emerging threats posed by quantum computing advancements.

The trends discussed herein underscore the dynamic and multifaceted nature of cybersecurity, emphasizing the necessity for continuous adaptation and innovation to counteract evolving cyber threats effectively.

10.9 Big Data and Analytics

Big Data refers to the vast amounts of structured and unstructured data generated continuously from various sources such as social media, sensors, mobile devices, and enterprise systems. The analysis of this data, termed Big Data Analytics, involves sophisticated computational techniques to uncover patterns, correlations, and insights that can inform decision-making processes.

The five primary characteristics of Big Data, often summarized by the five Vs, include Volume, Velocity, Variety, Veracity, and Value.

- **Volume** refers to the sheer quantity of data, often measured in terabytes or petabytes.
- **Velocity** denotes the speed at which data is generated and processed.
- **Variety** encompasses the different types of data, such as text, images, and video.
- **Veracity** highlights the accuracy and quality of data.
- **Value** signifies the potential insights and benefits derived from data analysis.

The emergence of Big Data requires robust and scalable storage solutions. Distributed file systems like the Hadoop Distributed File System (HDFS) facilitate the storage of large datasets across multiple machines. Data processing frameworks such as Apache Hadoop and Apache Spark are critical in managing and processing Big Data effectively. These frameworks employ the principles of distributed computing to perform large-scale computations across clusters of computers.

```
# Example of word count using Apache Spark

from pyspark import SparkContext
sc = SparkContext("local", "Word Count")
text = sc.textFile("hdfs://path/to/data.txt")
words = text.flatMap(lambda line: line.split(" "))
wordCounts = words.map(lambda word: (word, 1)).reduceByKey(lambda a, b: a + b)
wordCounts.saveAsTextFile("hdfs://path/to/output.txt")
```

The computational efficiency of Apache Spark, compared to traditional MapReduce implementations, makes it favored for iterative algorithms and real-time data processing. The Directed Acyclic Graph (DAG) execution engine allows Spark to optimize the execution plan, thereby ensuring better performance.

Data analytics encompasses descriptive, predictive, and prescriptive analytics. Descriptive analytics focuses on historical data to understand past behaviors and trends. Predictive analytics employs statistical models and machine learning algorithms to forecast future outcomes based on historical data. Prescriptive analytics suggests actions based on data analysis, often leveraging optimization techniques and simulation algorithms.

Machine Learning (ML) techniques, when applied to Big Data, facilitate the extraction of meaningful patterns and predictions. Algorithms such as classification, regression, clustering, and association are integral to ML-based analytics.

```
# An example of simple linear regression with scikit-learn

import numpy as np
from sklearn.linear_model import LinearRegression

# Sample data
X = np.array([[1], [2], [3], [4], [5]])
y = np.array([2, 3, 5, 7, 11])

# Model training
model = LinearRegression()
model.fit(X, y)

# Prediction
predictions = model.predict(np.array([[6], [7], [8]]))
print(predictions)
```

[13. 15. 17.]

Advanced analytics methods, such as deep learning, offer significant capabilities in handling unstructured data like images and natural language. Convolutional Neural Networks (CNNs) and Recurrent Neural Networks (RNNs) demonstrate remarkable performance in image recognition and time-series prediction tasks, respectively.

The integration of big data analytics into business processes allows organizations to gain a competitive edge. For instance, in the retail industry, analytics can optimize pricing strategies, inventory management, and personalized marketing campaigns. In healthcare, predictive analytics assists in personalized treatment plans and disease outbreak prediction.

The ethical considerations in Big Data analytics are paramount, especially regarding privacy and data security. Compliance with regulations such as the General Data Protection Regulation (GDPR) is mandatory to ensure that personal data is protected and used responsibly.

The landscape of Big Data and Analytics is rapidly evolving with advancements in technologies such as Quantum Computing, which holds promise for solving computationally intensive tasks more efficiently. Tools and platforms continually advance, providing more sophisticated, user-friendly, and scalable solutions for big data management and analytics.

Understanding the trends and tools in Big Data and Analytics is critical for software engineers and data scientists. As the volume and complexity of data continue to grow, the ability to analyze and derive insights from Big Data will remain a valuable skill, driving innovation and informed decision-making across industries.

10.10 Quantum Computing and its Implications

Quantum computing represents an area of computational advancement grounded in the principles of quantum mechanics. Fundamentally different from classical computing, quantum computing leverages quantum bits or *qubits*, which can exist in multiple states simultaneously due to the property of *superposition*. This section delves into the core concepts of quantum computing, its potential applications, and the implications for the field of software engineering.

A qubit can be in a state $|0\rangle$, $|1\rangle$, or any quantum superposition of these states, expressed generally as $\alpha|0\rangle + \beta|1\rangle$, where α and β are complex numbers satisfying $|\alpha|^2 + |\beta|^2 = 1$. This foundational difference from classical bits enables the execution of complex computational tasks more efficiently. For example, with n qubits, a quantum computer can simultaneously represent 2^n states, offering a parallelism that is not achievable with classical systems.

Due to *entanglement*, another quantum mechanical property, qubits that are entangled can exist in a state where the state of one qubit is dependent on the state of another, regardless of the distance separating them. This non-local correlation is fundamental to many quantum algorithms, providing an exponential speedup for specific types of calculations.

Quantum Algorithms

One of the primary interests in quantum computing arises from its ability to execute specific algorithms more efficiently than classical computers. Prominent among these algorithms are *Shor's algorithm* for integer factorization and *Grover's algorithm* for unstructured search.

Shor's algorithm exponentially reduces the computational complexity of factoring large integers, posing significant implications for cryptography, especially systems relying on RSA encryption. Implementing Shor's algorithm involves using a quantum computer to find the prime factors of a number N, thus breaking the RSA encryption within polynomial time, $\mathcal{O}\left((\log N)^3\right)$.

```
# Quantum Step: Quantum Fourier Transform (QFT)
n = ceil(log2(N))
qreg = QuantumRegister(2 * n)
creg = ClassicalRegister(2 * n)

circuit = QuantumCircuit(qreg, creg)
circuit.h(qreg[0:2*n])
circuit.append(QFT(num_qubits=2*n).to_gate(), qreg[0:2*n])

# Classical Step:
# Find periods using continued fractions
# Derive factors from periods
```

Grover's algorithm provides a quadratic speedup for searching an unstructured database or solving NP-complete problems by reducing the search time from $\mathcal{O}(N)$ to $\mathcal{O}(\sqrt{N})$.

```
# Initialize the qubits
grover_circuit = QuantumCircuit(N)
grover_circuit.h(range(N))

# Oracle implementation
grover_circuit.append(oracle_gate, range(N))

# Grover Diffusion Operator
grover_circuit.h(range(N))
grover_circuit.x(range(N))
grover_circuit.h(N-1)
grover_circuit.mcx(range(N-1), N-1)
grover_circuit.h(N-1)
grover_circuit.x(range(N))
grover_circuit.h(range(N))
```

Implications for Software Engineering

The advent of quantum computing necessitates a paradigm shift in several aspects of software engineering. One major area is security: cryptographic protocols need reevaluation, aiming to develop new standards, such as post-quantum cryptography, that are resilient to quantum attacks.

Another implication is the rethinking of algorithms and data structures. Classic time complexity measures might change under a quantum paradigm. Consequently, novel algorithms optimized for quantum computation are required, impacting algorithm theory and computational complexity.

Toolchains and development environments must evolve to integrate quantum programming languages and frameworks. Initial languages like Q# (Microsoft), Quantum Assembly Language (QASM), and higher-level abstractions (Python libraries such as Qiskit) facilitate the design and simulation of quantum circuits.

```
from qiskit import QuantumCircuit, transpile, assemble, Aer, execute

# Define a quantum circuit
circ = QuantumCircuit(2)
circ.h(0) # Apply Hadamard gate on qubit 0
circ.cx(0, 1) # Apply CNOT gate with control qubit 0 and target qubit 1

# Simulate the circuit
sim = Aer.get_backend('aer_simulator')
compiled_circ = transpile(circ, sim)
qobj = assemble(compiled_circ)
result = sim.run(qobj).result()

# Print the output
print(result.get_counts())
```

```
{'00': '0.5', '11': '0.5'}
```

Quantum computing introduces new vistas for optimization problems in many fields such as logistics, pharmaceuticals, and material sciences. Software engineering practices must evolve to create robust applications leveraging quantum computation paradigms. Robustness, error correction, and qubit coherence maintenance will be vital areas for future research.

Conclusively, as quantum computing matures, it will play an increasingly critical role in the evolution of computational methods, necessitating widespread adaptations in software engineering disciplines to harness its full potential. This emerging field will undoubtedly require skill augmentation and continuous learning to keep pace with its rapid development.

10.11 Future Directions in Software Engineering Research

Advancements in software engineering are driven by both technological innovations and evolving industry demands. Future research directions aim to address the limitations of current methodologies, enhance software quality and efficiency, and explore new computing paradigms.

Researchers are focusing on developing methodologies that better accommodate the increasing complexity and variability of software systems. Model-driven engineering (MDE) is gaining traction, emphasizing the use of models as primary artifacts in the development process. This approach enhances abstraction by allowing developers to focus on high-level specifications rather than low-level implementation details. MDE frameworks facilitate automated code generation and verification, leading to more consistent and error-free software.

Another significant direction is the integration of Artificial Intelligence (AI) and Machine Learning (ML) into software development processes. AI-driven development can significantly enhance the capabilities of tools for requirements engineering, design, coding, testing, and maintenance. For instance, natural language processing (NLP) can be used to automatically extract requirements from unstructured documents, while ML models can predict potential faults in code or optimize resource allocation in large-scale projects. The following snippet showcases a simple ML model used for bug prediction in Python:

```
import pandas as pd
from sklearn.model_selection import train_test_split
from sklearn.ensemble import RandomForestClassifier
from sklearn.metrics import accuracy_score

# Load dataset
data = pd.read_csv('bug_data.csv')

# Feature and target variables
X = data.drop('bug', axis=1)
y = data['bug']

# Split data into training and test sets
X_train, X_test, y_train, y_test = train_test_split(X, y, test_size=0.2)

# Initialize and train model
model = RandomForestClassifier()
model.fit(X_train, y_train)

# Predict and evaluate model
y_pred = model.predict(X_test)
accuracy = accuracy_score(y_test, y_pred)
print(f'Accuracy: {accuracy}')
```

The accurate prediction of bugs via ML models represents a significant leap in improving software reliability and reducing maintenance costs.

Blockchain technology is another burgeoning area of interest in software engineering research. Its immutable and decentralized nature offers promising applications in secure software development lifecycle (SDLC). Research is being conducted on how smart contracts can be employed for transparent and automatic enforcement of software development policies and agreements. Moreover, decentralized applications (DApps) built on blockchain offer new paradigms for developing secure and scalable systems.

With the proliferation of Internet of Things (IoT) devices, software engineering must evolve to address the challenges posed by these interconnected devices. Research in this domain focuses on scalable architectures, real-time data processing, and robust security mechanisms. Edge computing is emerging as a key enabler, allowing data processing to occur closer to data sources rather than relying solely on centralized cloud infrastructure. This reduces latency and bandwidth usage, essential for time-sensitive IoT applications.

Cybersecurity remains a paramount concern, and future software engineering research is increasingly directed towards proactive security measures. Techniques such as threat modeling, secure coding practices, and automated security testing are being refined and integrated into the development lifecycle. Moreover, the use of AI in cybersecurity is being explored to predict and mitigate potential threats effectively.

As quantum computing transitions from theoretical research to practical implementations, its implications on software engineering are profound. Current research is focused on developing quantum algorithms that can solve complex problems exponentially faster than classical algorithms. Software engineers must also explore new paradigms for designing and analyzing quantum programs, necessitating a radical departure from classical computing principles.

The importance of maintaining software quality in complex systems has led to the emergence of techniques like formal verification and software model checking. These methods mathematically prove the correctness of algorithms, ensuring that software behaves as expected under all possible scenarios. Tools supporting these techniques are becoming more accessible, making them viable for a broader range of applications.

The continuous evolution of software engineering requires professionals to stay abreast of emerging trends and innovations. Emphasis on lifelong learning and interdisciplinary collaboration is essential. Educational programs are increasingly incorporating these latest developments to prepare the upcoming generation of software engineers for future challenges. The following pseudocode illustrates the foundational steps for integrating continuous learning into a professional development plan:

Research in software engineering is a dynamic and evolving field that seeks to push the boundaries of what is possible. As the complexity of software systems grows, so does the need for innovative approaches to ensure their development is efficient, reliable, and secure.

10.12 Preparing for the Future: Skills and Education

The evolving landscape of software engineering demands that practitioners continuously update their knowledge and skill sets to remain relevant. This section delves into essential skills and educational pathways that can prepare individuals for the dynamic future of software engineering.

Technical proficiency remains foundational. Mastery of programming languages such as Python, Java, C++, and modern languages such as Swift or Rust is indispensable. Understanding the syntax, semantics, and idiomatic usage of these languages is crucial. Consider the following example in Python:

```
def add(a, b):
    return a + b

result = add(3, 4)
print(result) # Output: 7
```

Proficiency in these languages extends beyond elementary syntax; it encompasses knowing how to optimize code, handle exceptions, and implement best practices for maintainability and readability.

A deep understanding of algorithms and data structures is equally critical. Algorithms such as sorting, searching, and graph traversal should be second nature, along with data structures like arrays, linked lists, trees, and hash tables. Here's a simple example in C++ demonstrating the implementation of a binary search algorithm:

Algorithm 1 Develop Learning Plan

```
function develop_learning_plan
    identify_skills()
    set_learning_goals()
    select_learning_resources()
    allocate_time()
    monitor_progress()
    iterate_plan()
end function
function identify_skills    ▷ Identify the skills required for future projects
    pass
end function
function set_learning_goals ▷ Set SMART (Specific, Measurable, Achievable, Relevant, Time-bound) learning goals
    pass
end function
function select_learning_resources    ▷ Choose books, online courses, workshops, and conferences
    pass
end function
function allocate_time    ▷ Allocate regular time slots for learning activities
    pass
end function
function monitor_progress    ▷ Regularly assess progress towards learning goals
    pass
end function
function iterate_plan ▷ Update the plan based on new information and feedback
    pass
end function
develop_learning_plan()
```

```
#include <iostream>
#include <vector>
using namespace std;

int binarySearch(const vector<int>& array, int target) {
    int left = 0;
    int right = array.size() - 1;

    while (left <= right) {
        int mid = left + (right - left) / 2;

        if (array[mid] == target) return mid;
        else if (array[mid] < target)
            left = mid + 1;
        else
            right = mid - 1;
    }
    return -1;
}

int main() {
    vector<int> array = {1, 3, 5, 7, 9, 11};
    int target = 7;
    int result = binarySearch(array, target);
    cout << "Element found at index: " << result << endl;
}
```

Understanding and implementing key algorithms and data structures optimally is fundamental knowledge for any software engineer.

The paradigm shift towards DevOps and Agile methodologies necessitates familiarity with these frameworks. DevOps practices such as Continuous Integration/Continuous Deployment (CI/CD), infrastructure as code (IaC), and containerization with Docker and Kubernetes are crucial.

```
// Jenkinsfile for a simple CI/CD pipeline
pipeline {
    agent any
    stages {
        stage('Build') {
            steps {
                echo 'Building..'
                sh 'make' // Assuming a makefile is present
            }
        }
        stage('Test') {
            steps {
                echo 'Testing..'
                sh 'make test' // Assuming tests can be run with make
            }
        }
        stage('Deploy') {
            steps {
                echo 'Deploying...'
                sh './deploy.sh' // Custom deployment script
            }
        }
    }
```

```
}
```

Experience with cloud platforms such as AWS, Azure, and Google Cloud is becoming increasingly indispensable. The proliferation of microservices architectures demands a shift from monolithic application development toward distributed, loosely-coupled services. Mastery of API design, RESTful services, and familiarity with gRPC is necessary.

The integration of Artificial Intelligence and Machine Learning into software engineering practices requires knowledge in these domains. Developers should be adept with libraries such as TensorFlow, PyTorch, and scikit-learn. Consider the following classification example using Python's scikit-learn library:

```
from sklearn.datasets import load_iris
from sklearn.model_selection import train_test_split
from sklearn.ensemble import RandomForestClassifier
from sklearn.metrics import accuracy_score

# Load dataset
iris = load_iris()
X = iris.data
y = iris.target

# Split the dataset into training and testing
X_train, X_test, y_train, y_test = train_test_split(X, y, test_size=0.3)

# Initialize and train the RandomForestClassifier
clf = RandomForestClassifier(n_estimators=100)
clf.fit(X_train, y_train)

# Predict on the test set
y_pred = clf.predict(X_test)

# Print accuracy
print("Accuracy:", accuracy_score(y_test, y_pred))
```

Non-technical skills are equally vital. Effective communication, both verbal and written, enables clear articulation of ideas, requirements, and solutions. Collaboration and teamwork are essential in modern software development environments, where cross-functional teams are the norm.

Education in ethics and a strong understanding of the societal impacts of technology are becoming increasingly important. Professionals must navigate the ethical implications of their work, considering privacy, security, and the broader impact of technology on society.

Lifelong learning is a core tenet. Engaging in continuous professional development through courses, certifications, conferences, and workshops ensures one's skills remain current. Online platforms such as

Coursera, Udemy, and edX offer numerous courses tailored to emerging trends and technologies.

Finally, a robust portfolio demonstrating practical experience through projects, contributions to open-source initiatives, and involvement in coding communities can significantly enhance career prospects. A well-documented GitHub repository showcasing various projects, with detailed README files and comprehensive user guides, serves as a testament to a developer's skills and dedication.

By embracing continuous learning and maintaining a diverse skill set, software engineers can thrive amidst the accelerating pace of technological advancement.

Made in the USA
Monee, IL
05 November 2026

67814368R00193